MOTIVATION FOR ACHIEVEMENT

Possibilities for Teaching
and Learning

MOTIVATION FOR ACHIEVEMENT

Possibilities for Teaching and Learning

M. Kay Alderman
The University of Akron

 LAWRENCE ERLBAUM ASSOCIATES, PUBLISHERS
1999   Mahwah, New Jersey   London

Lawrence Erlbaum Associates, Inc., Publishers
10 Industrial Avenue
Mahwah, New Jersey 07430-2262

Cover design by Kathryn Houghtaling Lacey

Library of Congress Cataloging-in-Publication Data

Alderman, M. Kay.
   Motivation for achievement : possibilities for teaching
and learning / M. Kay Alderman.
        p.   cm.
   Includes bibliographical references and index.
   ISBN 0-8058-3077-4 (pbk. : alk. paper)
   1. Motivation in education. 2. Academic achievement.
I. Title.
   LB1065.A477 1999
   370.15'4—dc21   98-41907
                                                               CIP

Books published by Lawrence Erlbaum Associates
are printed on acid-free paper, and their bindings
are chosen for strength and durability

Printed in the United States of America
10 9 8 7 6 5 4 3 2 1

Contents

Preface

This text is designed for the use of preservice teachers and practicing teachers in graduate-level or in-service programs. The content is based on my belief that the current knowledge base in motivation offers hope and possibilities for educators—teachers, parents, coaches, administrators—to enhance motivation for achievement. The knowledge base from research and theory was chosen to help teachers understand motivation of students and themselves and to provide the basis for strategies to foster motivation for all levels of student performance, from those deemed academically at risk to those designated as honor students. The content is based on two roles teachers have for supporting and cultivating motivation in the classroom: (a) establishing the classroom structure and instruction that provides the environment for optimal motivation, engagement, and learning; and (b) helping students develop the tools that will enable them to be self-regulated learners.

Due to the proliferation of topics in motivation, there is no attempt to provide an historical perspective, nor to survey all documented theories. The theoretical and research orientation is based primarily on social-cognitive perspectives that have generated much research relevant for classroom practice. Motivational concepts have often been presented as either/or positions: intrinsic or extrinsic motivation; teacher control or student control; learner-centered or teacher-centered classrooms. This text attempts to strike a balance between the extremes. In the complexities of classroom motivation and learning, there are few either/or decisions. Instead the crucial decision is when to use what strategy.

FEATURES OF THE TEXT

The text contains features to aid the understanding of concepts and the application to practice. Much of the material has been field-tested with educators in my classes over a number of years. These include:

- Strategy Boxes: Guidelines and strategies for using the various concepts.
- Exhibit Boxes: There are two types: (a) forms that teachers might use for students (e.g., form for goal setting); and (b) examples of teacher beliefs and practices and samples of student work.
- Reflections: Questions to stimulate teachers' thinking about motivational issues inherent in the topics, their experiences, and their beliefs.
- Table and Graphic Illustrations: These serve as aids to understanding concepts.

Finally my experience as a teacher in public schools and in teacher education has influenced the choice of content and the perspective I bring to this text: a profound belief that schools and teachers can make a difference in the achievement of students. This is a belief I have tried to reflect throughout this text. To this end, a separate chapter is devoted to the motivational importance of teacher expectations and efficacy for student achievement.

OVERVIEW OF THE CHAPTERS

Chapter 1 begins with a consideration of motivation challenges and problems facing educators, followed by possibilities for addressing these problems and challenges. Central to problems and possibilities is the issue of motivational equality and inequality. This chapter concludes with a definition of motivation and the perspective for this text.

Part II is composed of four chapters that focus on the social cognitive processes that influence motivation. Chapter 2 presents the cognitive theory of attribution, the reasons individuals believe account for their own successes and failures, and those of other people. Attributional theory has generated extensive research since the 1970s. It deals with questions such as "How do one's beliefs about prior success and failure affect future expectations and actions?" "How can teachers help students who believe they cannot learn a given subject like math?" The attributional explanation for motivation is one that teachers, parents, coaches, and counselors find especially useful. As one student who had learned about attribution in another class cautioned his classmates, "You will never look at yourself the same way again after learning about attribution."

Chapter 3 explores the role of perceptions of competence or ability as a motivational factor. Perception of competence is explained from several points of view. The first is self-efficacy, which is the perceived competence about performing a specific task. The strength of one's self-efficacy helps determine which tasks are undertaken and in which task one persists. Another view of ability is self-worth, a theory that explains a motive to avoid failure and protect self-worth from a perception of low ability. This perspective can help answer the question: "Why don't students try?" A third perspective of perceptions of ability is that of achievement goal orientation. Students may approach tasks with the goal of improving their ability or proving their ability. Concepts of ability are related to standards for evaluation (individual and social comparison) and achievement anxiety, the final sections of this chapter.

Goal setting is the subject of chapter 4. Goals are crucial for achievement but they are usually given more prominence in athletics and work environments than in academic learning. This chapter deals with the following questions: "What are characteristics of goals that make them effective?" and "How can goal setting be used in educational settings?".

The perspective for chapter 5 is development and enhancement of student motivational capabilities. What are personal capabilities needed for motivation to learn? This chapter describes the components of self-regulation that equip students with the tools for self-management. These include a vision of the future, volitional control, learning and metacognitive strategies, self-instruction, and time and resource management.

Part III is composed of three chapters that focus on the environmental factors that affect student motivation. Chapter 6 presents two aspects of teacher motivation that are essential to optimum student motivation—teacher efficacy and teacher expectations.

These concepts deal with the following questions: "How do teacher expectations affect student motivation and learning?" "How are these expectations conveyed to students?" and "How do teachers' beliefs about their own effectiveness affect student motivation and learning? "

Chapter 7 is concerned with the effect of the social context on student motivation engagement. A positive social environment fosters in students a sense of belonging and membership. This is an especially important topic in view of the diverse population of students and the problems of inequality. Social context addresses the following questions: "What promotes a climate for a sense of membership?" "What is the role of peers and cultural diversity in establishing a positive classroom climate?" "How much choice and control should there be for optimum motivation?" "What is the role of cooperative learning in establishing a social support system?" and "What is the role of the teacher?"

Chapter 8 focuses on three instructional practices that affect student engagement and motivation—tasks, incentives, and evaluation. Task motivation is concerned with tasks and teacher practices that are more likely to engage students. Important questions are: "What type of tasks get students engaged?" "What is the teacher's role?" and "What is the role of interest?" The incentives section presents the current perspective on the relation between intrinsic motivation and extrinsic rewards. Important questions are: "How do extrinsic incentives affect intrinsic motivation?" and "What are the guidelines for using extrinsic incentives effectively?". Evaluation, the third factor, influences student effort and engagement. It includes decisions about the types of assessment systems that are most likely to increase or decrease student motivation and how teachers use factors such as effort to determine grades.

Chapter 9 presents guidelines for beginning the implementation of motivation strategies. This includes identification of concerns about implementation and describes a problem-solving approach for devising a plan. Finally, programs that offer possibilities for improving motivation and achievement are described.

—*M. Kay Alderman*

PART I

SETTING THE STAGE FOR MOTIVATIONAL POSSIBILITIES

CHAPTER 1

Motivation: Problems, Possibilities, and Perspectives

Education is, at least, the endeavor to get people to do things they could not previously do, to understand things they did not previously understand, and perhaps, to become the people they did not expect to become.
—Sockett (1988, p. 195)

The statement by Sockett expresses a basic premise about the role of motivation: It leads to possibilities for fostering the development of students' potential. A central theme of this book is that teachers have a primary responsibility in education to help students cultivate personal qualities of motivation that can give them resources for developing aspiration, independent learning, achieving goals, and fostering resiliency in the face of setbacks. Perhaps this responsibility is even more important in the context of the motivational problems and challenges faced in the home and in schools in the late 20th century.

This chapter begins by identifying motivational challenges faced by educators. This is followed by the identification of motivational perspectives that offer possibilities for addressing the problems and promoting optimal motivation. Next, a general framework for the role of schools and teachers in fostering optimum motivation is described. The last part of the chapter presents an introduction to the motivation perspective for this book and an overview of the remaining chapters.

PROBLEMS AND CHALLENGES: ACHIEVEMENT AND MOTIVATION

When you think of motivation problems, what comes to your mind? Do the following examples of motivational problems typify them?

3

- "I'm an underachiever and proud of it," an attitude reflected by Bart Simpson.
- Ms. Roger's Grade 3 students who failed to master their math facts and believe they can't learn math.
- Most students in Mr. Marshall's 10th-grade honor English class focus on making an A, but think they are not smart if they have to work for the grade.
- Ms. Sanders has been assigned the low track for English. As she looks over her curriculum, she thinks: "I'll omit the critical thinking exercises in the text because I know this group won't be able to do that type of thinking."
- A teacher in a low-income school says, "My students see themselves as victims of their circumstances. I don't want them to leave school with that attitude."

Motivation challenges such as these are described from two frameworks that are intertwined. The first perspective comes from the motivational research on the role of effort and ability as they relate to school performance. The second perspective reflects motivational inequality as it affects academic achievement. Many of the problems from this framework are grounded in the problems facing society. For both frameworks, schools are part of the problem and can offer possibilities for solutions.

Effort and Ability Framework

What kind of motivational problems reflect an ability/effort framework? This framework refers to beliefs about the respective contributions of effort and ability to performance. In the prior problems, Mr. Marshall's honor students reflect this framework when they devalue the role of effort in their achievement. In 1976, Covington and Beery wrote what has become a classic description of motivation problems in the schools. The problem, as they saw it, is that many school and classroom experiences act to undermine an individual's sense of self-worth because of a focus on ability and performance.

Student Ability.   Students become convinced that ability is the primary element for achieving success and a lack of ability is the primary reason for failure. The notions of ability is in comparison to other students. In competitive situations, the fundamental motivation for many students is to avoid failure and protect their self-worth from the perception that they have low ability. To protect their self-worth, some students adopt strategies to avoid the perception of failure. Two failure-avoiding strategies are setting unrealistic goals (either too high or too low) and withholding effort. Teachers often characterize these unmotivated students as apathetic or lazy. "I'm an underachiever and proud of it," reflects this pattern of self-worth protection.

Student Effort.   Others have cited student work habits, especially lack of effort, as a major motivational problem. Lack of effort was identified as the primary motivational problem by Glasser (1990). He described school as a place where students are not only *not* trying to do their best, but are expending much of their energy avoiding work. He contended that much of the widely reported school failure is a result of students failing to expend the effort to do high-quality work. These academic work problems can be seen in the following description of Ms. Foster's ninth-grade class.

> Ms. Foster says a large number of students are unmotivated. She describes this unmotivated behavior as: many students do not have goals; they sit passively in class; turn in no homework; don't keep up with their notebooks; do not take final exams or the state required proficiency tests seriously; resist new approaches to learning that require the use of critical thinking skills, preferring to use worksheets as they have in the past. Cooperative learning groups are described as generally unsuccessful either because of chaos or one person does the work. Learning aids such as manipulatives in math are not used because students don't keep up with the materials.

Another example of ability/effort as a motivational problem comes from a comparison of Japanese and Chinese students with U.S. students regarding the role of ability and effort in mathematical success (Stevenson & Lee, 1990). They found that U.S. students believed that innate ability was most important for success, whereas Japanese and Chinese students emphasized effort. Similar differences in beliefs were also found among their parents.

Still another example is student disengagement or lack of investment in learning in secondary schools (Newmann, 1992). Behaviors indicating disengagement range from severe (e.g., skipping, disruption, failure to do assignments) to behaviors that, on the surface, do not appear to be a motivation problem. This latter group of students behave well, attend classes, complete their work, but show little indication of pride in their work or commitment to learning. An example of disengagement is this student's comment:

> When you get home there's always something you can be doing with your friends besides homework so you just do enough to get a decent grade but you don't try to get your best grade, you do just enough to finish. (Newmann, 1992, p. 15)

Does it surprise you that disengagement also includes students who seemingly are succeeding in school?

These negative motivational patterns seen from the effort/ability framework may be fostered by school and classroom practices. One of the most prevalent is characterized as "the competitive learning game" (Covington, 1992). This game refers to classroom practices that force students to compete against each other for grades and recognition. Such practices include ability grouping, a limited range of accomplishments that receive rewards, and recognizing ability over effort. These topics are discussed in the chapters ahead.

Motivational Inequality as a Problem and Challenge

In 1979, Nicholls asserted that motivational inequality was prevalent in the schools. By *motivational inequality*, Nicholls meant that students who do not have optimum motivation for intellectual development are at a disadvantage compared with those who do. Students who have optimum motivation have an edge because they have adaptive attitudes and strategies, such as maintaining intrinsic interest, goal setting, and self-monitoring. There is evidence that this motivational inequality has increased rather than decreased in the years since it was first introduced (Tomlinson, 1993). Situations where motivational inequality is dominant are captured by the following scenario constructed from Maeroff's (1988) description of the climate found in some urban schools:

> The demands and expectations are low and students say they are unmotivated and see no reason to attend school. Low achievement is accepted as the norm. Teachers do not assign homework because they have little expectation it will be completed. Students see few examples of success; their sense of future is bleak and does not include academic achievement in any way. Students have no basis for an alternative view of academic achievement because they rarely come in contact with anyone other than similarly low achieving students. Some students don't have anyone at home to say "I'm proud you, keep up the good work." (p. 634)

The previous description illustrates a primary problem in school achievement—the large number of students at risk of failing academically. The students in this at-risk group predominantly come from families of poverty (Hodgkinson, 1993; Knapp & Shields, 1990). For example, Hodgkinson reported that almost one fourth of U.S. children live below the poverty line and are in danger of failing to fulfill their physical and mental promise. This does not mean, however, that the economically disadvantaged children are not motivated to learn in preschool and kindergarten (Stipek & Ryan, 1997). The authors found no differences in economically advantaged and disadvantaged preschool and kindergarten children on measures of motivation such as self-confidence and expectations for success. The difference in the two groups was on measures of cognitive competence, with economically disadvantaged children scoring lower than the advantaged group.

Ability Grouping. Unfortunately, in many cases the problems are compounded by school climate and teaching practices that may inhibit students from reaching their potential. One of these practices is the separation of students into groups based on their ability. When ability grouping is in place, many students are not exposed to rigorous subject matter that might better prepare them for college entrance examinations and college work, nor does it prepare them for jobs (Maeroff, 1988). In addition, the lower group is deprived of peer models of motivation strategies that would help them to achieve (Brown, 1993). Finally, teachers are likely to have lower expectations for this group and teach them accordingly (Oakes, 1985).

Cultural and Ethnic Diversity. Motivational inequality presents additional challenges for schools and teachers with the increasing ethnic and cultural diversity of the school population. Thirty percent of the school-age population is composed of students from a minority culture, with the proportion expected to increase in the future (Hodgkinson, 1993). The school where Ms. Foster teaches, composed of a student population of African-American, Anglo, and Hispanic cultures, is representative of the increasing diversity found in schools. The socioeconomic status (SES) ranges from middle and upper middle professional to a mobile, low-income population.

Why does the increasing diversity of the school population present a motivational challenge? One challenge for educators is the ethnic differences found in achievement, especially the underachievement of African-American and Hispanic students (Garibaldi, 1993; Mehan, Villanueva, Hubbard, & Lintz, 1996). A consistent and disturbing finding is that African-American students "generally earn lower grades, drop out more often, and attain less education than do whites" (Mickelson, 1990, p. 45). This is despite the fact that until Grade 4, there are no differences between the performance of African-American and White students (Simmons & Grady, 1990). What motivational factors play a role in these performance differences? One factor is a discrepancy between African-American students and their teachers with respect to aspirations, where teachers underestimated students aspirations and this in turn affected the type of education they provided students (Garibaldi, 1993). In addition, for minority students, there is sometimes negative peer pressure against behaviors associated with school success. These are referred to as *acting White or Anglo* behaviors (Fordham & Ogbu, 1986; Suarez-Orozco, 1989). Because this is a multifaceted problem, it is one that must be addressed by schools, teachers, parents, and the communities (Garibaldi, 1993).

Motivational Challenges Related to Educational Reform

Initiatives for reforming schools are occurring across the nation. What motivational challenges do various educational reforms present? School reform in most states has focused on raising standards through mandatory proficiency tests, which students must pass at various grade levels. However, raising standards has not increased student effort (Tomlinson, 1993). The extensive use of proficiency tests has motivational consequences for students and teachers. Do the pressures on students to pass these tests increase their motivation to learn or do some students give up in the face of failure? How does it affect teacher expectations? These questions are still largely unanswered.

Another reform initiative, Essential Schools, sees the roles of students as "workers" and teachers as "coaches" (Sizer, 1986). This has students working more on their own, frequently on long-term thematic topics and projects. Although these initiatives have the potential to increase student motivation, they also present challenges because this type of learning is more complex. Students need goals and persistence to work on and complete these semester-long, thematic projects.

Finally, inclusion—where special education students receive instruction in the classroom rather than in out-of-class programs—presents additional motivational challenges. Many of these students, such as students with learning disabilities (LD), have a long history of failure. A major motivational problem for these students is their belief that they cannot learn compounded by a lack of effective learning strategies. Thus, the challenge for teachers is to help them develop the motivational beliefs and learning strategies needed for success.

In response to motivation problems present in schools, a teacher observed, "They weren't like this 20 years ago." This is a refrain echoed in different ways by many teachers. Teachers are saying, "I don't know how to teach or motivate todays' students." The two recurring themes in the motivation problems described from these frameworks are: (a) students do not have tools like concentration, persistence, volition, goal orientation, delay of instant gratification, and strategies for acquiring and retaining new information needed to be successful; and (b) many teachers have not acquired instructional strategies to foster positive motivation.

REFLECTION. Have you thought about motivation problems and challenges from these frameworks? What problems do you view as the most challenging in your classroom? Your community?

MOTIVATION POSSIBILITIES AND GOALS

In view of the motivational challenges facing teachers, what are the possibilities for fostering positive motivation? To address the pervasive motivational inequality in schools, Nicholls (1979) proposed that optimum student motivation is a justifiable educational goal. Nicholls described *optimum motivation* as motivation that provides for optimum intellectual development. Collier (1994) also emphasized the importance of motivational factors in developing mental abilities: "Motivational factors determine not just the goals toward which people aspire but the way in which they seek out, process, and use information" (p. 8). Motivation is an important factor in the development of children's *resiliency*, which is the ability to bounce back successfully despite growing up in adverse circumstances (Gordon, Padilla, Ford, & Thoresen, 1994).

The following examples illustrate motivation possibilities:

• A comprehensive classroom management program implemented in an inner-city elementary school documented fewer discipline problems, increased student engagement, teacher and student expectations, achievement motivation, and academic self-concepts (Frieberg, Stein, & Huang, 1995).

• Ms. Toliver's eighth-grade math students in P.S. 72 have been recognized for their accomplishments. She tells students at the beginning of the year, "This is a new day and we will work from here. I do not believe in failure. Mathematics may be hard to learn—it takes dedication and hard work— but I let my students know two things from the beginning: (1) I am with them to teach, and (2) I expect to be met halfway" (Toliver, 1993, p. 39).

• From Day 1 in seventh-grade language arts, Ms. Adler establishes this expectation: "If you fail, it's not because you are not smart, but because you didn't use the right strategy."

• "Determination + Discipline + Hard Work = The Way To Success," formula for success in Jaime Escalante's classes (Mathews, 1988).

The possiblities reflected by these examples have a sound basis of support from the motivation knowledge base.

What Is Optimum Motivation?

A central theme in current motivation theories and research is the focus on developing self-regulated learners. Students who have self-regulation use both motivation and learning strategies (Zimmerman, 1994). According to Corno (1993), self-regulated learners have what is known as *volition*, or the ability to "maintain concentration in the face of obstacles." These learners will want to learn and do things to make learning happen and direct their own educational experience. Learners with these characteristics are more likely to continue to learn on their own.

Student motivation to learn was described by Brophy (1983) as more than simply doing enough to meet requirements but purposefully engaging in academic tasks by attempting to acquire the knowledge or skill involved in them. Similarly, Newmann (1992) contended that student engagement in academic work is critical to school success. Student *engagement* in academic work is defined as "psychological investment in and effort directed toward learning, understanding, or mastering the knowledge, skills, or crafts that academic work is intended to promote" (Newmann, Wehlage, & Lamborn, 1992, p. 12). A similar view of optimum motivation is a will to learn (Covington, 1992; Covington & Beery, 1976). Students with a *will to learn* are characterized as believing in themselves and in their ability to think for themselves. They also develop a sense of personal effectiveness and the belief that they cause their own achievements.

Ames (1992) described motivation from the perspective of a classroom structure that promotes optimum motivation. Features of a classroom that fosters optimum motivation are as follow: (a) tasks that are meaningful with reasonable challenge; (b) opportunity to participate in decision making and develop responsibility; and (c) an evaluation system that recognizes progress and mastery of content.

Although the motivation problems seem overwhelming and optimum motivation may seem like an elusive goal, the good news is that there is now a substantial knowledge base from motivation research and theory that will enable teachers to actively facilitate the motivation of students and establish a positive motivational classroom environment.

The School's and Teacher's Roles

What are the roles for schools and teachers in addressing these problems and in developing student motivation to learn? A primary assertion in this text is that motivation has to be explicitly addressed as part of instruction and socialization rather than treated as a by-product. This premise has been expressed in various ways. One example is the contention by Sockett (1988) that teaching qualities of personal capability, such as effort, perseverance, concentration, self-restraint, and punctuality, is a role of the school.

Stated in another way, the task for schools is to foster a will to learn and "the teacher's role is to encourage both confidence and high achievement in their students" (Covington & Beery, 1976, p. 5). The conditions for acquiring self-regulated learning and volition can be fostered in schools (Corno, 1993; Pintrich, 1995). Thus, teachers and schools have a specific responsibility to assist students in becoming self-regulated learners. Brophy and Kher (1986) maintained that teachers should be able to develop student motivation to learn by socializing students' beliefs, attitudes, and expectations concerning academic activities and by instructing their students in information-processing and problem-solving strategies. Newmann (1992) saw the teacher's role as one of engaging students in the hard work of school: the continuous cycle of studying, producing, correcting mistakes, and starting over again, like the following example:

> I like to work hard and I guess I'll just pound it into myself if I don't understand. If I don't understand something, I make sure that I work at it until I do understand, and I keep it up and I never give up. I'm not a quitter at all. (Newmann, Wehlage, & Lamborn, 1992, p. 14)

What are the types of motivational knowledge needed by teachers and schools to address these problems and foster optimum motivation? For teachers to fulfill their motivational roles, they need competencies in process skills and to be proactive decision makers (Rohrkemper, 1985). This means that teachers actively plan for motivation, not just react to motivation problems as they occur. With these process skills, teachers can diagnose the need for motivation strategies, determine the effectiveness of strategies, and fine tune or revise strategies.

Consider the following incident:

> A parent was in a teacher education program where she learned about the motivation strategies of goal setting and attributional feedback (described in chaps. 2 and 4). Her sixth-grade son indicated a desire to improve his reading grade and his mother said she would assist him. She had him set goals and provided him with feedback about his accomplishments. His grades began to improve. When the son was given his interim report, he saw that his grade was lower than he expected and he was very discouraged. The parent talked with the teacher, who explained that he had given lower grades than students were actually making on all interim reports. The teacher reasoned that students slacked off the last weeks of school and the lower grade would motivate them to work harder. After the parent explained that this had actually undermined the strategy she had been using with her son, the student was given his correct average. On his final report card, he had five As and one B—his best of the year.

This incident illustrates several points about understanding motivation and choosing strategies for enhancing motivation:

- The motivation knowledge base has not been widely disseminated in forms that provide teachers with the basis for effective strategy decision making. Thus, we might assume the teacher was unaware of other potential strategies for maintaining motivation.
- The motivational dynamics of success and failure must be understood, especially students' reactions to them. For example, the teacher had a misconception about how failure may affect student motivation.
- Some strategies are more powerful than others. Powerful strategies are likely to be more complex or involve combinations of motivational variables that increase the strength of a strategy, as in the prior incident where the parent combined goal setting and attributional feedback.
- In this example, one strategy appeared to facilitate motivation, whereas the other appeared to undermine it.

The knowledge base of motivation is so extensive that the crucial factor is making the best choice for a particular problem. If we have not learned the extensive motivational knowledge base, then our choices are limited. Chapter 9 presents a problem-solving model that will assist you in making decisions to enhance motivation for both yourself and your classroom.

REFLECTION.   What is your reaction to the previous scenario? What does it say about the importance of teachers having a strong understanding of motivation principles?

MOTIVATION PERSPECTIVES
FOR CLASSROOM LEARNING

The criteria for the selection of theory and research to be included in this text is to identify concepts that provide teachers with the most powerful tools for activation and persistence of their students' motivation. *Tool* in this sense means something that is used to perform an operation or that is necessary in the practice of a skill or vocation. As such, motivational tools may take two forms: (a) conceptual understanding (e.g., understand why a student may not try); or (b) the use of things (e.g., use an appropriate incentive). As you go through this text, begin building a motivational toolbox (Fig. 1.1). A form for this is provided in each chapter.

The goal of this text is to make the knowledge applicable and actionable (Argyris & Schon, 1974). Applicable knowledge tells what motivation concepts are relevant, whereas actionable knowledge tells how to implement motivation strategies in everyday practice. This means that learning a theory and learning a skill should not be viewed as distinct activities. Instead, knowledge must be integrated with action. For example, when a teacher learns the theory of learned helplessness, he or she learns to (a) explain this concept, (b) identify students displaying helplessness, and (c) select and devise strategies to help the student. The remainder of this section defines motivation and presents the perspective that reflects the content and organization of this text.

Defining Motivation

Our language is replete with terms that imply motivation, both from motivational theories and our everyday language. "Sam *tries* so hard," "Sarah took *responsibility* for her actions," and "there is no *incentive* for doing a good job at my work" illustrate three such motivational terms. However, what is motivation? Through the years, mtivation has frequently been described as having three psychological functions (Ford, 1992): (a) *energizing or activating behavior*—what gets students engaged in or turned off toward learning (Mr. Crawford's math students look forward to the new problem to solve each week); (b) *directing behavior*— why one course of action is chosen over another (Maria does her homework before playing Nintendo); and (c) *regulating persistence of behavior*—why students persist toward goals (Eddie continues to run cross-country even though he does not have a scholarship). These three functions can be explained differently by different motivation perspectives.

The motivation knowledge base that addresses these functions has greatly expanded from grand formal theories (e.g., achievement motivation, social learning) to a broad spectrum of motivational topics (Weiner, 1990). A unifying theme of these recent approaches is a focus on cognitive and emotional variables that influence achievement striving (Bandura, 1997; Graham & Weiner,

Motivational Toolbox

1. Important points to think about and lingering questions

2. Strategies I can use now

3. Strategies I want to develop in the future

FIG. 1.1. Motivational toolbox.

1996; Stipek, 1996; Weiner, 1990).[1] These cognitive and emotional variables are composed of self-focused thoughts such as beliefs about one's competence. These approaches include:

- causal attributions—reasons about why we succeed or fail;
- self-efficacy—beliefs about our competence to perform a task;
- learned helplessness—a feeling and belief about the hopelessness in a situation;
- thoughts about goals—the extent to which we focus on a goal to learn or as a reflection of ability;
- self-worth—a concern with protecting perceptions of our own ability.

The emphasis on the role of cognitions and self in motivation is accompanied by a recognition of the importance of the social nature of motivation in schools (Weiner, 1990), as well as the role of the environment (Bandura, 1986). The approach that captures these areas and forms the central core of motivation for teaching and learning is known as *social cognitive theory*.

Social Cognitive Approach to Motivation

Social cognitive theory assumes there is an interrelation between an individual's cognitive processes and the social environment (Bandura, 1997; Pintrich & Schrauben, 1992). This perspective of motivation interrelates: (a) personal factors or cognitive/emotional factors such as beliefs about ability; (b) environmental factors such as incentives and evaluation criteria used by the teacher; (c) and the behavior or performance of the person such as increasing effort after a low grade (Bandura, 1986; Dweck & Leggett, 1988). These three factors interact through a process that Bandura (1986) termed *reciprocal interactions* where each component affects the other two. The components are shown in Fig. 1.2.

A student's cognitive processes, such as belief about his or her ability, acts as an important mediator of motivation influencing both expectations for future performance and action taken. This is a complex, continuous interaction, but an example can make it easier to understand. The interactions of the three factors are shown in Exhibit 1.1 in the example of Martin and Marty who are both taking math.

---

[1]For an historical review of motivation theories, see Graham and Weiner (1996) and Weiner (1990).

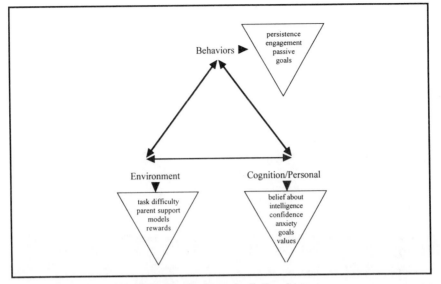

FIG. 1.2. Reciprocal relationships.

The two students had similar beliefs about their ability to learn math but experienced contrasting instructional environments. Their behaviors or actions were influenced by their beliefs and environment. These factors, in turn, influenced each student's subsequent beliefs about his or her ability in math and the actions he or she will take.

The content of the chapters in this text demonstrate the reciprocal influence of these factors: cognition, environment, and behavior. This motivation framework is the basis for self-regulation. Chapters 2 through 5 focus on the cognitive processes that influence motivation. The focus of chapters 6 through 8 is on classroom factors that affect motivation. The triarchic view offers teachers a range of possibilities for enhancing motivation for achievement because it considers what the student brings to the class and the environmental aspects that can be influenced by the teacher.

An important issue is whether this social-cognitive perspective is relevant for culturally diverse population. Graham (1994) asserted that motivation perspectives relevant for African Americans must incorporate the range of cognitive and affective factors that affect and guide behavior. This includes concepts such as causal attributions, expectancy for success, and their interrelations. Because of the overrepresentation of minority students in special education and low-track classes, motivational approaches for culturally diverse

---

Exhibit 1.1. A Social Cognitive Example

Cognition

Both Martin and Marty believe that either you have an ability to learn math or you don't. Furthermore, they believe that if you don't have the ability for math, there is nothing you can do.

Environment

Martin is in Ms. Jones' class. He is placed in the lowest math group. Ms Jones only gives this group part of the math curriculum. Because she thinks they won't be able to get it, she requires little homework completion.

Marty is in Mr. Crawford's remedial class. This class is structured so the students can develop their math skills. Students must get an A or a B on each test; if they fail, they must retake the failed tests until they pass with a B.

Behaviors

Martin spends less and less time on math. His confusion grows. He develops a dislike for math because the partial curriculum makes math seem very disconnected. His belief about his math ability has been confirmed. He will continue in the lowest math group until he is no longer required to take math.

Marty is surprised at the gradual improvement in her math scores. She chooses to spend more time now on her homework and is thinking about taking more math than planned. Marty is proud of herself, and she should be. Her belief about math ability begins to change.

---

groups must be especially sensitive to dynamics of failure or how individuals feel, think, and act in response to nonattainment of goals. These factors reflect a social-cognitive perspective.

In contrast, early motivation research was predominantly concerned with determining differences among ethnic groups—an approach that often led to misconceptions about the motivation of African-American students (Graham, 1994). Motivation for culturally diverse populations is more than comparing differences among different groups. An important aspect is to identify the motivational qualities that are neutral across cultures, are valued by those cultures, and that recognize individual differences (Sockett, 1988). Tharp (1989) observed that some motivational factors such as motivation for accomplishment, reward, and recognition receive relatively consistent support from parents and the community across cultures. Recent research (McInerney, Roche, McInerney, & Marsh, 1997) found that motivational profiles of Western culture and non-Western indigenous students were more similar than different. Therefore, research cultural perspectives on motivation will be integrated throughout this text as the topic indicates.

As you work your way through this text, you will come to understand the extreme complexities of initiating and maintaining a motivating classroom. The synthesis of research presented here provides a sturdy foundation of motivation building blocks to allow you to begin making informed decisions concerning the most effective motivation strategies.

REVIEW OF MAJOR POINTS

1. Educators are faced with motivational problems and challenges. One set of challenges stems from the ability/effort problem, where the focus on ability to the exclusions of effort leads some students to adopt strategies such as not trying to avoid the perception of failure.

2. Motivational inequality framework. Motivational challenges from the inequality framework include the number of students at risk of failing academically and the increasing diversity of the school population with the underachievement of African-American and Hispanic students. These challenges are compounded by ability grouping.

3. Other challenges are presented by school reform movements such as proficiency testing and inclusive school movement.

4. Optimum student motivation is a justifiable educational goal because the motivation knowledge base provides many possibilities for addressing problems and challenges. One role of teachers and school is to develop self-regulated learners and incorporate motivation and learning strategies.

5. Motivation is often described as having three functions: (a) energizing or activating behavior, (b) directing behavior, and (c)

regulating persistence of behavior. Current motivational topics focus around self-focused thoughts. Social-cognitive theory, which assumes a reciprocal relationship among an individual's cognitive/emotional processes, environmental/social factors, and the behavior or performance of the person, is the primary basis for this text. Similarly, the interrelationship of these factors is more appropriate for working with culturally diverse populations than previous comparative approaches.

PART II

SOCIAL-COGNITIVE PROCESSES THAT INFLUENCE MOTIVATION

This section moves from the problems and challenges to understanding the motivational processes students bring to the classroom—a first step in helping students develop self-regulation. The first three chapters in this section explain the social-cognitive processes of causal attributions for success and failure and the consequences of these beliefs, concepts of ability and evaluation of competence, and setting goals for accomplishment. They affect students' effort, persistence, and confidence in undertaking or avoiding tasks. As educators and parents, understanding these processes can open windows into understanding student motivation. These processes might be thought of as the building blocks of self-regulation. Chapter 5 presents additional components of self-regulation: possible selves, volitional control, learning and metacognitive strategies, and time and resource management.

CHAPTER 2

Attributional Beliefs and Motivation

Sylvia has been failing and has no confidence in herself to do the work. As a teacher, you believe that the main thing Sylvia needs is to experience success on the task. So you ask another student to help her with the task. Sylvia is able to complete the task successfully. You now expect her to be more confident. However, when you ask Sylvia about the likelihood of completing other similar tasks, she seems doubtful that she can do it. "I only did it the last time cause Sharon helped me."

When students like Sylvia lack confidence, a common response by teachers is to help them attain success on a task, as in the example. Although Sylvia has a successful experience, she still lacks confidence. What is the explanation for Sylvia's continuing low confidence? The motivation theory that can provide insight into Sylvia's response is attribution theory. *Attribution* is a cognitive theory that considers a person's beliefs about causes of outcomes and how those beliefs influence expectations and behavior. An understanding of attribution theory will help you:

- understand seemingly illogical beliefs of students (like Sylvia still having low expectations after experiencing success);
- understand and address lack of effort;
- identify strategies that can be used to help students succeed and gain in confidence; and
- understand your own causal beliefs about success and failure and how these influence student motivation.

Because attribution is concerned with causes given for outcomes, it is the theory of motivation that is most directly concerned with this question: "Why do people do what they do?" This question is

23

FIG. 2.1. Reasons given for a grade.

particularly important to teachers and students. Examples of the variety of causal explanations that students may give for their performance are shown in Fig. 2.1.

Attribution theory began with the common-sense psychology of Heider. Heider (1958) was interested in the reasons people give for an outcome such as success or failure on a task. The causes that people hold responsible for an outcome are important determinants of their future expectancies and behaviors. Heider identified two primary reasons that people use to explain their performance: *can* and *try*. Can refers to whether one has the ability to do a task, and try refers to how much effort a person puts forth. If we fail at a task, our expectations for future success differ depending on whether we attribute the failure to lack of effort (try) or to not having the ability (can) to succeed on the task. For example, if Cathy fails a math test and says "I'm just no good at numbers," it is unlikely that she will expect to improve in the future. Consequently, she will not try very hard in math classes. If Cathy fails and says "I didn't spend enough time studying," it is likely she will work harder on the next test.

ATTRIBUTIONAL PROPERTIES
IN ACHIEVEMENT SETTINGS

What are the properties of attributional thinking? Weiner (1979, 1985, 1986, 1992) generated much research that identified properties involved in attributional thinking in achievement settings. The properties include the specific reason for success and failure, different ways we view the reason, the source of the belief, and factors that influence change in expectations.

Descriptions of Attributional Thinking:
Content and Dimensions

What reasons for success and failure can teachers typically expect to find in a classroom? The research by Weiner initially identified four reasons most frequently given as the cause for success and failure in achievement settings: ability, effort, task difficulty, and luck. Subsequent research identified learning strategies as a fifth possible reason for success and failure (Clifford, 1986). These reasons are defined as follows:

- ability—how we rate our aptitude, skill, or knowledge ("I'm just not good at sports")
- effort—how hard we tried, including time spent
- task difficulty—how difficult or easy we believe the task to be
- strategy—the type of strategy used for learning (e.g., a prereading strategy).
- luck—the extent to which we believe luck was a factor

Ability and effort have typically been found to be the most frequent reasons for success and failure in achievement contexts (Weiner, 1992). Strategies were given by students only if teachers had emphasized the importance of strategy use for a successful performance (Clifford, 1986). If strategies were not emphasized, students did not consider them as a possible reason for their performance. However, in a course where strategy use was emphasized, strategies were the most frequent reason indicated by college students for success or failure (Alderman, Klein, Seeley, & Sanders, 1993).

The causes given for success and failure have been further classified into three dimensions or ways to look at causes (Weiner, 1979, 1992):

1. Attributions are classified according to an internal–external continuum. This refers to whether the cause is a factor within the person (ability or aptitude, effort, mood) or a factor outside the person (luck, task difficulty).
2. The second dimension is a stable–unstable continuum. The stability classification refers to whether the perceived cause has been a consistent or inconsistent one over time. Unstable causes for success or failure are those attributed to temporary or factors that can be modified.
3. The third dimension, controllable–uncontrollable continuum, refers to the extent we believe we have influence or control over the cause of an outcome. An uncontrollable factor is luck, whereas effort is generally believed to be controllable.

Table 2.1 presents attributional examples classified according to dimensions. The examples are from the student's perspective.

In this classification, if Cathy fails an exam and says "I did not try hard enough," we can infer that she believes that she can try harder—an internal–unstable attribution. Effort is sometimes perceived as stable as when we characterize ourselves as "basically lazy" or if we think "my 6 months of hard work paid off when I was chosen to be a member of the ensemble."

It is especially important for teachers to understand the stable–unstable dimension. Research typically found that students view ability and task difficulty as relatively stable. If Sylvia fails and says "I will never be able to learn math," she is referring to her math ability as stable. This is an internal–stable attribution and her reason for failure appears to be fixed. This is a self-defeating attribution for Sylvia. As teachers, we want students to think of ability as a skill or knowledge that is learnable—an unstable quality. For example, a student with poor writing skills who believes that writing is a stable ability, perhaps even innate, is not likely to revise drafts of papers or seek help, such as going to a writing lab.

Do students always have some idea of what determines success and failure? Apparently not. Alderman et al. (1993) found explanations such as "I don't know what happened" as explanations for a low grade and termed these as *mystery* attributions. In a study of causal factors given by elementary students, Butler and Orion (1990) found that attribution of test outcomes to unknown causes was more prevalent by students who were low achieving. Knowledge of how students use these attributions to account for success and failure in school settings (academic and sports) can help teachers predict students' expectancies and plan intervention strategies when needed.

Sources of Attributional Information

How do we decide what caused our success and failure? What cues do we use to explain whether an outcome was influenced by our ability, effort, or some other factor? Information comes from direct

TABLE 2.1

Examples of Attributions by Dimensions

| | Internal | | External |
	Controllable	Uncontrollable	Uncontrollable
Stable	• I've really improved my keyboarding skill due to my practice over the last 6 months. • Because I have consistently used the PQ4R, my grades have improved.	• I'm not good at math. • I can't draw a straight line.	• Mr. Jones' tests are impossible to pass. • I'm not a good writer because I never had a teacher who made me write.
Unstable	• I didn't overlearn material for the last exam. I wasn't well organized in studying. • "Success, success." I did better than I expected. I put my best efforts into passing and came up with good results. I studied until the terms became second nature.	• I was sick all week and couldn't study for the test.	• I got a good grade because my tutor helped me. • I made an A; the test was easy.

Note. There is no external-controllability column because, from the view of the student, external factors are uncontrollable.

and indirect cues (Graham, 1991). Some information comes from direct cues, like failing a test when other students succeeded. Information is also obtained from more indirect cues, often conveyed unintentionally, such as when a teacher communicates pity to a student who failed a test.

Direct Attributional Cues

One of the most important informational cues is the outcome of the task. Here students have a direct cue as to their performance. Another source of attributional information comes from comparing one's performance to that of others (Weiner, 1992). When most of the class fails a test, students are likely to attribute the failure to the difficulty of the task, not to their ability. However, if Sam failed and everyone else in the class made an A or B, he is likely to believe the failure was due to his low ability. If Sarah fails a test and a peer says, "I didn't study at all and I made an A," Sarah may take this as a cue that failure must be due to her ability. When a teacher sees students comparing grades on a test, information other than the test score is being communicated. An important role of the teacher is to help students interpret the possible reasons for test scores.

Indirect Attributional Cues

In school, feedback that students receive from teachers is a source of much information about ability. Graham (1991) identified three groups of feedback as sources of indirect cues: praise versus blame, sympathy versus anger, and help versus neglect.

Praise Versus Blame.   The praise or blame a student receives from a teacher can function as an indirect low-ability cue (Graham, 1991). The cue provided by praise or blame interacts with difficulty of the task and effort expended by a student. Praise acts as a low-ability cue when a student is praised for completing an easy task. A low-ability cue is also conveyed when a student fails a task but receives no blame, like lack of effort. The student can interpret this to mean, "There's nothing I can do about the failure." Chapter 8 presents guidelines for effective and ineffective praise.

Sympathy Versus Anger.   Did it ever occur to you that communicating sympathy to a student could be interpreted as evidence that he or she has low ability? Graham (1984) found that when teachers conveyed sympathy following poor student performance, the failing students took this as a cue that they had low ability. Obviously a statement like "I feel sorry for you because you didn't get any right" would be a low-ability cue. What might a teacher say that unintentionally conveys a message of low ability to a student? One student remembers a class being told, "All students have to do this except Holly and Ramon." Holly took her omission as a cue that she would not be able to do the task. In contrast, mild anger for failure can provide an indirect cue that one is able. For example, "You can do better than this. You handed this paper in with no editing," provides a cue to the student that he or she is capable of more.

Unsolicited Help. Another low-ability cue for students is unsolicited help by the teacher (Graham & Barker, 1990). Graham and Barker found that, regardless of whether a helper was a peer or teacher, other students judged the student who received unsolicited help as lower in ability than nonhelped peers. The important factor in this example is *unsolicited*. When the teacher gives help before it is requested, it suggests that the teacher knows the student will not be able to do it.

Ability Grouping. One powerful cue for ability that affects large groups of students is tracking according to ability groups. Students in both high and low tracks are defined by labels such as *high ability, honor, low achieving, slow,* and *average* (Oakes, 1985). These labels are powerful cues about one's ability. Oakes observed that students in the lower track are usually seen by others as dumb and also see themselves in this way. A label may have an adverse effect on students in the high-achieving class as well. Students in a high-track class may take this label as a cue that they naturally have high ability and assume inflated self-concepts. This belief can interfere with students working to develop their academic skills.

It is important that teachers be aware of the subtle cues that may have unintentional effects on students' perception of ability. Commonly accepted practices of generous praise, minimal blame, sympathy, and unsolicited help can sometimes be interpreted as "you have low ability" (Graham, 1991). Graham further suggested that these cues raise important questions pertinent to motivation of minority students, such as African Americans. For example, are minority students more likely to be targets for feedback that convey sympathy—thus receiving a cue for low ability?

Emotional Reactions Generated by Attributions

What emotional reactions might be generated by one's attributional beliefs about the causes of success or failure? How do these emotions affect motivation? Attributional beliefs produce emotional reactions such as pride, shame, hopelessness, guilt, anger, and pity (Weiner, 1985). According to Weiner, attribution to internal factors produces more pride and shame than does attribution to external factors. We experience more pride when we attribute success to ability and effort. Nicholls (1979) found that attribution to high ability following a success often triggers the emotion of pride. This is evident when a student makes a statement like, "I ran a mile; I'm so proud of myself." However, one experiences a greater sense of hopelessness when failure is attributed to ability: "I'll never be able to pass the proficiency test." This type of attribution is one that teachers want students to avoid because it affects the students' future expectations.

However, attribution to external causes tends to minimize achievement-related emotional reactions. If students say they succeeded on a test because they lucked out or people say that luck was responsible for their getting a job, their feeling of pride is minimized. Students might be happy if they made a good grade on an easy test, but would they feel pride as well?

Shift in Expectancies After Success and Failure

What role does attribution play in changing our goal expectancies for success and failure? In a typical change (without accounting for attributions), expectancies tend to rise after success and drop after failure (Weiner, 1986). This tends to confirm the saying that "success breeds success and that failure breeds failure." However, the decisive factor for change in expectancy is the reason given and how stable it is. How shifts in expectancies are affected by success and failure with the resulting attributions are shown in Fig. 2.2.

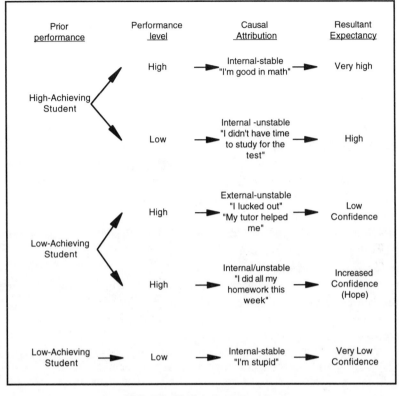

Prior performance	Performance level	Causal Attribution	Resultant Expectancy
High-Achieving Student	High	Internal-stable "I'm good in math"	Very high
	Low	Internal -unstable "I didn't have time to study for the test"	High
Low-Achieving Student	High	External-unstable "I lucked out" "My tutor helped me"	Low Confidence
	High	Internal/unstable "I did all my homework this week"	Increased Confidence (Hope)
Low-Achieving Student	Low	Internal-stable "I'm stupid"	Very Low Confidence

FIG. 2.2 Shift in expectancies.

REFLECTION.   Examine Fig. 2.2. What makes sense to you, what does not? What causes a student to continue to have low expectations after experiencing success?

The first two lines show students who have performed at a high level. The student attributes success to her math ability—a stable factor—thus her expectancy continues to be high. If she has a lower performance and attributes it to insufficient effort—an unstable, controllable cause—her expectancy also continues to be high.

What about a student who has a history of failure? Notice the third pattern in Fig. 2.2. Did it seem logical to you that a student continues to have low confidence after experiencing success? This was the case with Sylvia in this chapter's opening example. This is a pattern that has puzzled teachers. Intuitively, as in Sylvia's case, teachers know the student needs to be successful and will do something to help her attain success on a task. The critical aspect in this example is Sylvia's attribution. If the attribution for success is stable, external, and uncontrollable (e.g., helped by someone), there is no reason to believe that she can be successful next time. This can explain Sylvia's continuing lack of confidence.

The fourth line shows a student who has a history of failure, experiences success, and attributes the success to her effort in the form of practice. Her expectancy for success is on the rise. The example in the fifth line in Fig. 2.2 is the most difficult to change. The student has a history of failure and attributes failure to lack of ability. This student does not believe she can do anything to change her failure situation.

In summary, expectancies are more difficult to change when attribution for failure is made to a stable factor of ability than for an unstable factor of effort (Graham, 1991; Weiner, 1985). This belief pattern is known as *learned helplessness* and is discussed later in this chapter. As is seen, the crucial strategies for teacher intervention are to focus the student's attributions on (a) unstable, controllable factors of effort and strategy use; and (b) ability as knowledge or skills that can be learned. How this can be done is explained later in this chapter.

USING ATTRIBUTIONAL INFORMATION

The first step in using attributional theory is to learn to collect and interpret attributional statements made by students. Attributional information enables teachers to:

- Estimate the extent to which students will expend effort to attend help sessions, practice on needed skills, and so on.
- Give appropriate attributional feedback (i.e., effort, strategies, skills).
- Identify groups of students whose attributions may be especially self-defeating (e.g., females in math and science, students classified with learning disabilities, high-anxiety students).
- Identify *helpless* students to plan strategies for interventions.
- Develop attributional examples to help students understand determinants of success and failure.

Attribution Strategy 2.1 and Exhibit 2.1 suggest ways that teachers can gather information about student reasons for success and failure.

Attribution Strategy 2.1. Collect Attributional Information

- Simply ask students why they succeeded, failed, or improved.
- Some teachers elicit information by having students give their reasons after assignments or exams. See Exhibit 2.1 for an example.
- Attribution information can be obtained through the use of *learning logs* where students keep records and write about their goals, successes, and failures.
- Conduct an attributional task analysis of student performance. Is it because the student cannot or will not? A teacher may believe that a student is not performing well because she has low ability or is lazy. Instead the student may be performing low because she does not have the essential skills.
- Look for clues that will enable you to determine whether the student has the essential skills. Does the student have prerequisite knowledge or skills? Does the task require formal reasoning while the student is functioning at the concrete reasoning level? Does the student have the necessary learning or memory strategies?
- If the student cannot, then teach the prerequisite skill or guide student to the appropriate source of help.

Exhibit 2.1. Student Attributional Rating Form

Score on Test_____

My test score is a: success   nonsuccess

The reasons I received this score include:
1.
2.
3.

How I prepared for this test:
1.
2.
3.

This is what I plan to do next time:

INDIVIDUAL AND SITUATIONAL DIFFERENCES IN ATTRIBUTIONS

The beliefs one has about the cause of success and failure may vary according to age, cultural influences, gender, and type of task. How attributions are related to these factors are discussed in the following sections.

Situational Differences in Attributions

Does the particular type of task or situation influence a student's attributions? Frieze and Snyder (1980) had elementary school-age students judge the following tasks: art project, football, academic tests, and frog catching. Students gave different attributions for different tasks. Ability was believed to be more important for an art project and for winning or losing in football. However, task difficulty was more important for frog catching. The difference in attributions was explained as: Frog catching is an activity that students had no standards or criteria on which to judge their performance, whereas they are familiar with standards for art and football. For academic testing, effort was perceived as the most important cause. An important implication for teachers is to determine the type of attributions for success and failure that students make in their particular subject area or on different types of tasks. If students think ability is the key factor for success in an art project and believe they cannot draw a straight line, the teacher will have to plan instruction so that ability (drawing) is perceived as a skill that can be developed.

Developmental Differences in Attributions

Are attributional patterns associated with age or developmental stage? Indeed, there is a developmental trend in how the relationship between attribution and achievement is viewed, especially involving the respective roles of ability and effort (Nicholls, 1978, 1979). Younger children see effort and ability as the same and believe increased effort leads to increased ability. Prior to age 10, children believe that if two children attain the same outcome, the one who tried harder is the smartest even if he or she got the lowest grade. The child who made the highest grade is said to have tried the hardest even if he or she did not. Young children see ability as more modifiable than do older students.

As children develop cognitively, they increasingly make distinctions between effort and ability and become more accurate about the causes of success and failure. At about age 10, children begin to believe that a child who has low ability must compensate for it by increased effort. However, Nicholls and Miller (1984) pointed out that the developmental pattern of differentiating effort and ability can have negative effects on student motivation. If low achievement is attributed to ability, effort may be viewed as useless and students may actually decrease effort to protect self-worth. Thus, younger children have a more adaptive attributional pattern than older children by believing that increased effort should lead to increased success and ability.

The differentiation of effort and ability can have particularly debilitating effects on the motivation of adolescents who tend to see ability as the most important reason for performance outcomes (Covington, 1984). Because adolescents often judge their ability in comparison to the ability of their peers, this poses a new problem for teachers. Adolescents often equate expending more effort with having less ability. In the classroom, this translates to, "If you have to study a lot, then you must not be smart." Teachers may contribute to this by inadvertently giving more recognition to a student who succeeds with no effort than to one who worked for the success. This is further explained by self-worth theory in chapter 3.

Gender and Attributions

Do males and females differ in their explanations for success and failure? In some cases, yes. Overall, the attributions of girls reflect a lower expectancy pattern (Meece & Courtney, 1992). Studies that examined gender differences found girls are more likely than boys to: (a) attribute failure to their lack of ability even though their achievement is higher (Nicholls, 1979); and (b) make more external attributions (luck) for their successes. Girls tend to underestimate their performance, whereas males tend to overestimate performance (Frieze, 1980).

Gender differences in attributions for ability are particularly prevalent in subjects like mathematics (Wolleat, Pedro, Becker, & Fennema, 1980) and science (Licht, Strader, & Swenson, 1989), which have traditionally been gender typed. Although there may be no differences in actual performance, females tend to have a lower expectancy pattern for their ability. Where do these different expectations begin? Yee and Eccles (1988) found that parents hold different perceptions of their sons' and daughters' math success. Parents rated talent for math as the most important reason for their sons' successes, whereas effort was the most important reason given for their daughters' successes. What is the significance of crediting boys with math talent and girls with effort? When effort was believed to be responsible for success, the child was considered by the parent to be less talented in math. The authors suggested that parents may encourage their sons to continue to develop math talent. In contrast, they may have less confidence in their daughters' ability to be successful in math.

Attributions and Motivation Among Ethnic Groups

Do attributional explanations for success and failure act as an important motivational force in different ethnic groups? According to Graham (1989, 1994), because attributional theory considers the role of thought in determining behavior, it is particularly fruitful in examining motivation in different cultures and ethnic groups. Are attributional belief patterns similar among different ethnic groups? A comparison of poor African-American, Hispanic, Indochinese, and White fifth- and sixth-grade students found similar attribution patterns for all groups (Bempechat, Nakkula, Wu, & Ginsberg, 1996). All groups rated ability as the most important factor for success in math. Graham (1994) suggested that the important issue is to understand the motivational processes, such as attribution, operating within a particular ethnic group. The way in which children, regardless of ethnic group, conceptualize effort and ability is what is important.

Effort and Ability

Graham (1984) compared middle- and low-SES African-American and White students on attributions for failure following a problem-solving task. The middle-class children in both ethnic groups were more likely to attribute failure to lack of effort and maintained consistently higher expectancies for success after experiencing failure. For both groups, this is indicative of an adaptive attributional pattern following failure, similar to that found in research by Diener and Dweck (1978). The findings of this research study are important because they demonstrate the positive motivation pattern of African-American students—a pattern that has received little attention.

As mentioned in chapter 1, Stevenson and Lee (1990) compared beliefs of American and Asian students concerning the role of effort and ability for success in mathematics. They asked mothers in Minnesota, and Japan and Taiwan to assign 10 points among ability, effort, task difficulty, and luck to rank their importance in academic success and school performance. All the mothers assigned the points in the same rank order: (1) effort, (2) ability, (3) task, and (4) luck. Mothers in the United States scored ability and effort as about equal. In contrast, Taiwanese and Japanese mothers assigned effort a higher value than ability. Peak (1993) noted that, in Japanese elementary schools, ability is rarely mentioned whereas effort is consistently portrayed as key to success. In contrast, in the United States, students who try very hard are often labeled *nerd* or *grind*. This attitude is further described in chapter 7.

These perceptions of effort and ability take on increased importance when homework is considered in the context of effort. Japanese and Chinese students spend at least twice the amount of time and effort on homework than do American students (Stevenson & Lee, 1990). American teachers assign less and consider it less valuable. Peak (1993) pointed out that homework reflects teachers' beliefs on whether extra practice makes a difference and whether students are willing to engage in extra effort on behalf of their studies. American parents do not appear to consider good study habits as critical to academic success as do Asian parents.

Implications for Teachers

What can teachers draw from the attributional beliefs among different ethnic groups in terms of classroom practice? Graham (1989) emphasized the importance of teacher feedback in influencing concepts of ability and expectations of minority, low-SES students. Recall the previous discussion of indirect attributional cues. It is important to be aware of feedback that may indirectly convey to students that they have low ability. Graham (1994) suggested that in view of the number of African-American children in negative educational situations, it is especially important to be sensitive to how minorities feel, think, and act in response to nonattainment of goals. Bempechat et al. (1996), concluded that the essential factor is that teachers be aware of the ways students in different ethnic groups view effort and ability. Because similarities were found across ethnic groups, it was further concluded that educational interventions do not necessarily have to be targeted to children differentially based on their ethnic group membership.

Attribution guidelines to keep in mind for students of varying culture ethnicity and gender are presented in Strategy 2.2.

Strategy 2.2. Attribution Guidelines for Gender and Ethnicity

- Listen carefully to student expectations and attributions for performance to identify patterns of attributions that might be gender- or culturally related.
- As a teacher or prospective teacher, examine your own beliefs about competence for subjects like math and science that have been traditionally gender typed. If you are an elementary teacher, do you think of yourself as a math teacher? As a science teacher?
- Provide feedback that helps both males and females make more realistic estimates of their ability.
- Become familiar with cultural value for ability and effort. What is the relative value on effort and ability? The suggestions recommended in Strategy 2.1 can be used to become familiar with beliefs about ability and effort.
- Be prepared to discuss attributional beliefs and their implications with parents.
- Be especially sensitive to giving feedback that might be interpreted by students as sympathy and thus be interpreted as low ability.

TWO ATTRIBUTIONAL CONSEQUENCES: LEARNED HELPLESSNESS AND HELP SEEKING

It was established earlier that the reasons one gives for success and failure have consequences that influence both actions and expectations. Two areas of consequence that are of extreme importance to educators are learned helplessness and help-seeking.

Learned Helplessness

A student who has a history of failure and does not expect this to change will attribute failure to ability—an internal and stable factor. This pattern is characteristic of students classified as *learned helpless*. These individuals expect that their actions will be futile in affecting future outcomes. Consequently, they give up. Learned help-lessness was first investigated in young animals who had been presented with inescapable electric shocks in one situation; when placed in a different situation, they failed to try to escape or avoid the shock (Seligman & Maier, 1967). Animals that demonstrated no connection between their activity and avoiding the shock had learned to be helpless. It was further hypothesized that humans responded the same way; they were passive in situations where they believed their actions would have no effect on what happens to them. In this original explanation, helplessness was viewed as global—af-fecting all domains of one's life. Later research found that people may experience helplessness in one situation and not in others (Alloy, Abramson, Peterson, & Seligman, 1984). This means that a student may feel helpless in learning math but not in learning history.

Helplessness exists in achievement situations when students do not see a connection between their actions and their performance and grades. The important aspect of learned helplessness is how it affects the motivational behavior of students in the face of failure. The attributions a student makes for failure are a bridge between a student's willingness to try again or the student's tendency to give up.

Helpless and Mastery Orientation

In a now-classic study, Diener and Dweck (1978) identified two patterns of responses to failure following success in problem-solving tasks: a maladaptive helpless-orientation and an adaptive mastery-orientation. Children showed different response patterns to failure in their thinking, self-talk, affect, and actions. A comparison of the two response patterns is shown in Table 2.2. Keep in mind that the students in the study had the same failure experience while perform-ing the tasks, but there were two different patterns of response to the failure outcome. The thinking, self-talk, and actions of the help-less-oriented children formed a self-defeating pattern. When failure is attributed to lack of ability, there is a decline in performance. Attribution to lack of effort does not show this decline (Dweck & Goetz, 1978).

Are there ability differences in learned helplessness? Butkowsky and Willows (1980) compared good, average, and poor readers. They found that poor readers had lower expectancies of success on a

TABLE 2. 2

Helpless and Mastery Patterns
in Response to Failure

Helpless	Mastery
• Attribution to personal inadequacies such as deficient memory, problem-solving ability	• Attribution to effort
• Negative affect: dislike for task, anxiety, self-talk irrelevant to task, lack of positive expectation	• Remains optimistic: "I did it before, I can do it again"
• Decrease in effort	• Persistence in difficult tasks, looks for new strategies
• Avoids challenge	• Seeks challenge
• Performance declines in difficult tasks	• Maintains and improves problem-solving strategies

Note. Based on Diener and Dweck (1978) and Dweck and Leggett (1988).

reading task. Poor readers overwhelmingly attributed their failures to lack of ability (68% compared with 13% for average readers and 12% for good readers). They took less responsibility for success, attributing success more to task ease—an external cause—than did the good and average readers. In the face of difficulty, poor readers became less persistent—a self-defeating behavior.

Helplessness was also found when children studied new material that required them to read passages with confusing concepts. In a study by Licht and Dweck (1984), (a) half the children received material with a clear passage, and (b) the other half received a confusing passage. There were no differences between mastery orientation and helpless orientation when the passage was clearly written. In contrast, when the passage was not clear, most of the mastery children reached the learning criterion, whereas only one third of the helpless children did. This investigation is important because some academic subjects, like math, are characterized by constant new learning, which may be initially confusing to students. Mastery students will not be discouraged by the initial difficulty, whereas helpless students immediately lose confidence although they may be equally competent. When teaching new material, teachers can be especially alert for this pattern of helplessness in the face of initial difficulty.

Learned Helplessness and Students With Learning Disabilities

Are some students more prone to experience a sense of helplessness? Students particularly susceptible to the pattern of learned helplessness are those students who are identified as having learning disabilities (LD; Licht, 1983). Children with LD experience much failure over a long period of time on a variety of school tasks. As a result, these children come to doubt their academic abilities, with the accompanying belief that nothing they can do will help them be successful. This is followed by the self-defeating response of decreasing effort. Children with LD have been found to exhibit the following characteristics of the learned helplessness pattern (Licht, 1983):

- score lower than non-LD on measures of self-esteem and perceptions of ability;
- are more likely to attribute difficulty with tasks to lack of ability;
- are less likely to attribute failure to insufficient effort; and
- lower their expectations for future success and display greater decline in expectation following failure.

It is important for teachers to be aware of the characteristics of helplessness because learned helplessness may explain the students' apparent lack of motivation. How can a teacher identify a helpless pattern? What can a teacher do to lessen the likelihood of helplessness and help students who have this tendency? Butkowsky and Willows (1980) suggested that educators must begin to rethink failure as a necessary component of the learning process and not as a damaging experience to be avoided. Strategy 2.3 provides guidelines for assisting students who show patterns of helplessness.

Help Seeking

Do you ask for help when you need it or do you have the view, "I have to do it myself, no one can do it except me"? Why do teachers observe that students who are most in need of help do not attend help sessions when they are provided? This may reflect a view of help-seeking as dependence or independence. Nelson-Le Gall (1985) pro-

---

Strategy 2.3. Assisting Helpless Students

- Observe student reactions to failure to identify helpless patterns. Clues may be in what students say and how they approach tasks: (a) Are their explanations optimistic or pessimistic? (b) Do they easily give up or try new approaches? (c) Do they fail to try at all? (d) Are they generally passive?
- The past history of students may provide clues. Students who have a history of failure may be especially prone to helpless patterns.
- Teachers can anticipate new learning, in math or other subjects, which may be confusing at first to students. Then they can help students by:
  —establishing an attribution that all students can learn math;
  —attributing the learning to effort and ability such as "I understand conversion to metric now because I worked the extra problems and practiced the conversions everyday last week";
  —teaching the students learning strategies; and
  —structuring the material so it is more readily acquired by students;
- Attribution retraining is recommended for students who have a pattern of failure (Reid & Borkowski, 1987). This training is described in the final section of this chapter.
- The *LINKS MODEL* described in chapter 4 integrates several motivational concepts to address helplessness.

---

posed that, instead, we should emphasize the importance of seeing help-seeking as instrumental to achievement. We have learned from research that seeking help from others can have both negative and positive connotations (Newman, 1990, 1991). Help seeking is positive when students seek help to make a change in their learning. Help seeking also may be seen as threatening if the student thinks it is a sign of low ability. In this case, there is a personal cost to seeking help.

The attributional process is an important factor in whether help seeking is seen as positive or negative and consequently whether students attend academic help sessions. Ames and Lau (1982) identified factors that affected the extent that college students attended help sessions:

- Low-performing students were more likely to attend help sessions if they were given specific positive information about the effects of the sessions (e.g., "students who attended improved their performance").

- Students who attributed success to effort were more likely to attend.
- Students who did not seek help used more external attributions for failure, such as "tricky test questions," and used these external reasons as excuses.

Newman's (1990, 1991) investigations of help seeking among children in Grades 3, 5, and 7 has provided a fuller understanding of help seeking. For example, who seeks help, high or low self-esteem individuals? For all grades, the higher the perceived competence of the children, the less they felt there were personal costs to help seeking (e.g., being thought of as low ability). Students with low self-esteem were especially unlikely to seek help, whereas those with high self-esteem were more likely to seek help. Similar results were obtained by Nelson-Le Gall and Jones (1990) for average-achieving African-American children.

Newman also found differences between younger and older students in views about help seeking. Seventh graders were more aware than younger children that negative fallout might result from help seeking (e.g., embarrassment). However, older children were also more likely than younger to believe that smart classmates rather than "dumb" ones ask questions of the teacher.

Help seeking by college students showed a pattern similar to that of children. Karabenick and Knapp (1991) found that students with low self-esteem were more threatened by seeking help. One important and perhaps surprising finding was that students who use more learning strategies are more likely to seek help when needed, whereas students who use fewer strategies are less likely to seek help when needed. This attitude presents a double-bind for those needing help. Not only do they lack the necessary strategies for success, but they do not seek the needed study assistance. The authors concluded that students need to learn to judge when they need help and that help seeking should be included in learning strategy and motivation programs.

These findings on help seeking are important for teachers and counselors so they can plan ways to get students to attend help sessions or seek help in counseling when needed. Nelson-Le Gall (1985) emphasized the need to think of help seeking as an adaptive coping strategy rather than as a self-threatening activity. Some ways to accomplish this are listed in Strategy 2.4.

Strategy 2.4. Help Seeking

- The overriding task is to have students view help seeking, when needed, as a smart move instead of a dumb one.
- Establish a classroom climate where students are encouraged to ask questions.
- Document attendance and improved performance as a result of the help sessions and show this to students.
- Be sure students who have improved after attending help sessions attribute the improvement to the help sessions.
- Teach students a self-talk script to practice asking teachers for help in classes where they were having problems, as one middle school teacher did. See chapter 5 for self-talk examples.

TEACHER ATTRIBUTIONAL BELIEFS AND STUDENT PERFORMANCE

How do teachers' attributions for student performance affect student motivation? The beliefs that teachers hold about the role of ability and effort affect their responses to their students which, in turn, affect motivation. Weiner and Kukla (1970) conducted a study in which prospective teachers were given information about the ability level, usual effort of the students, and outcome and were asked to assign rewards.

REFLECTION.   How would you reward students with the following patterns of ability, effort, and success? Evaluate them on a 10-point scale from +5 (*highest reward*) to -5 (*maximum punishment*). Compare your evaluations with the results of the study and think about the reasons for your rating.

high ability	high effort	successful
high ability	high effort	failure
high ability	low effort	success
high ability	low effort	failure
low ability	high effort	success
low ability	high effort	failure
low ability	low effort	success
low ability	low effort	failure

Results reveal that the students who were characterized as having high effort were rewarded more for success and punished less for failure; those characterized as having low ability–high effort, success received higher rewards; and those with high ability–low effort failure received the most punishment. Weiner (1992) concluded that students who do not try evoke the most anger from teachers. Students who had low ability but tried hard and succeeded were viewed more favorably. He suggested that these findings might be explained in terms of our culture's value system, which tends to value the person who is able to overcome handicaps and succeed.

In another study, Medway (1979) examined the reasons teachers gave for the problems of students whom they had referred for psychological services. The results indicate that teachers held student characteristics to be more responsible for problems than what the teacher did. In addition, they attributed learning problems to the students' ability and behavior problems to students' difficulties at home. Consistent with the findings of Weiner and Kukla (1970), teachers placed more emphasis on effort cues in their responses to students. For example, teachers who attributed student problems to lack of effort gave more negative feedback to those students in the form of warnings and criticism. A study by Tollefson, Melvin, and Thippavajjala (1990) provided additional insight to teacher beliefs about effort. The reason most frequently given by teachers for unsatisfactory work was low effort. Although teachers indicated that low-effort students could improve, they viewed effort as stable, not expecting students to be successful in the long run.

Teacher attributions have also been examined as they relate to special education students. According to Palmer (1983), teacher attributions are influenced both by special education labels and previous performance of students. Generally, teachers attributed the failure of Educable Mentally Retarded (EMR) children to low ability and attributed the failure of children who have not been so labeled to either low effort or an external cause (Rolison & Medway, 1985). These studies suggest that the labels assigned to students may influence teachers' expectation for their performance. It is important to be aware of this possibility to avoid unrealistically low expectations. Awareness of beliefs about special education students is increasingly important as these students move into inclusive classrooms.

From these studies, it can be seen that teachers' beliefs about the causes of students' performance and behavior can affect the feedback and evaluation of these students.

REFLECTION.   Explore your beliefs about the role of effort and ability by thinking through Exhibit 2.2. What reasons do you give yourself for student performance and behavior? What cues do you use? Think about how these beliefs might influence your evaluation of students, your expectations, and the feedback you provide them.

Exhibit 2.2. Effort Reflection: Exploring Teacher Beliefs on Effort and Ability

OBJECTIVE: To make explicit your present view of effort and to operationalize effort in concrete terms

ACTIVITY

1. Compared to ability, state how important student effort is to you. Do you think of effort more as a character trait or as a habit that is learned?

2. List student behaviors that mean effort to you in your classroom.

3. List what you think students mean when they say they tried hard.

4. Compare your meaning of effort with that of students.

5. What is the reward for trying in your classroom?

6. Make a list of your effort strategies. These can be shared with your students.

ATTRIBUTIONAL RETRAINING

Types of causal attributions typically given by students to account for success and failure have revealed that attributions can be either adaptive or debilitating to one's future performance. What can be done when students display self-defeating attributions, such as thought patterns and strategies associated with learned helplessness? The most effective approach is known as *attribution retraining*. Retraining generally means an attempt to restructure a student's maladaptive explanations for failure and success to adaptive ones. The desired outcome is to increase student persistence and positive expectations. A number of different approaches have been developed: effort retraining, self-instruction, and antecedent information.

Effort Attribution Retraining

The importance of effort has been a central focus of attribution training. Many of these change programs involve two stages: (a) students achieve success; and (b) following success, students are taught to attribute success to effort.

Attributions to effort are emphasized because effort is internal, controllable, and usually perceived as unstable. In a groundbreaking study, Dweck (1975) carried out training for 12 children identified as *helpless*. Prior to training, all children showed a severe decline in performance following failure. The training experiment involved two conditions: (a) success only where children attained success with no attribution modification; and (b) success where children were taught to take responsibility for failure and attribute it to effort.

The results of the study reveal that children who were taught to attribute failure to insufficient effort continued to persist even after failure on the tasks. The subjects in the success-only treatment did not show any consistent improvement in their persistence after failure. This again explains the expectation pattern shown on Fig. 2.2 (and by Sylvia), where the student continued to have low expectations after experiencing success. No connection was made by the student between effort and success. Andrews and Debus (1978) modified the training procedures by adding positive reinforcement in the form of verbal praise for attributions to effort. Their results support Dweck's (1975) finding that students who attribute failure to effort persist longer. The authors suggested that systematic reinforcement for effort as given in this study may be used to enhance adaptive attributions.

Self-Instruction

Another approach to retraining taught eighth graders self-instruction procedures to change causal attributions (Reiher & Dembo, 1984).

Students were instructed to give themselves instructions such as, "I really want to do my best effort here," as they performed a task. The training was effective in getting students to attribute success and failure more to internal causes of effort and ability. They also persisted longer in the tasks over time. The authors concluded that the self-instruction procedures used to change attributions are feasible for teachers to use in the classroom. This training is described in chapter 5.

Antecedent Information

A more recent approach to attributional training has used antecedent information to precede and determine causal thought. Possible attributions for success are given to students in advance of a learning activity. In one study, college students were given antecedent information, via a videotape, for succeeding in a difficult class (Van Overwalle, Segabarth, & Goldchstein, 1989). In the tape, students who had taken the course previously are seen discussing their learning difficulties, the causes of the difficulties, and how they improved their performance. Students who saw the video models improved more than the control group on both the next exam and all exams the next year. The training was more effective for students who attributed their initial failure to intelligence; it had less impact on those who attributed their failure to strategies. This is a most important factor. By hearing the video models talk about difficulties they experienced and how they improved, the experimental students came to view intelligence as unstable—an adaptive belief. Strategies for providing antecedent attributions are presented in Strategy 2.5.

Strategy 2.5. Establish Antecedent Attributions

- Communicate the expectation that study strategies and effort are the key for learning (this minimizes unknown or mystery attributions when students say they do not know why they made a low grade). Supply students with strategic attributions when they do not have them for both success and failure.
- Establish a climate for help seeking; one aspect of being smart is knowing when to seek help. If needed, let students practice how to seek help though role-playing or a self-talk script asking the teacher for help.
- Establish that all students can learn the particular subject.

Retraining for Students With Learning Disabilities

Much attribution retraining has been directed toward students with LD because these students often display helplessness (Shelton, Anastopaulos, & Linden, 1985). The retraining procedure used models on audiotape. Prior to attempting each task, the children listened to a tape of another child attributing both success and failure to effort. It was found that training consisting of only 1 hour per week altered students' attributions and their task persistence in a positive direction.

The most powerful intervention occurs when attribution retraining is combined with cognitive strategy instruction (e.g., memory strategies and reading comprehension strategies such as summarization; Borkowski, 1988). Borkowski and colleagues have conducted a number of studies to address commonplace learning impairments in memory and reading comprehension of inefficient learners (learners who fail to use strategies where it would be helpful to do so). In one study, students with LD (ages 10–14) received six lessons about both reading summarization strategies and the role of effort in using strategies (Borkowski, Weyhing, & Carr, 1988). There were four groups in the experiment:

1. Reading Strategies Plus Complex Attribution (strategies and attributions in two phases; see Fig. 2.3),
2. Reading Strategies Plus Attribution,
3. Attribution Control, and
4. Reading Strategies Control.

Groups who received attributional training plus strategies scored significantly better on reading comprehension than the two control groups (about a 50% gain compared with 15%). The researchers

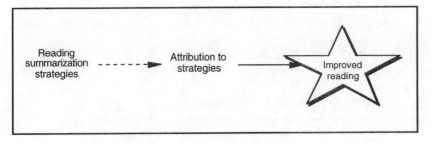

FIG. 2.3. Strategies plus attribution.

concluded that training students in strategies without simultaneous training in attribution is not effective for students who have lengthy records of poor self-esteem and negative attributional beliefs about the importance of personal control. Furthermore, the authors concluded that it is important to include specific attributional training in each content area. Otherwise students are likely to use the strategies only in the content area where they were trained. Based on a retraining procedure from this study, Fulk and Mastropieri (1990) developed steps for retraining strategies (Table 2.3). Examples of strategies taught included summarizing a passage in reading or solutions steps in math.

Guidelines for Attributional Feedback

The goal of attributional feedback is to focus the student on effort (operationalized), strategies, and ability/skill as the reason for success and on lack of effort or strategy use as the cause of failure. "That's great, Julie" does not give Julie specific information about her performance. Effort is operationalized by linking how the student tried to the improved performance (e.g., "Good job, you now

TABLE 2.3

Steps for Attribution/Strategy Training

Step	Strategy
1	Describe the purpose of the new strategy.
2	Describe the important role of effort in attributing outcomes to controllable causes.
3	Provide examples and nonexamples of how the strategy works.
4	Provide models of positive attributions combined with strategy use (e.g., "I got this one right because I used the strategy and tried hard").
5	Have students practice combined strategy–attribution sequence with feedback (e.g., "That's great! You worked hard to use the strategy and got the right answer").
6	Have students do independent practice of strategy with continued monitoring and corrective feedback as needed (e.g., "Remember to attribute your outcomes to your effort plus these steps").
7	Conduct formative evaluation.

Note. From "Training Positive Attitudes: I Tried Hard and Did Well," by B. J. Fulk and M. A. Mastropieri, 1990, *Intervention in Schools and Clinics, 26*, pp. 79–83. Copyright © (1990) by PRO-ED, Inc. Reprinted by permission.

know how to use the web browser to find a source"). The following are guidelines for attributional feedback:

- Give attributional feedback that links past achievement with effort to promote task involvement, skill development, and self-efficacy. Stressing only future achievement does not have same effect (Schunk, 1982).
- The sequence in which attributional feedback is given makes a difference. For difficult tasks, the early feedback should be to effort; as skills develop, the feedback should shift to ability (Schunk, 1984).
- Effort feedback is more productive for underachieving students (Ho & McMurtrie, 1991). Ability feedback may promote confusion for students who believe they lack ability.
- Cooperative learning has been found to facilitate more productive attributions. This may be even more effective if students are taught to give attributional feedback to each other. Strategy 2.6 gives ways to practice attributional feedback.

Strategy 2.6. Practice Attributional Feedback

- Providing students (or anyone else) with attributional feedback requires practice. Begin by writing attributional feedback statements for effort, ability, and strategy use for a successful experience, and then for failure. Examples of attributional feedback are:
  —Effort: "Julie, that's great, you got it right because of the extra practice you did in dividing fractions."
  —Ability: "Julie, that's great, you really understand how to divide fractions now."
  —Strategies: "Julie, you got it right because you applied steps in order, then checked your work."

When the Outcome is Failure

- Failure will occur and the attribution for failure is important in terms of the student's future expectation for success. If the student attributes her failure to "I didn't use the right strategy," she is more likely to be motivated to try again than is the student who believes she failed because "I'm not one of the smart ones." One must be cautious when assigning lack of effort as the cause of failure. Be sure the task was within the student's zone of proximal development (i.e., her capability of performing with assistance). When students indicate that they do not know why they failed, the teacher can suggest a strategy to be able to accomplish the task and in turn attribute success to the strategy. "Shannon, I noticed you did not carefully edit your essay and revise. When you attend to this, your essay will be much better."

DEVELOPING ADAPTIVE ATTRIBUTIONS

In summary, findings from the studies in attributional training offer possibilities for a set of tools for intervening in some of the most difficult motivational problems. Strategy 2.1 gave suggestions for collecting attributional information. With this information, a teacher can play a major role in devising strategies to help students develop adaptive attributions, which lead to persistence and higher achievement. This chapter concludes with Strategy 2.7, which has suggestions for helping students develop adaptive attributions.

REVIEW OF MAJOR POINTS

1. Attribution is a cognitive theory that considers a person's beliefs about causes of outcomes and how those beliefs influence expectations and behavior. Causes of outcomes include ability, effort, task difficulty, strategies, and luck. Three dimensions are internal–external, stable–unstable, and controllable–uncontrollable.

2. Knowledge of how students use these attributions to account for success and failure in school settings (academic and sports) can help teachers predict the expectancies held by students and plan strategies for intervention when needed.

3. Attributions are influenced by direct and indirect cues. A direct cue is results on a test. Indirect cues may be conveyed by teacher communication—praise and blame, sympathy and anger, and help and neglect—and labels like *high ability, low achieving, slow*, and *average*.

4. Attributional beliefs produce emotional reactions such as pride, shame, hopelessness, guilt, anger, and pity. Attribution to high ability after success often triggers the emotion of pride; a greater sense of hopelessness may be experienced when failure is attributed to ability.

5. Attributions play a role in changing goal expectancies for success and failure. The decisive factor for change in expectancy is the reason given and its stability. Expectancies are more difficult to change when failure is attributed to ability as a stable factor.

6. Attributions for success and failure are related to the cognitive level of children; younger children see effort and ability as the same and believe increased effort leads to increased ability. As children

Strategy 2.7. Developing Adaptive Attributions

Operationalize and Reward Effort

- **Make sure that you and your students have the same perceptions of effort; that you are in agreement about what *try* means**. Use Exhibit 2.2 to analyze beliefs about effort. At the beginning of the school year, have your students discuss the meaning of *effort* so there is a common agreement on what it means in your classroom.
- **"Take the magic out."** Give them a strategy. Emphasize effort as a strategy that can be developed. Operationalize effort as more than time spent on a task. Examples include: specific memory strategies, reading comprehension strategies, practice, and seeking appropriate help.
- **Productive Effort.** Help your students differentiate between productive and nonproductive effort. When a student does poorly and says "But I worked so hard," ask her to tell you what she did while working hard.
- **Link effort to outcome.** Establish an evaluation system so effort pays off for the student. Examples are: tie student practice/trials and homework to exam grades. Make effort the number of trials. Use feedback that specifies what the student did that led to success or failure. Make sure students see the relationship between homework and test scores.
- **Help students shift their criteria for success and failure from how their peers performed to their own prior performance**. Adolescents especially attribute success and failure to ability. "If you were smart, you would not have to study." Have them keep records of their test scores and other grades so they can see their own progress.
- **Focus on strategies and effort**. Praise or reinforce *mastery* attributional patterns. Begin this in the early grades. Use students' errors as an opportunity to teach them to handle failure, adjust strategies, or apply a stronger effort toward a particular concept.
- **Student Responsibility**. If test results are good, get students to say what they did that contributed to the grade; if bad, discuss what they might have done differently. Be sure this relates to a criterion or standard, not a comparison to other students.

Shift Perception of Ability From Stable to Unstable

- **Help students develop attributions that ability is a skill or content that can be learned through instruction, practice, and feedback** (e.g., math, computers, writing, reading, music, and tennis are all areas that one learns).
- **Make students aware that new learning is frequently confusing at first.** In particular, *helpless* students need to understand this because they are likely to believe they will never understand the new concept or procedure. Show them that learning is acquired in incremental steps. Proximal goals (chap. 4) and self-talk (chap. 5) are useful for this.
- **Have peers model antecedent attributions and coping strategies either through video or audio training**. Collect examples of attributions as indicated in Exhibit 2.1 and place them on bulletin boards and/or in student informational material.

develop cognitively, they increasingly make distinctions between effort and ability.

7. Gender differences identified in attributions for success and failure include the following: girls are more likely than boys to attribute failure to their lack of ability, although their achievement is higher, and make more external attributions (luck) for their successes; girls tend to underestimate their performance, whereas males tend to overestimate performance.

8. Similar attribution patterns have been found among different ethnic groups. A comparison of poor African-American, Hispanic, Indochinese, and White fifth- and sixth-grade students found that all groups rated ability as the most important factor for success in math. The ways in which children, regardless of ethnic group, conceptualize effort and ability is the important issue.

9. Learned helplessness, a consequence of attributional explanations, exists when individuals expect that their actions will be futile in affecting future outcomes. The important aspect of learned helplessness is how it affects the motivational behavior of students in the face of failure. Two patterns of responses to failure were identified: maladaptive helpless orientation and adaptive mastery orientation. Mastery students are not discouraged by the initial difficulty, whereas helpless students immediately lose confidence although they may be equally competent. Students with LD are particularly susceptible to a pattern of learned helplessness because they have experienced much failure over a long period of time on a variety of school tasks.

10. The attributional process is an important factor in whether help seeking is seen as positive or negative. For all grades, the higher the perceived competence of the children, the less they felt there were personal costs to help seeking. Students with low self-esteem were especially unlikely to seek help, whereas individuals with high self-esteem were more likely to seek help. It is important for teachers to emphasize the need to think of help seeking as an adaptive coping strategy rather than as a self-threatening activity.

11. The beliefs that teachers hold about the role of ability and effort affect their responses to their students. Students who do not try evoke the most anger from teachers, whereas students who have low ability but try hard and succeed are likely to be viewed more favorably.

12. Attribution retraining generally means an attempt to restructure a student's maladaptive explanations for failure and success to adaptive ones, with the desired outcome to increase student persistence and positive expectations. Approaches to attributional retraining include effort retraining, self-instruction, and antecedent information. The most powerful intervention occurs when attribution retraining is combined with cognitive strategy instruction.

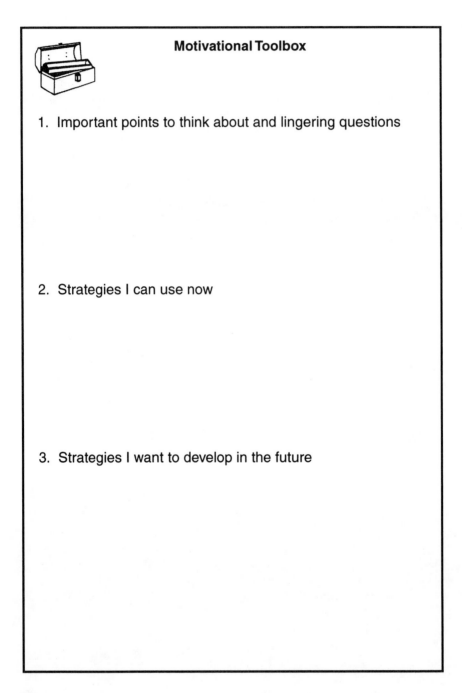

Motivational Toolbox

1. Important points to think about and lingering questions

2. Strategies I can use now

3. Strategies I want to develop in the future

CHAPTER 3

Concepts of Ability
and Motivation

Schools must ... foster a will to learn and to relearn ... students must be encouraged to believe in themselves and in the validity of their own thought processes ...they must develop a sense of personal effectiveness ... teachers must foster both confidence and high achievement in their students ... confidence and competence must increase together for either to prosper.

—Covington and Beery (1976, pp. 4–5)

The central concern in this chapter is students' perceptions and evaluations of their ability and how it affects their motivation. In every aspect of life, whether people are thinking about trying out for a play or an athletic team, worrying about taking a test, applying for a job, comparing themselves to other people, or deciding what courses to take, they are evaluating their ability. How students evaluate their ability has important implications for their expectancies for success in future tasks.

SELF-PERCEPTIONS OF ABILITY: AN OVERVIEW

Self-perception of ability is a major component of many current perspectives of motivation: perceived competence, expectancy-value, self-efficacy, self-worth, and goal orientation (Pajares, 1996). These beliefs about ability are closely related to the expectancies students have for success on an upcoming task and values they hold for the task (Bandura, 1986; Meece, Eccles, & Wigfield, 1990). When students believe they can succeed in a task or subject, they are more likely to undertake it and their value for it increases (Bandura, 1986; Mac Iver, Stipek, & Daniels, 1991).

An important question is whether children perceive themselves as equally competent in all areas. The prevalent view today is that children as young as age 8 can differentiate abilities among the domains of cognitive or academic competence, physical competence in sports, social competence with peers, and general competence (Harter, 1982). Self-perceptions of ability are not only domain-specific, but also distinct for different subject areas. Students might have a high self-concept of their ability in math, but a low one in language arts (Marsh, Byrne, & Shavelson, 1988).

The primary focus of this chapter is on social-cognitive perspectives of self-efficacy, self-worth, and goal orientation. Research on these three topics directly impacts teacher practice. Important in each of the theories are the criteria that one uses to evaluate competence. To begin this focus, consider the varying beliefs that students in Ms. Foster's science class hold about their capabilities. Some beliefs will help students improve and succeed in school, whereas others are likely to limit development of their capabilities. Although Ms. Foster is aware of some beliefs, she is unaware of subtle clues about other beliefs with their motivational implications. Beliefs about capability may be inferred by the statements and behaviors listed in Fig. 3.1. All the students made self-evaluations about their competences or abilities. However, there are important differences in the source of the evaluation and the confidence expressed by each student. Self-efficacy is the first area explored to better understand self-evaluations of competence.

SELF-EFFICACY: EVALUATION OF COMPETENCE

Self-efficacy is a judgment students make about their capability to accomplish a specific future task (Bandura, 1986). A key assumption underlying self-efficacy is that there is a difference between having the skills to perform a task and using the skills in a variety of circumstances. How does this assumption affect motivation? According to Bandura (1986), there are two types of expectancies in thinking about possible outcomes: outcome expectancy and self-efficacy expectancy. An *outcome expectancy* is an individual's anticipation that a given action can lead to a certain positive or negative outcome ("If I use effective learning strategies, I will make at least a B in the course").

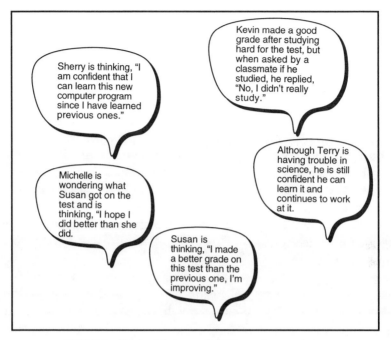

FIG. 3.1. Students' views of ability and competence.

An *efficacy expectancy* is a person's judgment of his or her capability to perform the skills required for the given outcome ("Will I be able to use the learning strategies needed to make a B in the course?") The most influential factor is the efficacy expectancy—how effective will *I* be? Self-efficacy judgments are important factors affecting motivation in areas ranging from academic tasks to career choice to athletic performance.

Self-efficacy may also reflect a social judgment of confidence or collective efficacy, as well as an individual one. *Collective efficacy* is defined by Bandura (1997) as "a group's shared belief in its conjoint capabilities to organize and execute the courses of action necessary to produce given levels of attainment" (p. 477). In a cooperative task, group members hold beliefs about the capability of the group as a whole to be successful, as well as their beliefs about their personal capability. More effective groups will have a strong sense of collective efficacy.

Self-Efficacy Influences in Academic Tasks

Self-efficacy judgments, whether accurate or inaccurate, help determine (a) which activities to undertake and which to avoid, and (b) how much effort we will expend and how long we will persist in the face of obstacles (Bandura, 1986). We are more likely to undertake tasks we believe we have the skills to handle, but avoid tasks we believe require greater skills than we possess. For example, students who have doubts about their math ability are likely to avoid taking math courses whenever possible. In addition, the stronger the self-efficacy, the harder individuals will try to accomplish a task. This is particularly important when facing difficulties (Bandura, 1986). Individuals with strong self-efficacy are less likely to give up than are those who are paralyzed with doubts about their capabilities.

How the belief one holds about ability influences strategies was illustrated in a study by Collins (as cited in Bandura, 1993). Collins selected children at low, medium, and high levels of math ability and gave them hard problems to solve. In each ability group, there were children who were confident about their math ability and those who had self-doubts. Children's beliefs about their capability, not their actual ability, proved to be the factor that differentiated the problem-solving strategies used by children in each group. Confident children chose to rework more problems and were quicker to abandon ineffective strategies than were children who had doubts about ability. In fact, perceived self-efficacy was a better predictor of positive attitudes toward mathematics than was actual ability. This confirmed that self-efficacy is not just a reflection of one's ability, but the beliefs one holds about that ability. As Bandura (1993) pointed out, people may perform poorly either because (a) they lack the skills, or (b) they have the skills, but lack the confidence that will allow them to use them well.

The level of self-efficacy is a key aspect in self-regulatory strategies used by students. Examples of research findings are:

- Students with higher self-efficacy set higher goals and expend more effort toward the achievement of these goals (Zimmerman, Bandura, & Martinez-Pons, 1992).
- Academic self-efficacy increases in subject areas as students progress through school (Zimmerman & Martinez-Pons, 1990).

- Students with higher self-efficacy use more cognitive and meta-cognitive strategies and persist longer (Pintrich & De Groot, 1990).

Is there an optimal level of efficacy beliefs? Bandura (1986) suggested that the most useful efficacy judgments are those that are slightly above what a person can perform on a specific task.

Sources of Self-Efficacy Judgments

What factors influence a people's beliefs about their capabilities? Beliefs about capabilities come from four sources of information: prior task accomplishments, vicarious experiences (observing others), verbal persuasion, and physiological states (Bandura,1986). These sources are not equally influential. They are described in order of their power to influence self-efficacy (see Fig. 3.2).

Task Accomplishments

Remember the students' thoughts at the beginning of the chapter. Sherry is confident that she can learn a new computer program because she was successful at learning one previously. That is an example of self-efficacy that is based on her personal experience—a successful task performance in the past. Personal experience is one of the most influential sources of efficacy information. It follows then that successes tend to raise efficacy expectations—whereas failures tend to lower them. It is especially detrimental to a sense of confidence if failure occurs early in the learning experience unless it is attributed to an internal–unstable factor, such as lack of effort (Bandura, 1986).

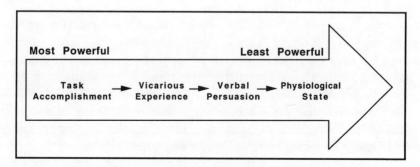

FIG. 3.2. Sources of self-efficacy beliefs.

Vicarious Experiences

A second source of self-efficacy beliefs comes from a vicarious experience, such as observing the performance of others. Although a vicarious experience is not as powerful as a previous successful performance, seeing a model is especially useful when individuals have limited skills or are attempting to learn a new skill. Students observing a model successfully perform in a threatening situation are more likely to develop an expectation that they can acquire the same skill. Not only is the model demonstrating the skill, but he or she is also demonstrating coping strategies, such as persistence or trying several ways to attack the same problem (Schunk & Hanson, 1985). Live models as well as video or audio models can be used to provide vicarious learning.

Verbal Persuasion

"You can do it." How many times have you heard those encouraging words when attacking a new problem? Verbal persuasion is most effective when people already have some degree of evidence that they are capable. Although telling a student "you can do it" is a widely used strategy, the effect on increasing efficacy expectations is likely to be weaker than feedback that comes from direct or vicarious experience. In other words, telling students they can learn to write is not as influential as the direct experience of successfully writing an essay. It is important to note that both positive and negative messages affect a sense of efficacy. However, negative messages have an even greater influence on lowering efficacy expectations than positive messages do on increasing efficacy (Bandura, 1986).

Physiological State

People also get information about their competence from the physiological responses of their bodies. Physical symptoms such as sweating or rapid heart rate may provide clues about efficacy (Schunk, 1989). Think about the last time you stood up to make a presentation. Too much anxiety in approaching a task may lead to either avoiding the presentation or negative thinking about your possible performance. Anxiety can interfere with perceptions of self-efficacy; this in turn interferes with performance.

How can knowing about sources of self-efficacy help teachers? Knowing the types of knowledge that students use for information about their capabilities can help teachers provide appropriate feedback and devise strategies to enhance students' self-efficacy. Remember what students *think* they can do is a better indicator of successful achievement than their actual ability.

Identification and Awareness of Efficacy Beliefs

How can teachers use self-efficacy knowledge to strengthen motivation and achievement? Pajares and Miller (1994) believed that identifying, understanding, and altering students' inaccurate efficacy beliefs will provide teachers with insight about student motivation that goes beyond teachers' awareness of students' prior knowledge in a subject. Teaching strategies that flow from this awareness of student efficacy can enhance self-efficacy and increase student achievement.

Students enter learning situations with different beliefs about their capabilities (Schunk, 1989). Are there areas where students' judgments of capability are consistently low or underestimated? Yes, mathematics is one area where beliefs about capability are influential. Researchers consistently find that females have lower self-efficacy in mathematics than males (Pajares & Miller, 1994; Randhawa, Beamer, & Lundberg, 1993). Pajares and Miller pointed out that actual ability in mathematics does not correspond to what undergraduate students believe about their capability. Instead of making choices on actual ability, students' beliefs about their capability are a critical factor in making career choices, as well as asking questions such as, "Will my major field require math?" "Will my teaching field specialty be math?" "I will be an elementary teacher because I know a lot of math won't be required."

Another area where students have consistently exhibited a low sense of self-efficacy is special education (Gresham, 1984). For example, when self-efficacy comparisons were made among mildly handicapped, nonhandicapped, and gifted children, mildly handicapped children experienced lower academic achievement and social self-efficacy than nonhandicapped and gifted children (Gresham, Evans, & Elliott 1988). Gresham (1984) explained that this persistent finding of low self-efficacy among mildly handicapped children is due to the history of academic and social failures they have experienced. Becoming aware of low self-efficacy leads to the next step, what might teachers do to promote self-efficacy of students?

Strengthening Self-Efficacy

What is known about strengthening self-efficacy? A range of strategies that can be used by teachers to enhance self-efficacy have been identified (Schunk, 1991a). Strategies that teachers can use to influence self-efficacy include: (a) goals and feedback, (b) rewards, (c) self-instruction for verbalization of strategies, (d) participant modeling, and (e) various combinations of these strategies. Keep in mind that self-efficacy, skill development, and strategy use go hand in hand—whether it be math problem solving, soccer skills, or expository writing. Students learn strategies that enable them to develop skills resulting in increased self-efficacy.

Goals, Feedback, Rewards, and Verbalization

Because task accomplishment is the most powerful source of self-efficacy information, an important approach is to use strategies that can strengthen task accomplishment. The strategies of goal setting, feedback, rewards, and self-talk or verbalization were used in various combinations to help students categorized as learning disabled or remedial to strengthen self-efficacy.

Schunk and Cox (1986) investigated the combination of strategy verbalization and effort feedback on the performance and self-efficacy of students with learning disabilities. While solving subtraction problems, students verbalized or said the task steps aloud to themselves; they were then given feedback that their successes were due to their effort. The combination of verbalization and effort–feedback led to problem-solving successes, higher self-efficacy, and subtraction skills. The authors believe the two strategies—verbalization and effort feedback—serve different purposes. Verbalization was useful for training students to systematically use the task strategy. Giving students feedback that effort is responsible for success communicated that they are developing skills and that they can continue to perform well with hard work.

The importance of feedback for enhancing self-efficacy may sometimes be overlooked by a teacher. Pajares and Johnson (1994) conducted a study in a language arts course for preservice teachers. The students received feedback from their teacher on attempting and completing writing tasks, but they did not receive feedback on their specific writing skills. The end of course assessment revealed that although the students improved on writing skills, their self-efficacy judgments about their skills did not increase. The authors concluded that when teachers note a growth or decline in skills (in this case, writing), it is imperative for them give the students feedback about their specific skill development. As emphasized earlier, students will make future judgments not just on their actual skills, but also on their perception of their competence in using the skill. These perceptions of self-efficacy are more likely to increase with specific teacher feedback.

Participant Modeling

Vicarious experience is the second most powerful source of self-efficacy. The most frequent form of vicarious experience for students is seeing a model (another student or teacher) perform a skill they are attempting to learn. Who is a more effective model, a peer or teacher or a mastery or coping model?

Peer or Teacher Model? Schunk and Hanson (1985) had students, ages 8 to 10, observe either a peer or teacher model solving fractions on a videotape. Children who had observed a peer model had higher self-efficacy and achievement scores on the math assessment than did students who had observed the teacher model. The authors concluded that the increase may have been because the children saw themselves as more similar to the peer model. The use of peer models is especially recommended for enhancement of self-efficacy among low-achieving students who are more doubtful about attaining the level of competence demonstrated by the teacher.

Mastery or Coping Model? Models can reflect either mastery or coping behaviors (Schunk & Hanson, 1985; Schunk, Hanson, & Cox, 1987). A mastery model demonstrates a task at a high level of expertise with a high level of confidence. In contrast, a coping model demonstrates the task along with the difficulties they experienced and the strategies (e.g., effort) they used to overcome the difficulties. The effectiveness of coping versus mastery peer models was compared by Schunk, Hanson, and Cox (1987). The two types of models demonstrated strategies as follows.

1. Peer coping model: Made errors at first and verbalized negative statements that reflected self-efficacy (e.g., "I'm not sure I can do

this"). The teacher then gave a prompt (e.g., "What do you do when denominators are the same?"). Next, the coping model made statements about how they overcame failure (e.g., "I need to pay attention to what I'm doing") and eventually performed at a mastery level.

2. Peer mastery models: Performed all problems correctly while working at average rate. Verbalized high self-efficacy and ability (e.g., "I'm good at this." "That was easy.").

Both mastery and coping peer models were more effective than adult models in raising children's judgments of capability. The children in this study demonstrated increased skill development and self-efficacy.

Modeling is a resource that is readily available in classroom. An alert, sensitive teacher can identify coping and mastery peer models in their classrooms and use them to strengthen the self-efficacy of many students.

Using Self-Efficacy in the Classroom

First, Pajares (1996) reminded us that there is no kit for enhancing self-efficacy. Nevertheless, the research findings provide teachers with resources to: (a) promote efficacy of all students, (b) target students where low-efficacy is apparent. The first step in using self-efficacy is to gather information about students' judgments of their competence. Zimmerman and Martinez-Pons (1990) suggested that self-efficacy measures can be used to better understand students with little motivation, as well as to identify areas of student giftedness. Strategy 3.1 suggests ways to gather information about student competence and strategies to enhance self-efficacy.

We have seen that self-efficacy beliefs about confidence to achieve a task are important motivationally, influencing whether students will attempt a task and the amount of effort and persistence involved in completing the task. The following two sections, self-worth theory and goal orientation, explain two other perspectives of judging ability and the influence on motivation.

REFLECTION.   Think about a self-efficacy story in your life—a story about how beliefs in your own capability helped you to accomplish a goal or overcome a setback. How can you use it to remind yourself of your own motivational resiliency?

Strategy 3.1. Developing Self-Efficacy

Use of Models

Choose peer models carefully. It is important to choose a peer who can be an effective coping model to highlight the importance of persistence and strategy use. Also be alert for influential students who spontaneously present themselves as mastery models. Ask them questions about how they worked out difficulties to elicit the coping strategies they might have used.

Act as a coping model. Although as a teacher, coach, or parent, one might easily be a mastery model, act as a coping model instead. For example, a ninth-grade writing teacher modeled beginning expository writing by composing a draft of an essay on an unfamiliar topic. She then put her draft on a transparency to demonstrate for her students the beginning stages of process writing.

Share self-efficacy stories. Write a self-efficacy story about how your self-efficacy beliefs helped you overcome a setback or failure. Have students write or tell self-efficacy stories.

Estimate the strength of student self-efficacy. Self-efficacy strength can be easily assessed by a scale developed specifically for the task in mind. Gathering this information is especially important in areas where low self-efficacy is likely, such as females and mathematics or when teaching a difficult topic. The following scale, with an example, is adapted from Bandura and Schunk (1981).

On a scale of 1 to 100, rate how sure you are that you can write a one-page document on a word processor and print it out.

Not sure at all   Very sure
1___ 10___ 20___ 30___ 40___ 50___ 60___ 70___ 80___ 90___ 100

Attributional feedback. One of the most important methods to increase self-efficacy is feedback to students that they are making progress on specific skills or strategy use. Think back to the previous chapter on attributions. Feedback about effort and strategies are more likely to increase self-efficacy. "Charles, the effort you showed by restudying the words you missed paid off. Look at your improvement."

Strategy use. Teach students specific strategies for remembering, comprehending, and problem solving. Always remember to link subsequent improvement to the specific strategies used by students.

Goal setting. Encourage students to have a specific goal in mind. Have them compare present performance to their present goal. When they see they have improved, it is likely to increase their sense of self-efficacy (Schunk, 1989). See chapter 4 for more explicit guidelines on goal setting.

Rewards. Rewards increase self-efficacy when they are tied to specific accomplishments (Schunk, 1989).

Teacher self-efficacy. Teacher beliefs in their own competence to make a difference in student learning influences student self-efficacy. Teacher self-efficacy is addressed in chapter 6 as teacher efficacy.

SELF-WORTH THEORY: SELF-PROTECTION
OF PERCEIVED ABILITY

The self-worth motive is based on the premise that a central part of all classroom achievement is the need for students to maintain a positive image of their ability (Covington, 1992). Students often believe that ability is the primary element for achieving success and lack of ability is the primary reason for failure. Their motive then becomes avoiding failure and protecting their self-worth from the perception that they have low ability. This self-protective motive is more prevalent during the adolescent years.

Attributional explanations are important components for the self-protection of ability. When students attribute a failure to putting forth little effort, the attributions serve to protect them from the explanation that they failed because of low ability (Brown & Weiner, 1984). This explains why Kevin, after making a good grade, claimed he did not study, when, in fact, he did. Kevin believes that if people were aware that he had to study to receive a good grade, they might think that he lacked ability. Ability and self-worth are often seen by students as synonymous. It is ability, often in the absence of accomplishment, that defines self-worth for them. For students who believe success is unlikely, the main priority is to avoid failure that is linked or attributed to ability through the use of failure-avoiding strategies (Covington, 1992; Covington & Beery, 1976).

Classroom Practices and Failure-Avoiding Strategies

The negative motivation patterns of failure avoidance are often fostered by school and classroom practices. Perhaps the most prevalent practice is the competitive learning game (Covington, 1992). The *competitive game* refers to situations that force students to compete with one another for grades and rewards. The following are classroom practices that force students to play the competitive game:

- offering insufficient rewards that force students to compete or give up,
- rewarding student ability and not effort,
- basing grades on how each student compares to other students, and
- forming groups based on similar abilities of students.

These practices are damaging to students who believe that ability reflects their self-worth. What are the failure-avoiding strategies used by students to protect themselves from the perceptions of others that they have low ability? The most common way to do this is to use low effort explanations. Low effort is demonstrated in behaviors such as false effort, setting goals too easy or too high, and cheating (Covington, 1992). These behaviors may seem logical to the student, but may seem irrational to a teacher or parent. They must be recognized as strategies, however—strategies to avoid failure.

False Effort and Nonparticipation

Students who do not try will always be one of the most frustrating problems for teachers. Self-worth theory helps explain why students may not try. If a student tries hard (spending extra time studying for a test) and then fails, he or she may attribute the failure to a lack of ability. This allows students to protect their self-esteem by denying that they tried hard. With false effort, students exert just enough effort to give the appearance of being interested or paying attention (Covington & Beery, 1976). Students can rationalize that if they really did try they would succeed. Tactics they might use to maintain this illusion of trying are:

- pretending to understand by answering only easy questions,
- trying to avoid the teacher's attention by keeping their eyes or heads down, and
- avoiding any work not absolutely required (Covington, 1992).

Effort has been called the *double-edged sword* (Covington & Omelich, 1979). This means that "students must exert some effort to avoid teacher punishment and personal feelings of guilt, but not so much effort as to risk incompetency-linked humiliation should they try hard and fail anyway" (Covington, 1984, p. 10). Students are often confused by teachers' contradictory responses to effort. On the one hand, teachers value and reinforce effort. On the other hand, when they are asked to predict which students will learn the most, they view ability, not effort, as the most important factor.

Self-Handicapping Behaviors

Another group of failure-avoiding strategies are known as self-handicapping behaviors by providing excuses for failure in advance.

Three forms are described here. One form of self-handicapping behavior is procrastination—where students irrationally put things off without good reason for a delay (Covington, 1992). This provides students with the excuse that "Because I studied at the last minute, I can't be blamed for failure" (i.e., "at least my ability can't be blamed"). Procrastination may take the form of (a) last-minute studying, (b) staying busy with little to show for it, (c) collecting resources for a project but never starting it, or (d) undertaking many activities but not allowing sufficient time for any of them. Research indicates that low achievers were more likely than high achievers to use self-handicapping strategies (Midgley, Arunkumar, & Urdan, 1996). No difference was revealed in strategy use by race or gender.

Goals that are too high or too low may be another failure-avoiding strategy (Covington, 1992; Covington & Beery, 1976). Covington and Omelich (1979) pointed out that setting unattainable goals allows students to "fail with honor." Such failure does not imply low ability. For example, if a student is taking 15 credit hours, holding a 30-hour-a-week job, and aspiring to make all As, it is no reflection on ability if he or she fails.

Setting goals so easy that one cannot fail is another failure-avoiding strategy. This occurs when students continue to choose tasks they have already mastered. Another example is the student who says before taking an exam, "I just hope I pass."

Through the lenses of self-worth theory, cheating can be viewed as another way to avoid failure. Because self-worth and ability are intertwined in the minds of some students, a competitive situation will often activate this strategy. Covington and Beery (1976) reported the following examples of this type of self-protection of ability from elementary school students who cheated:

> I know someone who studies hard for tests and cheats too. They feel really bad but it is better than being yelled at for bad grades. (p. 55)

> People cheat because they are afraid of doing poorer than other kids and feeling miserable for being different and behind. Some do it to be the best in the class or to move to the next group. (p. 55)

Academic wooden leg is when students publicly admit to minor weaknesses to protect themselves from greater imagined weaknesses. An example, according to Covington (1992), is admitting to test-taking anxiety because appearing anxious is preferable to appearing stupid.

Self-Worth, Failure-Avoiding Strategies, and Minority Students

For minority students, the focus on ability to achieve in school may bring other risks to perceptions of ability. Claude Steele (1992) first described the special risk faced by African-American students as vulnerability to racial stereotypes that leads to disidentification with school—a risk that entails double jeopardy. For African Americans, a low grade on a test might simply reflect incompetence in the subject. However, the low grade can be used by others to confirm a broader inferiority related to ethnicity or culture. Steele (1997) extended this explanation for self-worth protection to other categories of students in areas where there are stereotypic images, such as females in math. Students who are vulnerable to stereotypic judgments may resist the values and goals of school. For example, they might shift their basis for self-worth to other areas, such as peer relations. An example is the finding by Hare (1985) that the source of self-esteem for African-American boys depended more on peer relations than on school achievement.

What is it that contributes to this disidentification with schools and academic success? Steele (1992) explained that a major factor is the prevalence of images in society that lead to a devaluation of race—a devaluation based not necessarily on racism, but on images that do not give a full portrait of the African-American influence in U.S. society. This may be done in subtle ways. For example, teachers may fail to appreciate the best work or talent of a student. Steele described the case of Jerome to illustrate devaluation by teachers. As a third grader, Jerome showed exceptional talent in art. However, as Jerome moved to higher grades, little mention of his talent was made by his teachers. As a consequence, Jerome acts as if he does not care about his unrecognized talent. By not acknowledging his artistic talent, he is less vulnerable to the possibility that it will not be valued—a form of self-protection.

Steele (1992, 1997) identified several guidelines to address failure avoidance in minority students.

- Make students feel they are valued and that their culture is valued. Include minority experience in the mainstream curriculum, not limiting it just to separate programs or special times of the year.

- Stress that there are multiple intelligences or capabilities in school.
- Challenge students without overwhelming them by taking into account their present skill levels and pacing them so the challenge is achievable.
- Communicate to students that they belong in school and profess your belief in the potential of the student.
- Know the student beneath the stereotype.

Although Steele suggested these strategies for African-American students, they are useful for all students. Identification and disidentification with school for minority students are further discussed in chapter 7.

ACHIEVEMENT GOAL ORIENTATION

In self-worth theory, we saw the extent to which students, especially adolescents, might go to protect their concept of ability. A related framework, achievement goal orientation, explains contrasting views of the role of ability in learning (this is not to be confused with goal-setting theory, the topic of chap. 4). Consider the example of two students, Stephanie and Latrell, who are preparing a speech to be presented in class:

> Stephanie is thinking, "I've always been self-conscious about speaking in public and this will give me a chance to practice and develop my presentation skills." Latrell, in contrast, is thinking, "My teacher and classmates will be very impressed with my presentation ability after my speech is finished."

The two students have a different perspective about what the speech means in terms of their ability. How will this affect their motivation for the task? For example, how will each student respond when the teacher gives critical feedback in the early stage of preparation for the speech? Their responses will be quite different because they have different achievement goal orientations.

Contrasting Achievement Goal Orientations

Achievement goal theory integrates cognitive beliefs and emotions that focus on the purpose behind the outcome of a task (Dweck, 1986, 1992). Depending on the source of the research, the two contrasting aims of achievement have been labeled:

- learning goal————————performance goal[1] (Dweck, 1986; Dweck & Leggett 1988);
- task-involvement———ego-involvement (Nicholls, 1983, 1990);
- mastery goal————————performance goal (Ames, 1992; Ames & Archer, 1988).

The contrasting classes of goals have been described as "seeking to prove one's competence versus seeking to improve one's competence" (Dweck, 1992, p. 165). The two patterns represent a continuum affecting motivational factors such as effort, persistence, response to mistakes, and risk taking quite differently. Students, like Stephanie, who have a learning focus are seeking to increase their competence. Their feeling of competence comes from improvement through their own effort. Therefore, Stephanie is likely to see the corrective feedback as useful for developing her presentation skills. Students, like Latrell, who have a performance focus are concerned with looking smart or proving their ability and avoiding negative judgments of their ability. Their feeling of competence comes from doing better than others. Latrell is likely to see corrective feedback as implying that he lacks ability in speaking. The differing attitudes toward academic tasks are shown in Table 3.1.

Although the different goal patterns do not reflect differences in intellectual ability, the patterns do have a major influence on student achievement. The learning goal pattern is the more adaptive one, fostering long-term achievement that reflects intrinsic motivation (Ames, 1992; Heyman & Dweck, 1992; Meece, 1991).

Theory of Intelligence and Goal Orientation

What influences whether students are more likely to approach a task with a learning or a performance goal orientation? One important influence is the theory of intelligence, entity or incremental, held by students (Dweck & Leggett, 1988; Elliott & Dweck, 1988). According to this explanation, some individuals believe that intelligence is "something you have"—an entity. Other people believe intelligence is incremental and malleable, continuing to develop as one gains skills and knowledge. Children who have an incremental view of ability are more likely to adopt a learning goal focus (Bandura & Dweck, cited in Dweck & Leggett, 1988). After a failure, these

---

[1]For simplification, the terms learning and performance are used in this text.

TABLE 3.1

Contrasting Goal Orientations

Characteristic	Learning / Mastery	Performance / Ego
Value of learning	Has an intrinsic value for learning in itself. Goal to increase learning.	Learning is not an end in itself. Focus on looking smart and not looking dumb.
Effort/ability	Effort and ability are related. Effort enhances ability.	Ability is capacity. Effort means lack of ability.
Error/failure	A strategy was not effective.	Provokes fear of low ability.
Attribution	Uses effort/strategy attributions most frequently; ability least frequently.	Uses ability attributions most frequently.
Feedback	Used to judge progress and as self-corrective information.	Used to compare performance with another's.
Persistence	High persistence in difficult tasks.	Low persistence in face of difficulty.
Challenge	Seeks challenge.	Avoids risk taking and challenge.

Note. From Ames and Archer (1988), Dweck and Leggett (1988), and Nicholls (1983, 1990).

children prefer more challenging tasks and tend to persist and change strategies as needed.

Does this mean there are no ability differences? Nicholls (1989) pointed out that, although children are aware of each other's competencies, it is a motivation problem only when there is a performance/ego-involvement focus. Children should learn and teachers should keep in mind that differences in ability should not be interpreted as superiority of the higher ability.

REFLECTION.   In the previous chapter, Exhibit 2.2 asked you to compare your views about the importance of effort and ability. How did you judge these? Do you see contradictions in your beliefs? Are they related to your views of intelligence?

Effects of Goal Orientation on Student Achievement

Conceptions of ability and goal orientation have been found to affect a variety of student behaviors. Solmon (1996) created learning and performance goal structures for learning to juggle in physical education classes. In the learning condition, the teachers stressed short-term goals, individual challenge, and trying to improve over previous trials. A competition ladder was used in the performance condition, and the teachers stressed moving up the ladder and surpassing classmates. Students in the learning condition completed a higher number of difficult trials per minute and students worked harder with better practice habits. In the performance condition, teachers reported problems such as cheating, arguments, and off-task behavior. In addition, females reacted more negatively to the performance condition. The evidence demonstrates the effects of the goal orientation structure on students' motivation. The learning structure clearly supported more positive learning effects for students and teachers.

Other studies found that the particular goal orientation affected cognitive engagement and effort (Meece, Blumenfeld, & Hoyle, 1988). Fifth- and sixth-grade science students were assessed on goal orientation and cognitive engagement. Results indicate that students who placed greater emphasis on learning goals also reported more active cognitive engagement. Students with performance goals (pleasing the teacher or seeking social recognition) had a lower level of cognitive engagement.

The effect of a learning versus a performance focus on the memory performance of fifth and sixth graders was investigated by Graham and Golan (1991). When the emphasis was on ability, as in the performance goal situation, there was interference with memory for tasks that required a great deal of cognitive effort. Thus, learning that is potentially more meaningful or complex, requiring deep-level processing, appears to be the most vulnerable to the effects of performance goals. It is especially important for teachers to be cognizant of the influence of the particular goal orientation in complex learning situations.

The particular goal orientation was also found to influence help-seeking behaviors (Butler & Neuman, 1995). Second- and sixth-grade students were more likely to seek help when the task was presented to them as an opportunity to develop competence. When tasks were presented to students as a measure of their ability, they were less likely to seek help.

The two goal orientations are not mutually exclusive. A person can be motivated for learning and performance with the strength of each orientation being the determining factor (Schraw, Horn, Thorndike-Christ, & Bruning, 1995). A strong learning orientation can offset the debilitating effects of a strong performance orientation. Schraw et al. found that in a difficult college introductory course, students with a strong learning orientation attained higher achievement. They also engaged in a greater number of adaptive behaviors, such as using more study strategies and metacognitive knowledge. The deterrent to motivation occurs when the concern for performance is much stronger than the concern for learning or mastery.

It is important for teachers to recognize student goal orientations to better understand students' motivation and also assist parents in understanding their children. It is easy to misinterpret a strong performance goal orientation by a student as a positive form of motivation. What are student behaviors that may indicate their particular goal orientation? Strategy 3.2 gives examples that might occur in learning situations, and a successful intervention to promote adaptive patterns is shown in Exhibit 3.1.

Strategy 3.2. Recognizing Student Goal Orientation

A focus on performance goals may be indicated by the following examples:

Students or teachers believe that high achievers lose something when low achievers are successful.

Students keep track of their GPAs, not as a way of tracking their learning, but as a way to show how smart they are.

A student becomes visibly upset when asked by the teacher to rewrite a paper and construct more support for his or her thesis.

A student is visibly upset about receiving a grade of B on an essay exam and exclaims, "but I'm an A student."

A student focuses on making the highest grade in his or her group or class.

A middle school student who makes low grades for not turning in assignments, tells his parents that "The work is too easy; I already know that."

A focus on mastery goals may be indicated by the following examples.

A student compares his or her most recent test grade to previous grades to monitor progress.

Students do extra work without expecting a better grade.

A student asks for additional feedback on how to improve a paper.

A student chooses a challenging assignment.

Exhibit 3.1. A Successful Intervention

Bell and Kanevsky (1996) designed an intervention in a regular Grade 2 classroom to promote adaptive learning responses associated with a learning goal orientation. A purpose was to "establish sound foundation for motivation that is resilient to undermining forces of evaluation and difficulties inherent in academic achievement situations" (p. 2).

The intervention took place in math lessons with pattern-recognition tasks. The motivation instruction had three components occurring in seven sessions:

Learning goal. Students were told throughout the training that the goal was for them to learn. An example is "... don't give up and practice so you can learn" (p. 3).

Nature of learning was used to support the learning goal. An example is, "It often takes lots of hard work and lots of tries and lots of time and lots of mistakes before something is learned" (p. 3). These were referred to as good or helpful learning behaviors and listed on a poster called good learning reminders.

Attribution training was used to increase awareness of the role of effort and to assist students in using effort in learning. This had four parts represented on a poster: (a) I can learn, (b) Where to start? (c) What do I already know? and (d) Help?

The results indicate that the training was effective. Compared with the nontrained group, the trained group (a) chose more challenging tasks on posttest than on the pretest; (b) increased in effort attributions, whereas the nontrained group declined; and (c) increased their pattern-recognition scores, whereas the scores did not change for the nontrained group.

STANDARDS FOR EVALUATION OF COMPETENCE

Self-efficacy, self-worth motive, and goal orientation are strongly influenced by the criteria that students use to evaluate their own performance. Two kinds of standards may be used by students: social or individual comparison. *Social comparison standards* mean comparing the grade one receives to the grade of other students (e.g., "What did you make? I made 92"). *Individual comparison standards* mean comparing a recent grade to a previous performance or to the goals previously set (e.g., "I improved from a C to a B on this test"). These two standards are related to the goal orientation held by students (Dweck, 1986; Nicholls, 1990). The use of a social comparison standard is linked to a performance- or ego-focused goal. In contrast, an individual standard indicates a mastery or learning goal.

Social comparison standards can have strong debilitating effects on student motivation. The failure-avoiding strategies described earlier can be a consequence of social comparative standards. Covington and Beery (1976) noted that adolescents, in particular, obtained their perceptions of ability or lack of ability by comparing their performance with peers. They may be competent in a skill or in their knowledge, but never surpass a friend's or a sibling's performance. Therefore, they view themselves as less competent. A positive influence of social comparison occurs when a self-efficacy peer/coping model is effectively used. The student gains information about how to perform a skill by comparing his or her performance to that of the model.

The use of a group as a source for comparison has a unique influence. This effect on perceptions of ability is referred to as the *big-fish-little-pond effect* (BFLPE; Marsh, 1987; Marsh & Parker, 1984). Although students may be equally competent, when they compare themselves with more competent students, they might develop lower academic self-concepts. However, when they compare themselves with less competent students, they could perceive themselves as having a higher self-concept of ability. These effects are more likely to occur when there is school-wide differentiation in ability such as tracking. Marsh and Parker see implications for parents who are considering placing their children in high-ability schools. The development of a low self-concept of ability at an early age may be more detrimental than the benefits of attending such a school. However, if teachers and parents are knowledgeable of social comparison effects, especially as they relate to theories of intelligence and mastery and performance effects, the possible detrimental effects may be minimized.

Developmental Trends in Self-Concept of Ability and Standards

What do we know about the development of self-concepts of ability? Young children tend to overestimate their likelihood of success, but their evaluation of competence changes with age and experience (Stipek & Mac Iver, 1989). The overestimation of success by younger children may be moderated as they grow older and become more realistic. There is some evidence that self-perceptions of academic competence declines with age (Eccles, Wigfield, Harold, & Blumenfeld, 1993). These declines are assumed to be a result of both developmental changes and the classroom environment.

How does an individual choose one standard for comparison over the other? Comparative standards are related to stages of development (Veroff, 1969). Children begin with individual comparison, experiencing pleasure in their own accomplishments such as walking and climbing. Evaluation standards shift to social comparison in the early school years. In middle elementary school years, individual and social comparisons become integrated. Research suggests that skill development and life stage interact in the use of comparative standards as follows (Frey & Ruble, 1990):

- Young children can use both individual and social comparison when judging performance.
- Comparison to others is not likely to convey much useful information during periods when children are showing rapid improvement. Comparison to previous skills is most useful in this case.
- Social comparison is more useful at a beginning stage of learning. It provides more useful information when other beginners are available for comparison.
- Comparison to a similar peer is useful when attempting a new task or goal. A young child may observe another child to find out how to twirl a hula hoop. An older woman beginning a jogging program may use agemates' experience as a way to predict her potential for jogging.
- When performance reaches a plateau, there is less need for individual comparison. For example, when runners reach a plateau or performance diminishes, they may be more interested in comparing their performance to agemates. Research found that declining and older runners emphasized comparison with agemates and deemphasized comparison with their own performance.

Classroom Practices That Foster Positive Competence Evaluation

What can teachers do to increase a mastery goal orientation and reduce the prevalence of failure-avoiding strategies and performance orientation? First, be aware of practices that promote a performance or learning orientation. Ames and Ames (1991) listed practices that contribute to a negative motivation pattern (Table 3.2). Strategy 3.3 presents recommendations for reducing failure-avoidance and performance orientation practices in the classroom.

TABLE 3.2

Factors That Contribute to a Negative Motivation Pattern

Factor
• Public evaluation
• Reinforcing ability instead of effort
• Communicating low expectations
• Permitting students to be uninvolved in learning
• Reinforcing performance instead of learning
• Excessive emphasis on success and grades
• Lack of recognition (can't get it)
• Poor working/learning conditions (noise level, overcrowding, etc.)

Note. From "Motivation and Effective Teaching" by R. Ames and C. Ames, 1991, in J. L. Idol & B. F. Jones (Eds.), *Educational Values and Cognitive Instruction: Implications for Reformation*, Hillsdale, NJ: Lawrence Erlbaum Associates.

Strategy 3.3. Reducing Failure-Avoiding Strategies and Performance Orientation

Characteristics of Classroom Climate That Fosters Development of Competence:

Effort and strategies are emphasized and respected
Learnable intelligence is emphasized
Improvement is recognized in evaluation
Failure does not mean dumb
Meaningful learning is emphasized
All students are valued and treated with dignity
Social comparison through public recognition and comparative grading is deemphasized.

Specifically:

Introduce attributional antecedents that ability increases as one gains in knowledge and skills.
Give students opportunity to improve knowledge and skills through retesting and revising.
Instruct students in learning strategies.
Emphasize student progress. Give feedback that indicates progress in skill development.
Emphasize that effort is critical for improving ability.
Avoid labels and statements (*smartest, slowest*) that can be interpreted as a ranking by ability.
Use rewards to emphasize the learning accomplished by students. Arrange rewards so they can be attained for individual accomplishment, not in competition with another person. Use noncompetitive or cooperative learning structures to provide more possibilities for students to gain rewards because they are not competing for them.

ACHIEVEMENT ANXIETY

Self-evaluation of competency is also related to achievement anxiety. Anxiety has long been identified as a factor that has debilitating effects on school performance (Hill & Wigfield, 1984). It increases as students move through elementary into high school (Hill, 1984). As anxiety increases, it is more likely that students will have lower achievement. Key questions that relate to anxiety and achievement are: (a) What are the current explanations of the relationship of anxiety and performance? (b) How can teachers help students adapt?

Explanations of Achievement Anxiety

Does test anxiety cause poor performance? The answer may surprise you. According to Covington (1992), emotional factors such as stress and tension were previously believed to directly affect performance. However, the prevailing explanation is cognitive interference instead of test anxiety. Poor performance is thought to result from self-defeating thoughts that interfere with test preparation and test taking.

Cognitive Interference

How does cognitive interference work? This explanation suggests there is a cognitive skill deficit, with poor performance resulting primarily from inadequate study in the first place (Culler & Holahan, 1980; Tobias, 1985). The already limited capacity of humans to process information is further limited by distracting and self-defeating thoughts at every phase of learning (Tobias, 1985). Contrary to popular beliefs, test taking is only one phase affected by anxiety. Attention is affected prior to study. During study, self-defeating thoughts interfere with information processing. High-anxiety students have deficits in several study habit areas:

- self-monitoring—judging whether they are ready for an exam (Covington, 1992);
- organizing information into more meaningful patterns (Steiner, Wiener, & Cromer, 1971);
- distractibility—classroom disruptions and students' own worries (Eysenck, 1988).

From a skill deficit point of view, high-anxiety students need study and organization skills to overcome these deficits.

Motivational Explanations

Self-efficacy, self-worth protection, and goal orientation are related to achievement anxiety. Students who have a low sense of self-efficacy are more likely to experience the negative effects of achievement anxiety. However, high efficacy appears to protect a student from anxiety (Bandura, 1993). This reemphasizes the importance of identifying low efficacy students and providing strategies to increase their efficacy.

From a self-worth perspective, Covington (1992) theorized that achievement anxiety is a reaction to the threat of failure. A student who has not performed well in the past fears repeating the failure and being thought incompetent. Students who have good strategies and perform well are affected by anxiety if they have a performance goal orientation. Their self-worth is more dependent on perfection and they are more concerned with looking smart. A failure would destroy the perfection and their image. Covington characterized these students as overstrivers. They know how to get good grades, but this does not alleviate their fear that they may not really have ability.

Strategies for Alleviating Debilitating Test Anxiety

In view of the nationwide increase in competency testing of students and teachers, it is imperative that teachers and schools develop programs to help students manage achievement anxiety. For example, in some schools, teachers report that students do not take the competency tests seriously. This may be a failure-avoiding strategy by students. Helping students handle debilitating anxiety in the face of such testing involves interventions that help students develop information-processing and test-taking strategies (Hill & Wigfield, 1984; Tobias, 1985; Wigfield & Eccles, 1989) and learning to deal with failure in constructive ways (Rohrkemper & Corno, 1988). Guidelines for helping students handle achievement anxiety are found in Strategy 3.4.

Brown and Wahlberg (1993) developed motivational scripts for teachers to present to students prior to taking the Iowa Test of Basic Skills. Students who received the motivational instructions per-

---

Strategy 3.4. Strategies to Reduce Debilitating Test Anxiety

1. From the beginning, emphasize that test-taking skills are something we learn in school.

- Teach students how to activate prior knowledge.
- Set up practice tests.

2. During test taking, remind students:

- to sit where they can write easily,
- to pay attention to instructions both from teachers and instructions provided with the tests,
- what they are allowed to do (i.e., whether they can make notes, underline, or highlight),
- to go back and check their answers if they finish before time is up, and
- to pace themselves, neither rushing nor working too slowly. If they can't answer a problem, move on and come back later (Hill & Wigfield, 1984).

3. Give highly motivating instructions about the importance of doing one's best. Brown and Wahlberg (1993) used the following script:

It is really important that you do as WELL as you can on this test. The test score you receive will let others see just how well I am doing in teaching you math this year.

Your scores this year will be compared to students in other grades here at this school, as well as those in other schools in Chicago.

That is why it is extremely important to do the VERY BEST that you can.

Do it for YOURSELF, YOUR PARENTS, and ME. (p. 134)

---

formed better than students who received the standard instructions. The script is also found in Strategy 3.4.

The concepts of ability that are described in this chapter have important implications for educators. Regardless of level of ability, the important goal is to assist all children to reach their potential. This is the real meaning of *motivational equality* (Nicholls, 1989). Finally,

Merely having ability or having potential is not enough to enjoy success in school or in life. Talent and potential will be wasted unless children believe they possess ability and have the freedom to use and develop their talents. (Miserandino, 1996, p. 210)

MAJOR POINTS FOR REVIEW

1. How students evaluate their ability has important implications for academic motivation and expectancy for success. The prevalent view today is that perceptions of competence are not only domain specific, but distinct for different subject areas.

2. Self-efficacy is a judgment that individuals make about their own capability to accomplish a future task. It is not just a reflection of one's ability, but the beliefs one holds about that ability. Self-efficacy judgments influence which activities we choose to undertake and which to avoid, how much effort we expend and how long we persist in the face of obstacles.

3. Beliefs about one's capabilities come from four sources of information: mastery accomplishments, vicarious experiences (observing others), verbal persuasion, and physiological states. The most powerful source is mastery accomplishments or direct evidence.

4. Strategies that can increase self-efficacy are goals and feedback, rewards, self-instruction for verbalization of strategies, participant modeling, and various combinations of these strategies. Coping models who demonstrate the task, along with the difficulties they experienced and strategies to succeed, are more likely to increase self-efficacy than mastery or expert models. Peer models have been found to be more effective than adult models in raising children's self-efficacy.

5. The self-worth motive is based on the need for students to maintain a positive image of their competence. Ability and self-worth are often seen by students as synonymous. Their motive then becomes one of avoiding failure and protecting their self-worth from the perception that they have low ability.

6. Students protect their self-worth through the use of failure-avoiding strategies: false effort and nonparticipation, self-handicapping behaviors that provide excuses in advance, goals too high or too easy, cheating, and academic wooden leg. The tendency toward self-worth protection is influenced by classroom practices that promote competition among students. Practices include insufficient rewards that force students to compete or give up; rewarding student ability but not effort, and evaluation systems where grades are based on student comparison to other students.

7. Self-worth protection occurs when minority students protect self-worth by resisting the values and goals of school, purposefully choosing behaviors that are detrimental to academic success. For minority students, the focus on ability may lead to vulnerability to racial stereotypes, which leads to disidentification with school. It is important that teachers and schools to incorporate practices so that all students can identify with the goals of educational attainment.

8. Two contrasting achievement goal orientations—learning and performance—refer to the underlying purposes behind actions. Students who have a learning focus are seeking to develop their skills, with their feeling of competence coming from improvement. Students who have a performance focus are concerned with looking smart or proving their ability with their feeling of competence coming from doing better than others. The learning goal is the more adaptive motivation pattern in most circumstances.

9. A primary source of the particular goal orientation is whether intelligence is an inherent, fixed entity or incremental and malleable, continuing to develop as one gains in skills and knowledge. Learning goals are associated with the latter, although a person can be motivated for learning and performance. Learning goals have been found to be positively related to seeking help and use of strategies for complex learning.

10. Students' self-efficacy, self-worth motive, and goal orientation are strongly influenced by the criteria they use to evaluate their own performance. Two types of criteria are social comparison standards where the criteria is the performance of others, and individual comparison standards, where the criteria is the student's own previous performance or goals. The use of a social comparison standard is linked to a performance goal and individual comparison to a learning goal. Children begin with individual comparison, experiencing pleasure in their own accomplishments, such as walking and climbing, with evaluation shifting to social comparison in the early school years. In middle elementary school years, individual and social comparisons become integrated.

11. The prevailing explanation for achievement anxiety is cognitive interference, where poor performance is thought to result from self-defeating thoughts that interfere with test preparation and test taking. Students who have a low sense of self-efficacy are more likely to experience the negative effects of achievement anxiety, whereas

high efficacy appears to protect a student from anxiety. Interventions that help students develop information-processing and test-taking strategies help students handle debilitating anxiety in achievement situations such as competency testing.

Motivational Toolbox

1. Important points to think about and lingering questions

2. Strategies I can use now

3. Strategies I want to develop in the future

CHAPTER 4

Goals and Goal Setting

"Would you tell me, please, which way I ought to go from here?" asked Alice. "That depends a great deal on where you want to get to," said the Cheshire Cat.

—Carroll (1963, p. 59)

Have you used terms such as *aim, aspiration, purpose,* or *intent*? These are terms we often hear that imply goal setting. *Goals* have been defined simply as "something that the person wants to achieve" (Locke & Latham, 1990, p. 2). "Goal setting theory assumes that human action is directed by conscious goals and intentions" (Locke & Latham, 1990, p. 4). There is an important distinction between goal setting theory and goal orientation (chap. 3). *Goal setting* refers to a specific outcome that an individual is striving to achieve, whereas *goal orientation* refers to a type of goal orientation or underlying purpose behind the strived-for goal (Dweck, 1992). The focus of this chapter is on the importance of goal setting for achievement outcomes.

A coach would not think of starting a season without emphasizing both team and individual goals. Goals are a standard component of many, if not most, employee evaluation criteria. What about goal setting in classroom learning? Although teachers have goals in mind, how often are these made explicit? How often are students encouraged to set goals for themselves? From a motivational viewpoint, goals and goal setting play a central role in self-regulation (Schutz, 1991). Goal setting influences learning and motivation by providing a target and information about how well one is doing. This chapter describes types of goals, the motivational effects of goals, the properties of goals that enhance motivation, the relationship between goals and feedback, and applications of goal setting to the educational settings.

MOTIVATIONAL EFFECTS OF GOAL SETTING

Goals are cognitive representations of a future event and, as such, influence motivation through five processes (Locke, Shaw, Saari, & Latham, 1981; Locke & Latham, 1990). More specifically, goals:

- direct attention and action toward an intended target. This helps individuals focus on the task at hand and marshal their resources toward the accomplishment of the goal.
- mobilize effort in proportion to the difficulty of the task to be accomplished.
- promote persistence and effort over time. They provide a reason to continue to work hard even if the task is not going well.
- promote the development of creative plans and strategies to reach them.
- provide a reference point that provides information about one's performance.

GOAL CONTENT AND MULTIPLE GOALS

When an individual sets a goal, what is the focus of the goal? A goal may be a vague idea that is difficult to communicate or it may be a clear vision. The focus of a goal can be a product, such as making an A on an exam, or a process such as using steps for writing an essay. Although a number of goals may be operating at the same time, people tend to function with core goals—a set of one to five personal goals that guide behavior (Ford, 1992). Schutz (1994) identified three core goals that tended to be the most important for preservice teachers—family, occupation, and education. Most of their reported activities centered around these three goals.

What is the importance of this multiple goal perspective? When we set one goal, others may be activated (Ford, 1992). For example, when an adult returns to school to pursue a master's degree, the degree is a goal. This goal may activate others at the same time to move to a better pay scale, expand social contacts, and learn new ideas to improve teaching. As this example demonstrates, the activation of one goal does not preclude the activation of another. However, multiple goals can be especially problematic among adolescents. Wentzel (1989) asked adolescents to list what they try to achieve in their classes. From these responses, she compiled a list of

12 goals. Students were then surveyed to determine how often they tried to achieve each of the 12 goals in their classes. Comparisons made between low, medium, and high GPA groups indicated that the groups valued goals differently. The high GPA group ranked being a successful student, getting things done on time, and being dependable and responsible highest among the 12 goals. In contrast, the low GPA group ranked having fun and friends highest. Only 19% of the low group indicated that being a successful student was a goal. This raises an important question. How can the school or teacher influence student goals? Can the low GPA group who ranked fun as the highest goal be encouraged to put more emphasis on goals associated with achievement?

One possibility for teachers is to emphasize that learning tasks may have multiple outcomes or goals. As goal rankings in the previous study indicate, high GPA students were more likely than low and medium GPA students to try to accomplish several goals at the same time. Ford (1992) pointed out that when a person has more than one reason for participating in an activity, motivational power is increased, providing a type of motivational insurance. For example, in a second study, Wentzel (1991) concluded that a goal of trying to interact with peers is not, in and of itself, detrimental to classroom learning. The pursuit of both social responsibility and academic goals was most related to achievement. Thus, for students who generally focus more on fun and friendships than on learning and self-improvement, it may be possible to use the multiple goals principle to facilitate meaningful engagement. For example, cooperative learning provides opportunity for multiple goals—academic, social skills, peer interaction, and responsibility. Cooperative learning in the social context is further explained in chapter 7.

Some educators are beginning to broaden the possible types of goals by expanding the types of learning outcomes that are possible in school. Ellison (1992) used the seven types of intelligences—logical/mathematical, linguistic, musical, spatial, bodily/kinesthetic, interpersonal, intrapersonal—proposed by Gardner (1983) as goal targets for fifth graders. The steps included the following:

- Began goal-setting conferences with students in September by asking, "Have you thought about your goals for the year?" Gathered information from parents about their children's strengths and areas of difficulty.

- Began with goal setting for intrapersonal intelligence (capacity for understanding self), focusing the goals on confidence, responsibility, and self-management.
- Self-evaluation of goals occurred in February with affirmation, refocus, and celebration of goals followed by teacher redirection where indicated.

Exhibit 4.1 shows an example of a student goal (Ellison, 1992).

Exhibit 4.1. Goal Setting: A Student–Parent–Teacher Process

Student's Name _Sally Schubert_ Grade _5_ Teacher _L. Ellison_

Intrapersonal: self-confidence, responsibility, self-management, ethics ...
Feel good about school.

Interpersonal: relationship with others, respect, multicultural understanding, solving problems...
Make new friends.
Have fun! Be relaxed.

World-understanding: science, social studies, visual arts, media, multicultural, global studies ...
Learn about Germany.

Linguistic: reading, writing, speaking, media ...
Read faster.
Improve cursive.

Logical-mathematical: math, visual, problem solving ...
Learn chess.

Spatial: visual arts, geometry, spatial reasoning ...
Improve watercolor skills.

Bodily-kinesthetic: physical education, dance, coordination ...
Practice running.

Musical: vocal, instrumental, cultures ...
Practice flute.

Other goals: your life beyond the classroom ...
Stay in own bedroom.
Tell adults if you get uptight!

Signatures: student, parent, teacher ...
Jill L. Ellison + Rick   Sally Schubert

From "Using Multiple Intelligences to Set Goals" by L. Ellison, *Educational Leadership, 50*(2), p. 71. Used by permission of the Association for Supervision and Curriculum Development. Copyright © 1990 by ASCD. All rights reserved.

If multiple goals are to be productive, they must be coordinated and not in conflict. When people attempt more goals than they can handle, one or more of the goals may result in failure or one may become dominant. For example, fun may overcome being a successful student. The crucial factor is helping students balance their goals.

PROPERTIES OF GOALS
THAT ENHANCE MOTIVATION

How difficult or specific should goals be? Goals by themselves do not automatically lead to more effective task performance. However, certain properties of goals affect task performance: distal or proximal, difficult or easy, specific or general, assigned or self-chosen, and commitment to the goal.

Long- and Short-Term Goals

What is the relation between long- and short-term goals? Target goals, mission goals, ultimate goals, end goals, distal goals, and "Begin with the end in mind" (Covey, 1989, p. 97) are all phrases that imply long-term goals. Long-term goals keep us directed toward our ultimate target. Short-term goals, also known as proximal goals or subgoals, are the stepping stones to the long-term goal. As stated previously, the content of a goal is something we want to accomplish. The issue is not whether a long- or short-term goal is more effective. Each has a role and they complement each other in contributing to achievement and self-regulation. This relation is illustrated in Fig. 4.2.

The interrelationship of these goals is illustrated in a study that compared the effects of proximal and distal goals on children's self-efficacy and mathematics performance (Bandura & Schunk, 1981). Third graders were assigned to one of three conditions.

1. Proximal goal group: Children were told they could consider setting a goal of completing at least six pages of work each session.
2. Distal goal group: Children were told they might consider setting the goal of completing the entire 42 pages by the end of the seventh session.
3. No goal group: Goals were not mentioned to the children.

The results indicate that children who set attainable subgoals progressed at a more rapid pace, achieved mastery in math, and increased their self-efficacy. The proximal group also displayed more

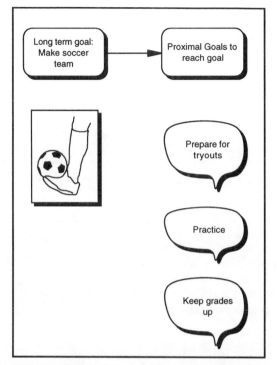

FIG. 4.1. Proximal goals leading to long-term goals.

competence and displayed the most intrinsic interest in solving the problems. The authors concluded:

> Self-motivation can best be created and sustained by attainable sub-goals that lead to future larger ones. Proximal subgoals provide immediate incentives and guides for performance, whereas distal goals are too far removed in time to effectively mobilize effort or direct what one does in the here and now. (Bandura & Schunk, 1981, p. 587)

Points to keep in mind for goal setting include:

- Distal goals help keep the larger picture in mind. However, focusing on the distant future may lead one to procrastinate more.
- When one sets distal goals, there is a tendency to break them up into proximal goals, but teachers cannot assume all students will do this (or even ourselves).
- When planning long-term projects, students need to see the relationship between what they are doing in class from day to day and the long-term goal.

In summary, both proximal and distal goals affect motivation and performance. Exhibit 4.2 shows a form for setting long-term goals. Exhibit 4.3 is a form for proximal goals that can be adapted for various age groups. Strategy 4.1 give ways the forms can be used.

Exhibit 4.2. Long-Term Achievement Goal Form

LONG-TERM GOAL

Long-term goals keep us focused and give us direction and a purpose for accomplishing the short-term goals. State a long-term goal using the following format:

1. One important goal I want to accomplish over the next 6 months to 2 years is:

2. This goal is important to me because:

3. Specific steps I will take to accomplish these goals are:

4. Possible blocks, both external and personal, to accomplishing this goal are:

5. What I can do to lessen these are:

6. Those to whom I can go for help are:

Exhibit 4.3. Proximal Goal Form

PROXIMAL GOALS AND PROGRESS

This form is a way to set goals for each week and to monitor your progress. Make the goals as specific as possible.

PLANNING

1. My specific learning goals for this week are:

2. Actions or steps I will take to accomplish these goals are:

3. How I will know I have accomplished my goals is by:

4. Possible blocks, both personal and external, that may interfere with my accomplishing these goals and how I can overcome them are:

5. Those I can go to for help with my goals are:

6. How confident I am that I will accomplish these goals:

not confident   very confident
0_____25

EVALUATING

7. How satisfied I am with my previous goal accomplishment:

highly   neutral   highly
dissatisfied   satisfied
0_____12_____25

8. Reasons for accomplishing or not accomplishing my goals are:

Strategy 4.1. Using Goal Forms

- *Long-Term Form.* Students can be asked to complete this form at the beginning of a semester. It might be used to help students think about multiple goals and their priority.

- *Proximal Goal Form.* This form can be adapted as needed for different age levels. I have had undergraduates use this form weekly. For the first few times, the teacher gives feedback. As students learn criteria for effective goals, they might be paired as *goal buddies* to give feedback to each other. Feedback is most often needed for making the goal more specific and specifying action steps. The identification of how to overcome blocks is very important. The evaluation phase elicits attributions for why they did or did not attain the goals.

Goal Difficulty and Challenge

Which is more effective, easy or difficult goals? Did you predict easy goals? Surprisingly, harder goals lead to a higher level of performance than do easy goals if the task is voluntary and the person has the ability to achieve the goal (Locke & Latham, 1990). People tend to expend more effort to attain a goal they perceive as difficult. However, the goal must not be so difficult that it seems to be unachievable because most people will avoid an impossible task.

In a study with school children, Schunk (1983a) investigated the effects of goal difficulty on the performance of children who were deficient in arithmetic division skills. One group received difficult goals and another group, easier goals. The children in the more difficult goal group solved more problems and sustained greater task motivation than the less difficult goal group.

Establishing the level of goal difficulty—challenging, yet realistic—that will help students perform their best is a balancing act for teachers. Goals should not be so rigid that necessary adjustments cannot be made. If the standard for goal attainment is too difficult or rigid, there is likely to be a of drop-off in motivation. As described in chapter 3, setting an unachievable goal is one mechanism that individuals might use to protect a sense of self-worth. In addition, students may need help in setting realistic goals. Schunk (1991a) recommended setting upper and lower limits and goal conferences as means of helping students set realistic goals.

REFLECTION.   Think about what a realistic goal means to you. How much risk is involved in your goals?

Goal Specificity

Specificity is another property of goals that affects performance. Specific goals have clear standards for accomplishment (e.g., "My goal is to read the story and have my summary finished for literature class tomorrow"). General goals are vague with a nonspecific outcome (e.g., "My goal is to catch up with my assignments"). It has been demonstrated that specific goals result in higher performance than either no goals or general goals (Locke & Latham 1990). A descriptive analysis of weekly goals set by college students in learning logs over the course of a semester found differences in types of goals by student grades (Alderman, Klein, Seeley, & Sanders, 1993). The A group had more than twice as many specific goals as the B and C groups. Examples were (a) specific goals (e.g., "I want to make 36 out of 40 on the next test"), and (b) general goals (e.g., "I want to make a good grade on the next test"). The reason that specific goals increase task performance is because they provide a guide for the type and amount of effort needed to accomplish the task (Bandura, 1986). A specific goal is more likely to motivate an individual to higher performance than are good intentions. The proximal goal form (Exhibit 4.2) is useful for helping students learn to set specific, short-term goals.

Goal Commitment

What affects strength of commitment for goals? How does this affect goal attainment? Goal commitment is our determination to pursue a course of action that will lead to the goal we are aspiring to achieve (Bandura, 1986). Strength of goal commitment will affect how hard one will try to attain the goal. Goal commitment is affected by the properties described thus far: difficulty and specificity. For example, when goals are too difficult, commitment declines, followed by a drop-off in performance (Locke & Latham, 1990). Commitment is also affected by goal intensity, goal participation, and peer influence.

Goal Intensity.   Commitment is related to goal intensity, or the amount of thought or mental effort that goes into formulating a goal and how it will be attained (Locke & Latham, 1990). This is similar to goal clarification because when we clarify a goal, we are involved in a conscious process of collecting information about the goal and task and our ability to attain it (Schutz, 1989). In a study of fifth graders, Henderson's study (cited in Locke & Latham, 1990) found that students who formulated a greater number of reading purposes with more detail and elaboration attained their purposes to a greater extent than did students with superficial purposes. Although there was no difference in IQ scores of the groups, the students who set more goals with elaboration were better readers. It stands to reason that the more thought that is given to developing a goal, the more likely one will be committed to the goal.

Goal Participation. How important, motivationally, is it for people to participate in setting of goals? This is an important question because goals are often assigned by others at home, school, and work settings. The state imparts curriculum goals to teachers, who in turn impose them on students. A sales manager may assign quotas to individual salespersons. Letting individuals participate in setting goals can lead to greater satisfaction. Nevertheless, telling people to achieve a goal can influence self-efficacy because it suggests they are capable of achieving the goal (Locke & Latham, 1990).

To investigate the effects of assigned and self-set goals, Schunk (1985) conducted a study of sixth-grade students with learning disabilities who were learning subtraction. One group was assigned goals (e.g., "Why don't you try to do seven pages today"). A second group set goals themselves (e.g., "Decide how may pages you can do today"). A third group worked without goals. Students who self-set goals had the highest self-efficacy and math scores. Both goal groups demonstrated higher levels of self-regulation than the control group without any goals.

Nevertheless, Locke and Latham (1990) concluded that self-set goals are not consistently more effective than assigned goals in increasing performance. The crucial factor in assigned goals is acceptance. Once individuals become involved in a goal, the goal itself becomes more important than how it was set or whether it was imposed. Because, in work and schools, goals are often assigned by others, it is important that the assigned goals be accepted by participants. Joint participation in goal setting by teachers and students may increase the acceptance of goals.

Peer Influence.   One factor where teachers might be influential in promoting goal acceptance and commitment is peer influence. Strong group pressures are likely to increase commitment to goals (Locke & Latham, 1990). This group cohesiveness is more often found on athletic teams. Obviously the coach wants a strong commitment to the team goals. In the classroom, group goals may aid the commitment of students working in cooperative learning groups and thus lead to a higher quality of work.

RELATIONSHIP OF FEEDBACK AND GOALS

It is important to reemphasize that goals initiate a self-evaluation process that affects motivation by providing a standard to judge progress (Bandura, 1986). This simply means two comparative processes are needed: goal and feedback or knowledge of results about progress. Locke and Latham (1990) described the relationship between feedback and goals as:

> Goals inform individuals as what type or level of performance is to be attained so that they can direct and evaluate their actions and efforts accordingly. Feedback allows them to set reasonable goals and to track their performance in relation to their goals, so that adjustments in effort, direction and even strategy can be made as needed. (p. 197)

This process is shown in Fig. 4.2.

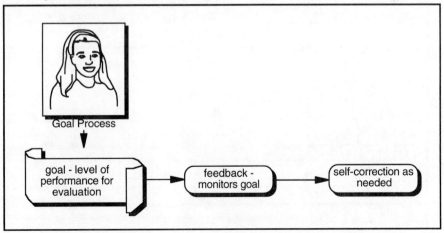

FIG. 4.2. Relation between goals, feedback, and self-correction.

What factors make it more likely that feedback will occur? Proximal goals give more opportunity for knowledge of results because individuals can monitor their performance and make corrections as needed. When people see a discrepancy between their goal and their performance, what are the effects on subsequent performance? This was investigated in studies by Bandura and Cervone (1983, 1986). The results indicate that the more dissatisfied high self-efficacy individuals were with their performance, the more they increased their effort for future tasks. The motivational influence of goal discrepancy is apparent in the log entry in Exhibit 4.4 when the student said, "I didn't finish two of my goals. I think I have to get a few priorities straight."

Exhibit 4.4. Log Entries Showing Relation Between Goals and Feedback

Third Week

Got 32/40 on exam. First read chapters, then did reviews in study guide. Reviewed class notes but should have done before last night. Know could have done better if I had put more time in it. I know B in any course is OK, but for me an A is my goal.

Next Entry

My first chance to do homework all week. I worked on my bulletin boards [for another class]. I guess setting achievable goals does help. It's kind of like giving a test to yourself. Even though no one else knows about it you still feel like you failed if you don't achieve it. Next week I'm going to achieve these goals:

1. Have my correct chapters read for each class.
2. Get all the information I need for my bulletin board.

Next Entry

So far so good. I've kept up on my reading and finished two out of three programs. My goals from last week are almost achieved. On to new ones. I'm going to actually start my bulletin board. I've discovered that setting achievable goals makes you realize that even though it seems like there is a mountain of work, you can get it done, one step at a time.

Next Entry

I didn't finish two of my goals. I think I have to get a few priorities straight.

Next Entry

- I started to implement the PQ4R technique we were taught in class. I read the overview, topic headings, and summary. I didn't ask questions, but I did use the study guide. I improved my grade to a 36 this time. I'm very happy about that, not only because of the score, but because I tried to use this technique and it started to work. (*Note.* "Preservice teachers as learners in formation: Metacognitive self-portraits," by M. K. Alderman, R. Klein, S. Seeley, & M. Sanders, *Reading Research and Instruction, 32*, pp. 38–54. Copyright © 1993. Reprinted by permission.

Which should be the focus of feedback—achieved progress or deficiencies? Bandura (1993) emphasized feedback on progress. When feedback emphasizes progress, personal capabilities are highlighted. This enhances self-efficacy and aspirations. In contrast, feedback that emphasizes deficiencies undermines the self-regulatory processes.

CLASSROOM INTERVENTIONS IN GOAL SETTING

What type of goal setting interventions have been applied in classroom settings and what was the outcome? Interventions that have been conducted at elementary, secondary, and college levels and with students with learning disabilities are described in the following sections.

Elementary and Secondary Achievement

Gaa (1973, 1979) investigated the effects of individual goal-setting conferences on both elementary and secondary students' achievement. After being tested on reading, first- and second-grade children were assigned to one of three experimental conditions: conferences with goal setting, conferences without goal setting, and no conferences. All students received the same reading instruction. The children in the goal conference group met with the experimenter once a week and received a list of reading skills. In the first meeting, children were given an explanation of goals and how they related to reading. In each conference, children checked the goals (skills) they would work on during the week and rated their confidence in their ability to achieve goals. The conference group also met weekly with the experimenter, but they did not set goals or receive feedback.

To assess the differences between the groups, both groups participated in goal-setting conferences. On follow-up assessment, the goal-setting group scored higher on the reading achievement posttest, set fewer goals, but achieved more of the goals they set. Gaa concluded that practice and feedback in goal setting leads to more realistic goals and helps students be more accurate in goal setting. He explained that the goal conference group may have set fewer goals because they had learned to focus their effort on the goals to be accomplished. Two ways of assisting elementary students are shown in Strategy 4.2.

Strategy 4.2. Goal Setting for Elementary Students

- Lois Peak (1993) described a way that goal setting is taught to children in Japan. At the beginning of a new term in elementary schools, students are encouraged to think about their past performance and set a personal goal for the coming term. Next they develop a plan for reaching it, write their goals down, and post them on classroom walls. Students are periodically assigned a brief essay to describe their progress toward their goal of self-improvement. At the end of the term they write a final essay describing their success and the difficulties they encountered and read it to the class. When the students have finished reading their essay, the teacher finds a few words of praise and the entire class applauds.

- Goal Interview. Five steps are used to assist children to formulate a goal:

1. Ask students to tell or write a story about something they want for themselves (e.g., a dog, complete chores, be friendly).
2. Ask students to tell why they want the particular thing (motive).
3. Ask students to tell how they will attain the goal.
4. Ask students what could stop them from getting the goal (obstacle).
5. Ask students to tell about overcoming the obstacle. (Goldman, 1982)

Goals were used to help students in a middle school ESL class self-evaluate portfolios (Smolen, Newman, Walthen, & Lee, 1995). Students established personal goals based on self-evaluation of their work. Index cards were distributed to students every Monday. The students wrote a new goal on one side of the card and the evaluation on the other side. Students were able to write their own goals after several weeks of modeling, demonstration, and practice. Student were encouraged to choose goals from strategies that were posted in the room. The student goals gave the teacher a window into the students' progress. An example of a student's goal is shown in Exhibit 4.5.

Gaa (1979) conducted a second study with high school students. The focus for this study was process goals. Process goals were the actions or steps to accomplish the product (e.g., the paper). Tenth-grade students were assigned to one of three groups: the goal-setting group received weekly individual goal-setting conferences and set short-term goals toward the attainment of the final goal; a second group received individual conferences but set no goals; the control

---

Exhibit 4.5. Bao's Goal Card

The Front of Bao's Card

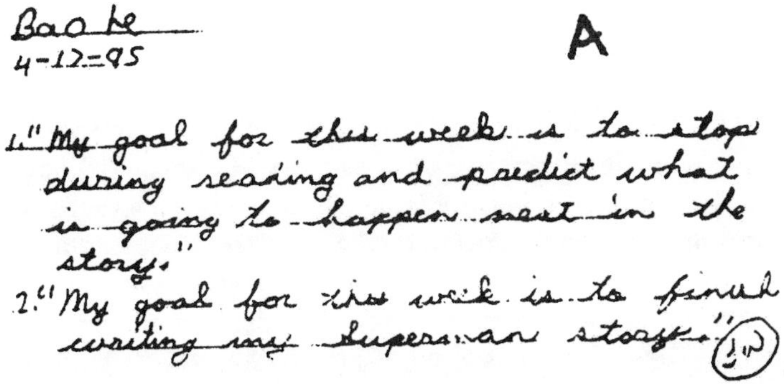

Bao he
4-12-95   **A**

1. "My goal for this week is to stop during reading and predict what is going to happen next in the story."

2. "My goal for this week is to finish writing my Superman story."

The Back of Bao's Card

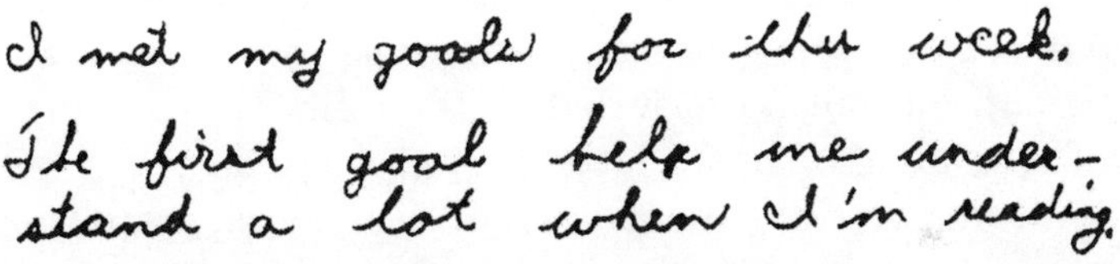

I met my goals for this week. The first goal help me understand a lot when I'm reading.

From "Developing student self-assessment strategies," by L. Smolen, C. Newman, T. Walthen, & D. Lee, *TESOL Journal*, 5(1), 22–26. Copyright © 1995 by TESOL, Inc. Reproduced with permission.

---

group received the same instruction but received no goals and participated in no conferences. The goal-setting group scored higher on an English achievement test and viewed themselves as more in control of their achievement outcomes. Their attribution for goal attainment was more to themselves than to external factors.

College Students

Which will enhance college students' performance more—being trained in goal setting or time management? At the undergraduate level, Morgan (1985, 1987) conducted two experiments to determine whether goal setting could enhance the performance of college students. In the first study, there were four groups (Morgan, 1985):

1. The subgoal group was trained to set and monitor study subgoals for concepts from assigned readings (e.g., "My goal is to learn the difference between assimilation and accommodation").
2. The time group was trained to monitor time spent studying.
3. The distal group focused on a single goal.
4. The control group only met to take the assessment.

The group that self-monitored the concept subgoals outperformed groups that monitored time or study or distal goals. Although the group that self-monitored study time actually increased study time and spent more time than the subgoal group, their performance was not significantly better than the control group. This surprising outcome was explained by Morgan: Although subgoals bring about more effective use of time, it is what one does with the time that is most important.

In the second study, Morgan (1987) compared groups on goal setting alone, self-monitoring alone, and a combination of self-monitoring and goal setting and two control groups. All three experimental groups performed better than the control groups. However, contrary to expectations, the combination goal-setting and self-monitoring group did not perform better than either procedure alone. Morgan's explanation for the latter finding was that goal setting and self-monitoring are intertwined and difficult to separate from each other. If one component is in place, it sets the other in motion.

Students with Learning Disabilities

The positive effects of goal setting have also been found to work with students who have learning disabilities (LD; Tollefson, Tracy, Johnson, Farmer, & Buenning, 1984). Seventh-, eighth-, and ninth-grade students with LD were trained to set realistic goals and expend effort to attain goals. Students were first taught goal setting by how many basketball goals they could make. Following goal-setting training, students set goals in spelling or math—their most difficult subject. Goal contracts were combined with attributional retraining. At the beginning, the students did not set realistic goals (only seven were classified as realistic goal setters). After the training, a significant number (79%) set realistic goals. Students also increased their attributions to effort and decreased their attributions to luck. The training process is described in Strategy 4.3.

Strategy 4.3. Learning to Set Realistic Goals

- **Basketball game.** There are three choices for distance: long, medium, and short. Each student selects a preset distance and is allowed three tosses into a wastebasket, predicting in advance how many baskets they would make. They keep records of their predictions and scores.
- **Baseball game.** Four lists of words were made for each student: easy (a single), moderately difficult (a double), difficult (a triple), and very difficult (a home run) words. Students were then given words that matched their level of spelling ability. To begin an inning, students chose the type of hit they wanted and recorded their prediction. Students then spelled the word orally; correct words were a hit and incorrect words an out. The students kept records of their actual outcomes. Each team is given 2 minutes at bat or three outs, whichever comes first. (Tollefson et al., 1984)

In another study, Graham, MacArthur, Schwartz, and Page-Voth (1992) taught fifth-grade students with LD a strategy for setting both product and process goals for writing an essay. The plan the students followed was:

1. choose a product goal (e.g., purpose of paper);
2. develop a process goal for how product goal would be attained;
3. write while continuing the plan;
4. develop and organize notes prior to writing; and
5. evaluate progress in meeting goals.

A mnemonic was used to help students remember: *PLANS* ("Pick goals, *L*ist ways to meet goals, *A*nd make *N*otes, *S*equence Notes" ; Graham et al., 1992, p. 327). After students learned the strategy, they wrote longer essays with improved quality.

GUIDELINES AND STRATEGIES FOR GOAL SETTING IN THE CLASSROOM

Positive effects of using goal setting in classrooms have been described. However, how proficient are students at goal setting if they are not taught? Bergin (1989) studied high school students' goals in out-of-school learning activities. The findings indicate that few of the students used effective goal-setting techniques. Only 12% listed subgoals that would be necessary to attain the goal. In addition the majority of the goals were general, not specific.

Goals can play an important role in increasing student competence and motivation. Teachers or coaches should not assume that students know how to set effective goals. Strategy 4.4 presents guidelines for using goal setting and describes a lesson.

Strategy 4.4. Guidelines for Using Goal Setting in the Classroom

- Present tasks and assignments to students as goals to be accomplished. These can be broken down into proximal goals.
- Have students keep a record of goals set and their performance (e.g., their test scores) so they can monitor their performance. Graphing their performance would allow students to see their progress (Harris & Graham, 1985).
- Help students identify obstacles that might interfere with goal accomplishment.
- Teach students who are procrastinators to set proximal goals and monitor them.
- Have cooperative learning groups set goals for their next work sessions and evaluate their goals from the most recent work sessions.

Goal-Setting Lesson

This is a lesson I have used to teach proximal goal setting to teachers, undergraduates, and high school students, including those with developmental handicaps. The steps are based on a model for stating and refining goals (Doverspike, 1973).

1. First the teacher models with a think-a-loud. "Here is a goal (on transparency or chalkboard) that is too general and idealistic. You are to help me revise it so it is cognitive, realistic, and specific. The goal is 'I want to have great study habits.'"
2. Students give ideas for the revision by identifying general terms and substituting new terminology. Mark out the original terms as new ones are decided on.
3. The revised goal might read: "I will improve my reading comprehension by learning PQ4R." Possible subgoals are: "I will practice each part one at a time" or "I will monitor my progress after each test."
4. Have each student write a goal, then, in pairs or triads, help each other refine their goals to be more cognitive, specific, and realistic.

REFLECTION.   Why might goal setting sometimes be scary for students?

COMBINING MOTIVATIONAL PROCESSES

Motivational processes have been examined in chapters 2, 3, and 4. Principles from these processes can be combined as strategies for interventions. The LINKS model is one such combination.

The LINKS model was designed to break the low-expectation cycle associated with learned helplessness (Alderman, 1990). The steps combine goal setting, attributional retraining, self-efficacy, and learning and metacognitive strategies as sequential steps to be used to break the low-expectation cycle of *helpless* students. These steps are shown in Fig. 4.3.

A key assumption of this model is that a successful experience is not enough. Students must attribute success to a controllable factors—their ability or operationalized effort—if their expectation and confidence is to increase.

Link 1: Proximal goals. The first link to success is to set a goal for performance. How does a teacher decide this starting point or proximal goal? Determine where students are or establish a baseline. The baseline can be determined by pretests (formal or informal), teacher observation and by the analysis of student errors. Teachers and students can then jointly decide on the proximal goal.

Link 2: Learning strategies. The students' second link to success is to develop the necessary learning strategies to accomplish the task. It can be assumed that low-achieving students fit the category *inefficient learners* (Pressley & Levin, 1987). An inefficient learner is described as any student who fails to apply learning strategies where they would be beneficial. In this link, the student is taught the necessary learning strategies to accomplish his goal. Examples are memory strategies, reading comprehension strategies, and metacognitive knowledge about when to use them.

Link 3: Successful experience. Success in this link is defined as a learning goal rather than a performance goal. The focus is on "how much progress I made," not on "how smart I am." The proximal goal serves as the criterion for successful experience. Success is not the final link, however. The student's attribution for the success must link his or her personal effort or strategy to the successful outcome.

Link 4: Attribution for success. In Link 4, students attribute success to their personal effort, strategies, or ability. The teacher's role is to help students make the appropriate attribution. Inter-

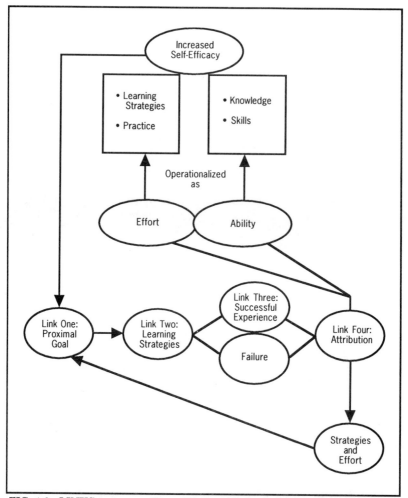

FIG. 4.3. LINKS to success. From "Motivation for At-Risk Students," by M. K. Alderman, *Educational Leadership, 48*(1), pp. 28–29, Used by permission of the Association for Supervision and Curriculum Development. Copyright © 1990 by ASCD. All rights reserved.

nal–unstable attributions are easiest to change. Because students control their own effort, this is the likely starting place for attribution for success. For this attribution to be effective, effort must be operationalized. This means, What did the student do when he tried? Effort might be: completing all homework, correcting errors, extra practice, redoing an assignment, going to a help or review lesson, or using the appropriate learning strategies. Students must also attribute success to ability operationalized as knowledge/skills. This model then goes full circle. Students who have succeeded and attributed the success to their own effort or ability have concrete performance feedback that, in turn, will lead to increased self-efficacy. Increased self-efficacy in turn leads to increased confidence about goal accomplishment with an increase in teacher efficacy.

REVIEW OF MAJOR POINTS

1. Goals and goal setting play a central role in self-regulation, influencing learning and motivation by influencing motivation through five processes: direct attention and action, mobilize effort, promote persistence and effort over time, promote the development of creative plans and strategies to reach them, and provide a reference point that provides information about one's performance. The focus of a goal can be a product or process.

2. People tend to function with core goals—a set of one to five personal goals that guide behavior. This multiple goal perspective is important because when we set one goal, others may be activated. If multiple goals are to be productive, they must be coordinated and not in conflict.

3. Properties of goals that affect task performance are: distal or proximal, hard or easy, specific or general, assigned or self-chosen, and commitment to the goal. The distal long-term goals keep us on our ultimate target. Short-term goals, also known as proximal goals or subgoals, are the stepping stones to the long-term goal. Harder goals lead to a higher level of performance than do easy goals if the task is voluntary and the person has the ability to achieve the goal. Specific goals result in higher performance than either no goals or general goals.

4. Goal commitment is our determination to pursue a course of action that will lead to the goal we are aspiring to and is related to goal intensity. Intensity is the amount of thought or mental effort that goes into formulating a goal and how it will be attained.

5. Although letting individuals participate in setting goals can lead to greater satisfaction, telling people to achieve a goal can influence self-efficacy because it suggests they are capable of achieving the goal. The crucial factor in assigned goals is acceptance. Once

individuals become involved in a goal, the goal becomes more important than how it was set or whether it was imposed.

6. Feedback is important because goals initiate a self-evaluation
process that affects motivation by providing a standard to judge
progress. Feedback allows the students to set reasonable goals and
track their performance in relation to their goals so that adjustments
in effort, direction, and even strategy can be made as needed. When
feedback emphasizes progress, personal capabilities are highlighted.
This enhances self-efficacy and aspirations.

7. Goal setting has been found to be effective at all levels of
schooling and with students with LD. However, some research indicated that few students use effective goal-setting techniques. An
important role for the teacher is to teach students how to set goals.

Motivational Toolbox

1. Important points to think about and lingering questions

2. Strategies I can use now

3. Strategies I want to develop in the future

CHAPTER 5

Developing Student Self-Regulatory Capabilities

The best moments occur when a person's body or mind is stretched to its limits in a voluntary effort to accomplish something difficult and worthwhile. Optimal experience is thus something we make happen....These periods of overcoming challenges are what people find to be the most enjoyable times of their lives.... By stretching skills, by reaching toward higher challenges, such a person becomes an increasingly extraordinary individual.

—Csikszentmihalyi (1991, p. 6)

The content of this chapter focuses on the personal capabilities needed for motivation to learn. *Empowerment, self-agency, self-motivation*, and *self-determination* are terms used to describe the personal capabilities that enable students to be independent learners and develop a core of resiliency. A framework for the development of personal capabilities is *self-regulation*. This refers to the degree to which individuals are active participants in their own learning, characterized by their goal-directedness and self-initiated actions that involve self-control (Zimmerman, 1994).

SELF-REGULATORY CAPABILITIES AND ACADEMIC SUCCESS

How much do capabilities such as concentration, self-discipline, effort, determination, and patience contribute to a student's academic success? To what extent does the absence of these qualities contribute to a student's academic failure? The contrast between two first-grade students illustrates the importance of these qualities for school success (Greenspan & Lodish, 1991). Albert and Angela are first-grade students seated at their desks working with colors. These students will illustrate the importance of these qualities for school success (Greenspan & Lodish, 1991).

Albert	*Angela*
• is circling letters that go with pictures (with obvious pride);	• is scribbling different colors on her paper and is restless when finished;
• is attentive, smiles warmly as Ms. Miller walks by;	• is sitting half on, half off her chair with a puzzled expression on her face and doesn't ask Ms. Miller what to do;
• Although he cannot quite read directions, figured out what to do from teacher's facial expression, posture, and words.	• grabs Brad's marker, pesters him, and is sent to time-out.

Albert clearly has an edge over Angela in behaviors that will help him be academically successful. The capabilities that Albert demonstrated are characterized by Greenspan and Lodish (1991) as the "ABCs of school learning." The "ABCs" have four elements: (a) attending and focusing, (b) establishing positive relationships, (c) communicating and, (d) being able to observe and monitor oneself.

Many students like Albert first learned these qualities at home. What is the school's role with the Angelas who lack these qualities? Although personal qualities such as attentiveness and concentration, effort and persistence, self-restraint, and punctuality are valued by teachers, Sockett (1988) suggested that there does not seem to be a concerted effort by schools to help students develop them. Instead there is often a belief that these qualities are unteachable.

REFLECTION. What are your beliefs? Are qualities such as these teachable? Do you teach any of these qualities?

Let's look at another student. The following description is from a college application written by Lilia who overcame insecurities of parental divorce, bulimia, and a short time in Juvenile Hall.

With the help of AVID [a program designed to help students have a greater chance to go to college] I am taking two AP classes which I never dreamed possible. I know the joy of learning and the sense of accomplishment which comes with doing the best I can.... One of my philosophies is if at first you don't succeed, keep trying until you do, which is one of the reasons I have taken the ACT once and the SAT twice.... I plan to apply the strength and determination that have enabled me to be successful in high school throughout my college career. (Mehan, Villanueva, Hubbard, & Lintz, 1996, pp. 1–2)

Lilia demonstrates personal characteristics and behaviors of self-regulation. Yet self-regulation is a social-cognitive phenomenon that also includes the environmental influence. The school had a role in providing the environment for Lilia's development of the capabilities that enabled her to have a chance to go to college (The AVID program is further described in chap. 9.). Chapters 6, 7, and 8 describe the teaching motivation, social climate, and instructional practices that help cultivate students' development of self-regulated learning characteristics.

OVERVIEW OF SELF-REGULATED LEARNING

What are the personal capabilities that will help students seize and make the most of their opportunities? Active participation, planned or automatized approaches to learning or work performance, and self-awareness of performance are hallmarks of self-regulation (Zimmerman, 1994). One example where these self-regulatory strategies play an important role is the approach used by skilled writers to the writing process (e.g., intentionality, making outlines, keeping daily records, and revising; Graham & Harris, 1994).

The cognitive processes presented in chapters 2, 3, and 4 form the basic blocks of self-regulation. Self-regulated learners have (a) adaptive attributional beliefs, accepting responsibility for their learning; (b) a strong sense of self-efficacy; (c) a belief that effort will lead to increased success; and (d) tools for setting effective goals. Other qualities of self-regulated learning presented in this chapter are a vision of the future, volitional control strategies, cognitive and meta-cognitive strategies, and the essential tools of self-instruction (self-coaching), self-monitoring, and time and resource management.

VISION OF THE FUTURE AND POSSIBLE SELVES

Students in a high school dropout-prevention program (Farrell, 1990, 1994) were asked this question; What expectations do you have for yourself? The following are responses from three students in the program.

> *Cathy*: "I want to ... I don't know what profession I want to be ... , but whatever I choose to do I wish to succeed and to have a family and to be the best I can be." (Farrell, 1994, p. 15)

> *Roberta:* "There are so many things. I want to be a singer or a teacher, a stewardess, psychologist." (Farrell, 1994, p. 15)

> *Michael*: "The thing that scares me most is ... having no future. That really scares me.... One of my greatest fears is growing up and bein (sic) a bum." (Farrell, 1990, p. 14)

Cathy and Roberta have a positive vision of what they want their futures to be like. In contrast Michael is fearful about his future prospects. The views of the future expressed by these students illustrate the concept of *possible selves*. Possible selves are how we think about ourselves and the future (Marcus & Nurius, 1986). As depicted in Fig. 5.1, possible selves include the ideal selves we would like to become as well as a self we are afraid of becoming. For example, African-American adolescents were asked to list hoped-for possible selves and feared selves (McCready, 1996). Hoped-for selves included doctor, dancer, cosmetologist, and social worker. Feared selves included drug dealer, homeless, and working at McDonalds. The possible self we envision can be seen as a symbol of hope, as it is for Cathy and Roberta, or a reminder of a bleak future, as it for Michael. A visual representation of possible selves is shown in Fig. 5.1.

How Important Is the Vision of the Future for Motivation?

A vision of a possible self is the first step in developing self-regulation. It sets planfulness in motion and acts as an incentive for present behavior (Borkowski & Thorpe, 1994; Marcus & Nurius, 1986).

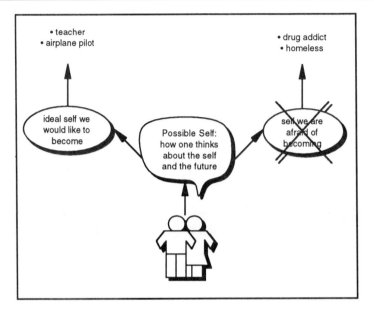

FIG. 5.1. Possible selves.

Sometime in your past, *teacher* became a possible self for you. Your hopes of becoming a teacher guided decisions such as choosing to go to college and sacrificing financially in order to do so. Or, if you are now teaching, your vision of becoming an even better teacher is guiding your decision to continue to learn.

What if a student has a fearful view of the future as Michael does? The absence of possible selves is viewed as a serious motivational problem affecting other components of self-regulation. A primary characteristic of underachieving older students and adults is the absence of a vision of the future (Borkowski & Thorpe, 1994). When students' views about the future are unclear, their current behavior is more likely to be governed by whatever is happening at the moment. Remember the students in chapter 4 whose primary goal in school was *fun*. Their immediate concern with fun deters them from the academic preparation needed for college preparation or work opportunities. If students have not developed a future vision or are not committed to academically supportive short- and long-term personal goals, they are likely to show little self-regulation of their study behaviors. The failure to develop multiple, positive selves in early childhood may create a condition in which there is little long-term motivation for pursuing current and complex problem-solving activities (Borkowski & Thorpe, 1994).

How Are Possible Selves Developed?

The formation of possible selves is influenced both by developmental and sociocultural factors (Day, Borkowski, Dietmeyer, Howsepian, & Saenz, 1992). For young children, the future is vague. However, as they develop, the future becomes more clearly defined. Interactions with our social environment—including parents, media, people we admire, peers, and school experiences—have a formative influence on possible selves. The influences of others can have positive or negative effects on possible selves. The track star Carl Lewis formed an image based on Jesse Owens (Marcus & Nurius, 1986). Now, many track athletes are probably forming an image of a possible self based on Carl Lewis. However, students in the potential dropout population were neither viewed as student nor as worker by the peers and adults in their lives (Farrell, 1990). Consequently, these students did not see themselves in these roles. Welch and Hodges (1997) contended that if an academic identity is not in place, students will be limited in their expectations for themselves. Perhaps Cathy and Roberta were influenced by someone in their family or school to form the positive vision of the future, whereas Michael did not have this positive influence.

Possible selves are also influenced by our attributional history and self-efficacy judgments. A combination of ability and effort attributions for success is thought to help create more positive possible selves (Borkowski & Thorpe, 1994). If our prior explanations for success and failure were primarily attributed to uncontrollable factors, we are not likely to envision the future with much hope. In addition, the possible self may be dominated, temporarily, by negative possibilities resulting from a defeat, loss, or lapse of will power. Seeing these setbacks as temporary is essential for our motivation for the future (Marcus & Nurius, 1986).

Self-efficacy beliefs that are linked to an envisioned possible self are likely to be influential for career choices (Borkowski & Thorpe, 1994). A student who has a strong belief in her math ability is more likely to expend the effort and persist, and is more likely to include math in her career aspirations. The importance of helping students develop adaptive attributions and strong self-efficacy beliefs is underscored by their influence on a positive view of the future.

Helping Students Develop a Vision of the Future

What role can schools and teachers play in helping students develop possible selves or a vision of the future? Two programs are described: (a) a project to help make possible selves more concrete for elementary children, and (b) a project designed to help Hispanic students succeed at college.

Possible Selves Project: Elementary Students

An intervention was designed specifically to help elementary age (Grades 3–5) Mexican-American students think about their hopes and fears as they related to academic and occupational achievement (Day et al., 1992; Day, Borkowski, Punzo, & Howsepian, 1994). The intervention consisted of three critical components across eight lessons, with *Lesson 1* composed of ground rules.

- In *Lesson 2*, the metaphor "Possible-Me Tree" was used to make possible selves concrete for the students. The possible-me-tree has four strong branches that represent four areas of life: (a) family and friends, (b) free time, (c) school, and (d) work. Each type of branch had two types of leaves: green for hopes for the future and red to represent their fears of the future. The "Me Tree" was introduced through artwork by asking students to imagine they were trees and explaining a growing tree as having a strong trunk made of healthy parts of the self (knowledge and skills), sturdy branches (the four areas of their lives), and the two types of leaves to represent their hopes and fears for the future (motivational aspects of hopes and fears were explained). Students then constructed a tree out of felt material, generated leaves for each branch, and discussed why unhealthy trees (weak trunks, fragile branches, few leaves) hindered their ability to reach their goals. The students added leaves to their trees as they saw new possibilities and fears for themselves.
- In *Lessons 3–6*, students were given instruction and practice in three self-regulatory strategies to achieve their goals: "think ahead to the schoolwork you need to do; think while doing school work; think back over what you have learned" (Day et al., 1994, p. 80).

Students contrasted good and poor learners, and used the concrete representation of a time machine to practice the three strategies. This was followed by enacting a situation where students forgot a homework assignment, failed the test on it and a consequent discussion of failure. Finally, students were given an assignment to use the time line, practice the three strategies, and discuss their feelings of success.

- *Lessons 7 and 8* focused on the connection between hoped-for and feared selves and doing well in school. The time machine was used to project their future to the year 2010 and what they hoped to be doing then. The students role-played specific jobs they might be doing—both enjoyable jobs and jobs they might hold as a result of not graduating from high school.

Throughout all lessons, students were helped to form linkages between what they are doing in school currently and future occupations with the connections between proximal and distal goals.

The results reveal that students who received the intervention increased their understanding of the characteristics of good learners and the three self-regulatory strategies of think back, think now, and think ahead. Furthermore, they improved their knowledge of the importance and value of education for future occupations and financial security. Their hoped-for future selves included more higher prestige jobs.

The possible-me training was adapted by Gibson (1998) for seventh-grade students. The results indicated that the students listed fewer hoped-for future selves after training, but their selves were more realistic.

A Program for High School Students

At the secondary level, "Programa: Latinos Adelantan De Nuevo" (PLAN) was developed to help Hispanic students develop a vision of the future (Abi-Nader, 1990). This was a comprehensive program designed to address the belief held by many inner-city minority students that they have no control over their lives and are therefore powerless to shape their future. Consequently, these students lack motivation, are unable to set goals, and are indifferent about the importance of school. This may be have been the case with Michael.

One implicit goal of PLAN was to help students create a vision of the future. Several components of the program were used for this goal: assignments with stories in literature, mentors, and future talk. For example, students read *The Monkey's Paw* by William Jacobs. This is a story about a family who used a mysterious paw to get wishes to come true, but with ill-fated results. Students were given a follow-up assignment to present 3-minute speeches about their own dreams and wishes. In the speech, they were to imagine their future, talk about their dreams, and explain how they would achieve them.

PLAN also provided mentors and models for the students by having Hispanic college students and professionals make presentations once a month for seniors. Mentors were former PLAN participants and they attributed their success to the skills they learned in the program. Hearing these stories helped students see that it was possible for people like themselves to go to college.

An important role for teachers in the PLAN classroom was the initiation of a pattern of future-oriented classroom talk. Teachers focused on the future during discussions in four types of activities:

- *preparation* (e.g., planning a visit to a local university and learning how to fill out a financial aid form).
- *description* of situations students are likely to encounter in college (e.g., in reference to a term paper assignment, "I just want you to learn how to do it … I don't want surprises when you go to college"; Abi-Nader, 1987, p. 195).
- *storytelling* about PLAN graduates and their success in college. Teachers told stories and provided examples of role models who successfully completed the program. The examples included a display of good papers by former students. Because some students had difficulty identifying with success, a story of a student who struggled and finally made it was included (a coping model).
- *providing a rationale* for PLAN'S skill-building exercises (e.g., giving students an example of why public speaking is an important skill for college and work interviews).

The teacher's talk during these activities took place in the indicative mode, "when you go to college," rather than conditional mode (e.g., "if you go to college"). The PLAN approach has been effective. Students in PLAN graduate from high school and most earn full-tuition scholarships to college (Abi Nabor, 1991).

One strategy that can help students develop a vision of the future is the use of models. Suggestions for using models to help students develop a vision of the future are shown Strategy 5.1.

Strategy 5.1. Providing Students With Models for a Vision of the Future

1. Do not assume that all students will identify positive models on their own, as one teacher discovered. Students were asked to look in the newspapers to find examples of successful people. The teacher was surprised to find that the largest number of examples selected by students was a professional athlete who had been arrested on drug charges and a movie actress who had been arrested for fighting with police. Expose students to positive models and have them identify characteristics and strategies of the model that led to success.
2. Bring in people with whom students can identify as models of success. Be sure the models describe the strategies that helped them achieve their success.
3. Use stories of inspiration from fiction, autobiographies, and movies for discussion.

REFLECTION.   What are stories with examples of personal capabilities that have inspired you? What are stories that might inspire your students?

VOLITIONAL CONTROL:
DIRECTING MOTIVATION AND EFFORT

One of the most important components of self-regulation is volition. *Volition* is "the tendency to maintain focus and effort toward goals despite potential distractions" (Corno, 1994, p. 229). In everyday life, we use a number of terms that imply volition: *will, will power, discipline, self-direction,* and *resourcefulness*. These terms all imply the ability to buckle down to difficult tasks (Corno, 1993). The following example illustrates volition:

> Elissa, a college student, is a single parent with a 7-year-old child, Shanell. She finds it very difficult to study in the evening. There are constant distractions, such as her child needing help with homework. She remembers that the Urban League Center has a program of supervised homework for students in the evenings. She takes Shanell to the center two evenings a week while she studies in the library.

Elissa demonstrated the use of volitional strategies by finding a way to study while providing a resource for her child.

The Function of Volition in Self-Regulation

Volitional strategies protect goals by directing and controlling one's energy toward them. Elissa was protecting two goals at the same time: her need to take care of her family responsibilities and her need for academic success. Refer to the proximal goal form in Exhibit 4.3. First you planned a goal. The volitional component, Number 4 on Exhibit 4.3, asked you to list possible barriers and how you will overcome them. The actions you take to overcome the barriers are volitional strategies. Volition is responsible for making sure the goal is enacted. When goals are easy, volition is not necessary. Volitional strategies protect goals by: (a) focusing attention, (b) prioritizing and completing goals, (c) handling distractions, and (d) managing effort (Corno, 1993).

What are volitional challenges faced by students? There are many distractions in and outside of school, including social pressures, that can deter students from goal accomplishment. Challenges and distractions include:

- juggling athletic or musical practice with time needed for homework;
- the belief that a task is too easy, too difficult, or boring;
- goals that are not valued;
- complex assignments and long term projects;
- doing homework;
- classroom or home environment full of distractions; and
- juggling work hours with homework requirements.

Each of these items may seem trivial to adults, but such distractions and conflicts can have serious effects on the volition of children and their performance in academic areas.

Homework presents students with difficult volitional challenges because of many possible distractions; its success depends on students being able to handle distractions. Homework distractions were the subject of a study by Benson (1988), who asked sixth-grade students to list distractions that disturbed them the most when doing homework. The phone and television were the most frequent distractions listed by students. Others were people, general noise such as appliances, and background music. Students were also asked to list solutions for the distractions. A primary solution suggested by the students was to get their parents to help them. The researchers concluded that the students tended to place the responsibility on others or the environment to control distractions, not on themselves. However, the act of listing the distractions and solutions appeared to help students see how they could be more responsible for finding solutions.

Guthrie et al. (1996) suggested that children reading at home need volitional strategies such as having a system with a time and place, finding and keeping materials, decisions about what and what not to read, and knowledge of potential obstacles.

Volitional Control Strategies

What are volitional control strategies? They are strategies that exercise overt and covert control over our actions and thoughts. Covert control of metacognitive, emotional, and motivational strategies are used to control self-defeating thoughts. Overt strategies control the self by controlling the environment including persons within that environment (Corno & Kanfer, 1993). Examples of each of the five types of strategies reported by seventh-grade students and teachers are shown in Table 5.1 (Corno & Kanfer, 1993). If students are to be academically successful, they need volitional strategies to keep them working at goals although there are other things they want to do. How can teachers help students develop strategies to manage distractions?

Helping Students Acquire Volitional Strategies

Interventions to help students acquire volitional strategies have been conducted from the first-grade level to community college level. First-grade students were taught to reduce distractibility during reading group work (McDonough, Meyer, Stone, & Hamman, 1991). The students were taught how to set goals, not distract themselves, and not distract their classmates. Manning (1988) taught first and third graders to control off-task and disruptive behaviors in the classroom. The approach used to teach them was cognitive self-instruction, which is described later in this chapter.

A volitional enhancement program was implemented to help community college students develop volitional strategies (Trawick, 1991). The program consisted of four 70-minute lessons geared toward the control of external and internal environments. The four

TABLE 5.1

Volitional Control Strategies Exemplified by Students and Teachers

Strategy	Student	Teacher
Covert		
Metacognitive control	Think of first steps to take and get started right away. Go back over my work before I turn it in to make changes that will improve it.	Keep a running tab of times I have to speak to X about behavior. Reflect immediately after a lesson on how it went and make mental notes on what to do differently next time.
Motivational control	Pat myself on the back for good work. Tell myself, "Concentrate on this work because..." Think through ways to carry out this task that will be more fun, more challenging, or more reassuring to me.	Keep my mind on grading these papers when I'd rather be doing something else. Plan ways to make my teaching better whenever I have spare moments for thought (e.g., while driving, in the shower, walking).
Emotional control	Count to 10 before I blow up. Remember I have lots of things I can draw on to help myself; I've done this kind of thing before.	Wait 5 seconds before speaking when angry. Marshall my inner resources and remember I've been through more than this and made it.
Overt		
Control the task situation	List the things I can do to get to where I want to go.	Redefine my goals so they are more realistic for me.
Control others in the task setting	Move away from noise and distractions. Ask friends for help.	Establish rules for student behavior and enforce them. Call teacher study groups to cooperatively resolve problems. Give roles to students who need special attention.

Note. From "The Role of Volition in Learning and Performance," by L. Corno and R. Kanfer, 1993. In L. Darling-Hammond (Ed.), *Review of Research in Education* (pp. 3–43). Washington, DC: American Educational Research Association. Copyright © 1993 by the American Educational Research Association. Adapted by permission.

lessons were: (a) control of task and setting, (b) control of others in the task situation, (c) self-monitoring to control attention; and (d) motivational control such as attributional statements.

Interviews with eight subjects found that the most important change students made was gaining control over their study environment. They were better able to handle distractions from friends, siblings, and others. Changing the external environment was easier for students than changing their covert metacognitive processes. From this finding, it is suggested that when helping students acquire volitional control, they need more time and practice for covert metacognitive strategies.

A planned volitional curriculum to help students in acquiring strategies was described by Corno (1994). Class activities developed for the curriculum are shown in Strategy 5.2. These can serve as a starting point for helping students acquire volitional control strategies.

Strategy 5.2. Activities in Volitional Enhancement Curriculum

1. Teacher and students list possible distractions when studying.
2. Teacher and students make a master list of the most frequent distractions and categorize them as to where they occurred or if they were distracting thoughts.
3. List ways that students usually handle distractions; then match the response with the distraction. Evaluate how well it works. The most effective way is to refocus on the task.
4. Teacher models and demonstrates both effective and ineffective responses to a distracting situation.
5. Teacher leads students through 20-item quiz requiring identification and classification of more effective strategies.
6. Using written scenarios, small groups of students role play more effective strategies for handling distractions. Peer audience evaluates actors' strategies.
7. Teacher reminds students that he or she will be looking for evidence of students using strategies to handle distractions and doing their work. Select key tasks to observe. Record amount of time on tasks by groups and individuals. Students self-evaluate; then results are discussed with students.

Source. Adapted From "Student Volition and Education: Outcomes, Influences, Practices" by L. Corno, 1994, in D. L. Schunk & B. J. Zimmerman (Eds.), *Self-Regulation of Learning and Performance*, pp. 229–254. Hillsdale, NJ: Lawrence Erlbaum Associates. Copyright © 1994. Adapted with permission.

LEARNING AND METACOGNITIVE
STRATEGIES

Self-regulated learners know a large number of learning strategies such as reading comprehension and memory strategies. They also understand how learning strategies work, know when to use them, and can evaluate their effectiveness. These latter processes are known as metacognitive strategies (Borkowski & Muthukrishna, 1992). Learning and metacognitive strategies enable students to acquire and master academic content. Although it is beyond the scope of this text to make a full description of learning strategies, a basic sets of learning and metacognitive strategies is presented in the following sections.

Learning Strategies

Two lists of learning strategies are presented. The eight categories of learning strategies proposed by Weinstein and Mayer (1986) form a useful starter set. This list ranges from simple strategies like rehearsal to elaboration, which is essential for deep-level processing. These are listed in Table 5.2.

TABLE 5.2

Eight Categories of Learning Strategies

Strategy	Description
1. Basic rehearsal	Repetition
2. Complex rehearsal	Copying or highlighting text
3. Basic elaboration	Creating a mental image or pictures that connect items
4. Complex elaboration	Extending learning by summarizing or relating to prior knowledge
5. Basic organization	Grouping or categorizing items
6. Complex organization	Creating outlines and graphic organizers that show relationships
7. Comprehension monitoring	Self-questioning to check undertanding
8. Affective and motivational	Use of self-talk to reduce anxiety

Note. From "The Teaching of Learning Strategies" by C. E. Weinstein and R. E. Mayer, 1986. In M. C. Wittrock (Ed.), *Handbook of Research on Teaching* (3rd ed.). New York: Macmillan. Copyright © 1986 by Macmillan. Adapted by permission.

A set of cognitive strategies that really work for elementary school students in reading comprehension were identified by Pressley, Johnson, Symons, McGoldrick, and Kurita (1989). The strategies are:

- summarization—the ability to make a concise summary by constructing a sentence, short paragraph, or visual map.
- mental imagery—constructing a visual representation of the content.
- story grammar—the knowledge of how a story is structured.
- question generation—constructing questions that capture main ideas.
- question answering—answering questions on content such as at the end of the chapter.
- prior knowledge activation—strategies to recall previously acquired knowledge.

Keep in mind that many secondary and even college students may not be proficient in these reading comprehension strategies. In this case, a teacher's role becomes one of helping students become self-regulated learners by explicitly teaching these strategies, beginning one at a time. For more explicit descriptions of learning strategies, see Gaskins and Elliot (1991); Pressley et al. (1989); Pressley, Woloshyn, and Associates (1995); and Wood, Woloshyn, and Willoughby (1995).

Metacognitive Strategies

Metacognition, characterized as a "tool of wide application," generally refers to the knowledge and beliefs about one's cognitive processes and the monitoring and control of these processes (Flavell, Miller, & Miller, 1993). If students are to learn independently and manage their lives, metacognitive strategies are essential.

Metacognitive knowledge and strategies can be subdivided into three categories: person, tasks, and strategies (Flavell et al., 1993). Examples in each category are:

- *Person.* Knowledge and beliefs about memory and how it works; beliefs about intelligence (e.g., some students believe a good memory is something you have or don't have).

- *Task.* An awareness that some tasks are more difficult than others and the evaluation of task difficulty and amount of time needed for task completion (e.g., planning a project and estimating the time needed and comparing it with the time available).
- *Strategies.* Decisions concerning which strategy will work the best for different types of tasks (e.g., which strategy is best for an essay test and which for mastering the table of elements in chemistry?).

Metacognitive strategies that help students take control of their learning are often lacking in low-achieving students (Gaskins & Elliot, 1991). As teachers, we often do this metacognitive work for students instead of helping them acquire the strategies to help themselves.

SELF-MANAGEMENT THROUGH SELF-MONITORING AND SELF-INSTRUCTION

Two tools used by self-regulated learners to manage actions and thoughts are self-instruction and self-monitoring. As humans, we use self-instruction when we talk to ourselves to guide our behavior. Self-monitoring occurs when we observe and evaluate our progress. These two strategies are often used in tandem. For example, a student might use self-instruction to remember how to carry out a series of steps in a problem and then use self-monitoring to keep track of and evaluate his or her progress.

Self-Instruction

An important tool in cognitive self-regulation is self-directed talk to control thought and actions (Harris, 1990; Rohrkemper, 1989). Self-instruction can be covert, silently talking to ourselves, or overt, speaking out loud. It is useful for control of behavior, development of metacognition, and treatment of academic problems (Meichenbaum, 1977). Examples of self-instruction are: (a) Elissa silently reminding herself not to panic when she sees a test question that is unfamiliar; and (b) Angela repeating out loud, "I must stay in my seat until I finish my colors."

What is the source of self-directed speech? Its roots are in Vygotsky's (1962) explanation of the development and role of speech in children. It begins in early childhood, when young children talk out

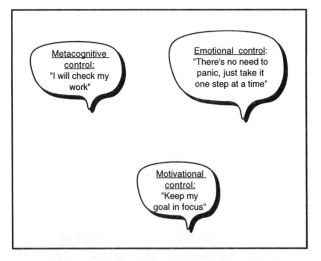

FIG. 5.2. Overt and covert self-instruction.

loud to themselves, even in the presence of others. This is initially guided by others' speech. Vygotsky explained that young children talk to themselves or use private speech to direct their own behavior. At about age 6 or 7, children become aware that it is not appropriate to talk out loud to oneself. Self-speech then becomes covert or silent (see Fig. 5.2).

As a self-regulatory process, self-instructional speech can take six forms (Graham, Harris, & Reid, 1992). These forms can help students understand the task, generate strategies for accomplishing the task, manage anxiety, and evaluate progress. These forms may be used independently or in combination as needed. Table 5.3. shows the forms with examples of each.

Teaching Students to Use Self-Instruction

Self-instruction has been used for a variety of goals, including positive classroom behavior, composition skills, and problem solving. It is particularly useful for helping students with learning disabilities to develop academic competencies (Graham et al., 1992). The instruction for self-talk can be geared to an entire class or to individual students (Manning, 1991). Self-instructional training typically begins with modeling by the teacher, followed by practice by the students. The steps for teaching are described in Strategy 5.3.

TABLE 5.3

Forms and Examples of Self-Instruction

Forms of Self-Instruction	Examples
1. Problem definition statements	I made a D on my first exam. What can I do? Was it how I studied? How can I improve?
2. Focusing attention and planning	I have to figure out a better way to study. The text is hard for me so I have to find a way to understand what I'm reading.
3. Strategy statements	I will try the SQ3R that the teacher gave us.
4. Self-evaluation and error correction statements	I tried to summarize what I have read so far and I still don't understand. I need to call one of my classmates to see how she is doing with this.
5. Coping and self-control statements help students overcome difficulties or failure	Although I don't understand it yet, I don't need to panic. I can always ask my teacher.
6. Self-reinforcement	My friend asked me questions and I could answer them. I'm ready for this test.

Note. From "*Making the Writing Process Work: Strategies for Composition and Self-Regulation,*" by S. Graham and K. Harris (1996). Cambridge, MA: Brookline. Copyright © 1996 by Brookline. Adapted by permission.

Strategy 5.3. Steps for Teaching Self-Talk

1. Explain the importance of self-talk. Discuss with students how talking to themselves can be either positive or negative. For example, self-statements such as "I can't do it" are self-defeating. "I'm not stupid, I just didn't use the right strategy," is a step in a positive direction. Ask students to give examples of their self-talk and classify them according to positive or negative.
2. Model self-instruction. A coping model, teacher, or peer can show how they have used self-talk to improve performance. Students might be given a self-talk script and then develop their own.
3. Select tasks and have students practice self-talk. Gradually fade the modeling and prompting when they can do it on their own. Cues are provided through cue cards and posters until students perform independently.

Source. Based on Graham et al. (1992) and Manning (1991).

The following research study shows the effectiveness of self-instructional training. First- and third-grade students who had a history of inappropriate classroom behavior were selected for the intervention to increase appropriate classroom behavior (Manning, 1988). The training targeted behaviors that students needed to decrease (e.g., out of seat, daydreaming, disturbing others) and behaviors students needed to increase (e.g., staying seated, listening, concentrating, keeping hands and feet to self). The training was conducted two times per week, 50 minutes per session, for 4 weeks. The training components were:

- *Modeling.* Students viewed adult models in class and video tapes of peers. The models used self-instruction to improve work habits like raising a hand instead of screaming out an answer.
- *Guided practice.* Students practiced behaviors through games, role play, and the completion of incomplete scenarios.
- *Cueing.* Students were given cue cards with reminders to do the behaviors in the classroom. Cueing was continued until students used behaviors without prompts.

The self-instruction training group was compared with a control group that did not receive self-instruction at three time periods—immediately following training, after 1 month, and after 3 months. The experimental group demonstrated greater on-task and less disruptive behavior at all three intervals than did the control group. The improved behavior was also observed by the teachers.

There are many ways students and teachers can use self-instruction as a self-regulatory strategy. Self-instruction can be used:

- as a volitional strategy to remind oneself to concentrate on work;
- to remember steps in academic tasks like problem solving or writing;
- to control attention and on-task behavior;
- to cope with anxiety and failure; and
- as part of attributional retraining.

Self-Monitoring

Self-monitoring requires a student to selectively attend to specific actions such as on-task behavior or processes such as attributional thoughts. It contains two components that go hand in hand: self-recording and self-evaluation (Zimmerman, 1995). Self-recording is a record of cognitions or actions being monitored by a student. The methods of recording include tally sheets, charts, graphs, and narrative logs. A student can evaluate the frequency or duration of a behavior like how long she was able to stay at her desk studying or a student can evaluate her accuracy by rechecking her solutions before turning in her homework. An example of a form for self-monitoring of homework goals is shown in Exhibit 5.1.

Exhibit 5.1. Self-Monitoring Homework

1. Did I write my assignment down?   Yes   No
2. What do I need to take home?
   a. _____
   b. _____
   c. _____
3. Time I will do my homework _____
4. Completion of my homework   Yes   No
5. What did I not understand?

Students who cannot monitor their own learning are at a great disadvantage. They are likely to continue to make the same mistakes. Self-monitoring serves as a tool for self-improvement and enhances learning in several ways (Zimmerman, 1995). It:

- increases selective attention by focusing students on a limited number of responses;
- helps students determine how effective a performance was;
- lets students know how effective a learning strategy was and encourages them to find a better one; and
- enhances management and use of time.

Record keeping was a strategy used by inner-city students who demonstrated characteristics of self-regulation (Wibrowski, 1992). One student reported:

> I keep a list of the words, I got wrong....When studying from a textbook, if I find something important, I get a piece of paper and just write down the name of the person and what he or she did or something like that and I have a study sheet. (p. 78)

Self-monitoring and recording are particularly important for students who have difficulty paying attention. Fifth- and sixth-grade students were taught to self-monitor study strategies in an individualized mathematics program (Sagotsky, Patterson, & Lepper, 1978). They periodically recorded "+" on a grid if they were actually working on the math and "-" if they were not. Students increased in study behaviors and math achievement. Self-regulatory components were used by Alderman (1985) to prepare high school seniors for a final exam in physical education (Exhibit 5.2).

Exhibit 5.2. Physical Education: A Self-Regulated Structure

First Day of Class

- *Self-Evaluation and Goal Setting.* Students complete a self-evaluation of health/physical fitness, competence level, and interest in various activities and then set goals for the year.

First 9-Week Grading Period

- *Weekly Self-Tests and Record-Keeping.* Students completed tests in physical fitness and recorded scores in team notebook.
- *Goals for Final Exam.* Based on feedback from self-tests. Students were asked to set a realistic aerobic goal. Choices included jog, walk, or jump rope. Instructor met with each to discuss the goal.

Second 9-Week Period.

- *Practice Schedule.* Students practiced three times a week and recorded practices on individual record cards.

Final Evaluation

- *Self-Evaluation.* Students evaluated learning with comments such as, "I learned to set a goal and accomplish it."

Source. Adapted from Alderman (1985).

Personal Note: I kept a daily log while writing this text. I recorded such things as: reading and notetaking completion, work on drafts, where I should begin the next work session, and ideas. When I began a new work session, I knew where to begin; this kept me from repeating a task. More important, it led to better organization, use of my time, and goal setting.

RESOURCE MANAGEMENT STRATEGIES: TIME AND ENVIRONMENT

Self-regulated learners manage their time and environmental resources to accomplish their goals. Strategies to budget time and manage resource are presented in this section.

Time Management

The term *time management* is somewhat misleading. There are only 24 hours in a day and we cannot change that. We can only manage ourselves in how we use the time. Covey (1989) reminded us that the most important factor is how we prioritize time use. Does a high level of motivation ensure that students will manage their time well? No, according to research findings from studies of college students (Zimmerman, Greenberg, & Weinstein, 1994). Students often failed to regulate time even if they were motivated. Self-reports of time management were more strongly related to the achievement of college students than were their SAT scores (Britton & Tessor, 1991).

Time use was also found to be the second most important self-regulated learning strategy used by inner-city high school students interviewed by Wibrowski (1992). Students reported two types of time strategies: time budgeting (planning time use) and time accounting (awareness of time use). The following report reveals one student's use of time:

> After school, I usually go home, I relax for about one hour and then I do my homework until I'm finished and if it is before 8 or 9 o'clock, I just relax and then go to sleep at around 10 o'clock. Or I just get up at about 6:30 and about 6:45, I call my mom, then I have breakfast, then I leave, then I get on the train for about 30 minutes, then I get to school, I go the cafeteria and talk to my friends till about 8:40. (p. 75)

Successful students indicated the time they spent studying or the time of day they studied. They were also aware of specific times that different activities take place.

Time budgeting is related to the processes of attributions for success and failure and self-efficacy perceptions (Zimmerman et al., 1994). A student who believes she is failing math because of ability is not likely to plan time to study math. However, a student who believes that writing improves through the process of feedback and revision will plan time for this to occur. An important factor in the self-regulation of time use is the quality of self-monitoring. When students are not aware that they are not learning, they are not likely to plan or adjust their use of time.

Our use of time is frequently based on habits, not on specific plans. Training students in time-budgeting strategies requires helping them become aware of their use of time and strategies to plan and prioritize their time use. Strategies for helping students learn how to use time effectively are found in Strategy 5.4.

Strategy 5.4. Strategies to Help Students Learn Effective Time Use

1. Discuss time use with students. The statement "I don't have time" can be discussed for attibutional meaning.
2. Have students record their time use both daily and weekly to determine how they are using time.
3. Next, have students make a personal time schedule.
4. Ask students to estimate time needed to complete various types of activities in and out of school.
5. Give examples of how you plan time for your lesson planning, grading, and other responsibilities.
6. Use computer software with calendars where available.
7. Make a calendar for your students to fill in with assignments for their classes.

Environment Management

Environmental control is concerned with study areas, noise levels, appropriate materials, and people (Gaskins & Elliot, 1991). Environmental management includes effective strategies to assist learning and strategies to reduce interference with learning. Organization is a crucial strategy that helps students control environmental factors. Some students need explicit instruction in organizational strategies. For example, when teachers at The Benchmark School initially generated a list of strategies needed by middle school students, organization was overlooked. However, they found that students needed to be taught how to organize their notebooks, notes, and handouts. Although several class periods were devoted to this early in the school year, the students were found to need a "refresher course" after a month or so. Explicit teacher explanations for organization can be found in Gaskins and Elliot (1991).

Organizational strategies are taught early in Japanese elementary schools (Peak, 1993). During the first weeks of first grade, students are taught a series of steps by which they prepare themselves to study. For example, they are first taught how to lay out materials on their desk and then they practice laying out the materials. They are also taught a routine to use at home in the evening to be sure all their equipment and book bag is ready for the next morning.

Management of study areas requires establishing a place where one can concentrate. One self-regulated characteristic of self-regulated high school students was the arrangement of the physical setting where they studied (e.g., isolate myself from anything that distracts me; Zimmerman & Martinez-Pons, 1986). Teachers can have students discuss and generate a checklist for a home and classroom study environment. Then, have the students evaluate how their personal environments compare with the master list.

SELF-REGULATION FOR FAILURE ADAPTATION AND RESILIENCY

One of the most important aspects of self-regulatory capabilities is the potential for dealing with failure and building resiliency to setbacks. Bandura (1997) reminded us that our pathways to goals and tasks are likely to be strewn with obstacles. It is not the failure and disappointments that are crucial, but the response to the setbacks. Failure is a part of school—failing tests, not being the valedictorian, not placing in the state music competition, not making the starting team or the drill team, criticism of one's work in art, losing the election for student council representative, and not understanding the reading time after time. A student's failure might be small—making his or her first B—from the view of a teacher, but a crisis from the student's perception. As described in chapter 2, when setbacks occur, some individuals abandon their efforts, prematurely giving up their goals, whereas others look for more effective strategies and try harder. One important role for teachers is to help students develop adaptive strategies to handle failure. What are these strategies?

Bandura (1997) contended that an optimistic belief in one's efficacy is a necessity in dealing with setbacks. This is related to adaptive attributions for success and failure—a learning goal view of ability and intelligence, volitional strategies to overcome obstacles, positive self-talk, and support from key people. As Rohrkemper and Corno (1988) contended, "Rather than shielding students from learning stress, we seek to teach them how to adaptively respond and learn from it" (p. 311).

Self-regulatory capabilities that have been described are not magical, nor are they learned simply by attending school. Examples of students who did not possess these capabilities have been presented in this and previous chapters:

- students in Ms. Foster's ninth-grade class, who did not have the goals or learning strategies, nor the social skills for cooperative learning;
- Angela, a first grader who was inattentive and off-task; and
- community-college students who lacked volitional strategies.

Self-regulatory strategies for students like Angela need to begin in the early grades. If there is no intervention, her inattentive/withdrawn and disruptive behavior will likely continue and it will become increasingly difficult for her to be engaged in learning (Finn, Pannozzo, & Voekle, 1995). Three components of self-regulation are particularly important for focus in the early years: self-control processes, beliefs about personal control, and hoped-for future goals (Borkowski & Thorpe, 1994).

Students who have developed these personal capabilities have also been presented:

- Albert, a first grader who is attentive and independent in figuring out what to do;

- Lilia, who has a vision of college and has determination to succeed; and
- inner-city students with self-regulatory strategies.

REFLECTION.   Make a list of your own self-regulatory strategies. Describe the characteristics of a self-regulated learner in your classroom.

The capabilities of self-regulation are needed by all students, whether they are high or low achieving. Students who have these qualities of personal capability will have a foundation for resiliency. Resilient students possess qualities such as a sense of purpose and future planning, social and help-seeking skills that enable them to gain support, and the ability to act independently (Benard, 1993). Teachers can influence the development of these capabilities by working directly on: (a) intellectual skills, (b) self-evaluation, (c) skills in interpersonal relations, (d) activity levels, and (e) self-efficacy and hopefulness (Reynolds, 1994).

For competence development and motivation, students must have a responsive environment, but personal agency beliefs are often more fundamental (Ford, 1995). Classroom climate and instruction that supports the development of these personal capabilities are presented in chapters 7 and 8.

REVIEW OF MAJOR POINTS

1. *Self-regulation* refers to the degree to which individuals are active participants in their own learning.

2. A vision of a possible self—how we think about ourselves and the future—is the first step in developing self-regulation. Motivationally, possible selves act as incentives for future behavior, with the absence of possible selves viewed as a serious motivational problem. Development of possible selves is based on social environment, attributions, and self-efficacy beliefs. Interventions to help students develop possible selves or visions of the future have been developed at elementary and secondary levels with promising success.

3. *Volition*, the "tendency to maintain focus and effort toward goals despite potential distractions," is important for self-regulation because it protects goals.

Students encounter many volitional challenges such as homework; its success depends on students' handling distractions. Volitional control strategies are covertly used to control self-defeating thoughts and covertly and overtly used to control the self by controlling the environment. Interventions to help students acquire volitional strategies have been developed from first-grade level to community-college level.

4. Self-regulated learners possess learning and metacognitive strategies. Learning strategies range from simple strategies like rehearsal to elaboration, which is essential for deep-level processing. Metacognitive strategies include knowledge and strategies of the person (knowledge and beliefs about memory and how it works), tasks (evaluation of task difficulty), and strategies (decisions about which strategy will work the best for different types of tasks).

5. Self-regulated learners use self-instruction and self-monitoring to manage actions and thoughts. Self-instruction is used when we talk to ourselves to guide our behavior and can be covert (e.g., silently talking to ourselves) or overt (e.g., speaking out loud). Six forms of self-instructional speech can help students understand the task, generate strategies for accomplishing the task, manage anxiety, and evaluate progress. Self-instruction has been used for a variety of goals, including positive classroom behavior, composition skills, and problem solving; it is particularly useful for helping students with learning disabilities develop academic competencies. Self-instructional training typically begins with modeling by the teacher, followed by practice by students.

6. Self-monitoring is the observation and evaluation of our progress. It contains two complementary components: self-recording and self-evaluation. It requires a student to selectively attend to specific actions, such as on-task behavior or processes such as attributional thoughts.

7. Self-regulated learners manage their time and environmental resources to accomplish their goals. Students can be motivated but fail to regulate their time. Training students in time-budgeting strategies requires helping them become aware of their use of time and strategies to plan and prioritize their time use.

8. Environmental control is concerned with study areas, noise levels, appropriate materials, and people and strategies to reduce interference with learning. Organization is a crucial strategy that helps students control environmental factors.

9. Self-regulatory strategies for students need to begin in the early grades with self-control processes, beliefs about personal control, and hoped-for future goals. Students who have these qualities of personal capability will have a foundation for resiliency. Resilient students possess qualities such as a sense of purpose and future planning, social and help-seeking skills that enable them to gain support, and the ability to act independently.

Motivational Toolbox

1. Important points to think about and lingering questions

2. Strategies I can use now

3. Strategies I want to develop in the future

PART III

THE CLASSROOM CLIMATE FOR OPTIMAL ENGAGEMENT AND MOTIVATION

This section moves from motivational processes to the classroom context. A classroom where students are engaged does not just happen, but is the result of interactions among students, teachers, and curriculum. The following three chapters focus on teacher expectations and confidence, the social climate of the classroom, and instructional components that affect engagement.

Teachers' beliefs about their potential effectiveness in teaching in various conditions and their expectations about abilities of diverse students have been identified as powerful influences on students' achievements. An essential element is that students of diverse populations experience a shared sense of membership with the school and classroom. Challenges for the teacher are to establish conditions that allow for optimal work conditions, provide safety for all students, and time facilitate development of personal responsibility. Three interrelated components comprise the classroom instructional focus: task, incentives, and evaluation.

CHAPTER 6

Teacher Motivation: Expectations and Efficacy

Miss Bailey, a language arts teacher in a high poverty middle school believes "The average student, no matter what his social or economic status, wants to be better when he leaves the classroom than when he walked in.... I try to provide the tools for them to do that. I teach every student like I was teaching the president of the United States ... when more than half of our students are at risk, we are all at risk.
—Rust (1992, pp. 1G, 6G)

How does a teachers' confidence affect their teaching practice and student motivation and achievement? This chapter focuses on two related areas that reflect teacher confidence: teacher expectations and teacher efficacy. *Teacher expectations* deal with what teachers expect students will be able to accomplish. *Teacher efficacy* refers to a teacher's confidence about teaching in a way that can bring about student achievement.

TEACHER EXPECTATIONS

Since the publication of Robert Rosenthal and Lenore Jacobson's (1968) *Pygmalion in the Classroom*, the topic of teacher expectations and self-fulfilling prophecy has been of great interest and controversy. The Rosenthal—Jacobson research was designed to manipulate teacher expectations and determine if these manipulations affected student achievement. Students were given a general achievement test, but teachers were told that it was a test that would identify certain students as late bloomers—students who would make large achievement gains during the year. In fact, the students identified as late bloomers had been chosen at random, not on the basis of any test scores. At the end of the year, those students who had been labeled late bloomers showed greater gain on achievement test scores than did the others. Rosenthal and Jacobson explained this gain as a self-fulfilling prophecy. A self-fulfilling prophecy occurs when "an originally erroneous expectation leads to behavior that causes the expectation to come true" (Good & Brophy, 1994, p. 84). This interpretation meant that the gains students made on achievement test scores were a consequence of expectations the teachers held for the students. There was much criticism of this study because later studies failed to find the same results (Claiborn, 1969). This led to further investigations to determine how expectations influence performance.

Teacher Expectations and Teacher Expectation Effects

Teacher expectations and teacher expectation effects are differentiated by Good and Brophy (1994). *Teacher expectations* are defined as "inferences that teachers make about the future academic achievement of students based on what they know about these students now" (Good & Brophy, 1994, p. 83). *Teacher expectation effects* are defined as "effects on student outcomes that occur because of actions that teachers take in response to their expectations" (p. 83). Teacher expectations can lead to positive or negative effects. Two types of teacher expectation effects have been identified: self-fulfilling prophecy effect and sustaining expectation effect (Cooper & Good, 1983; Good & Brophy, 1994).

The Self-Fulfilling Prophecy Effect. The self-fulfilling effect occurs when a teacher forms different expectations for students early in the year and uses different instructional practices with different results. Good and Brophy (1994) described the process as follows:

1. The teacher forms different expectations based on some student characteristic.
2. Because of these different expectations, the teacher behaves differently toward various students.

3. The teacher's behavior tells students what behavior and achievement the teacher expects from them.
4. If this treatment persists and if students do not resist or change it in some way, motivational patterns such as their aspirations and self-efficacy are likely to be affected.
5. With time, students' achievement and behavior will conform more and more closely to that originally expected of them: High-achieving students continue to achieve, whereas low-achieving students gain less.

The fact that teachers have different expectations for students does not by itself lead to a self-fulfilling prophecy. The expectation affects how teachers respond to the students and, in turn, the students are more likely to behave in the expected manner.

Sustaining Effect. A sustaining effect occurs when a teacher has an existing expectation about a student and continues to respond to the student in the same way although the student's behavior changed. This response maintains the behavior. An example is where a student has a history of misbehavior and then begins to behave more positively. The changes go unnoticed by the teacher, who continues to respond to the student in the same way, reinforcing the old behavior.

Expectations need not become sustaining or self-fulfilling effects. Brophy (1985) explained that a low expectation may have a positive outcome when a teacher is aware of low academic performance of a student, but is unwilling to accept it. The teacher may take extraordinary measures to see that the student achieves some success. Rose (1995) described a teacher who was aware of the low performance level of students but was not willing to accept it:

> Teachers will say either "we can't lower our standards" or "this poor child is reading below grade level" so I'll need a third or fourth grade book. But what you need to do is to make that eighth grade book *accessible*. (p. 17)

Although as a teacher you will be aware of student behavior and achievement, it is how you respond to students and how you teach as a result of the awareness that make the difference. Consider the example of two first-grade students (Goldenberg, 1992) whose low expectations led to high performance and high expectations led to declining performance. Marta and Sylvia were Spanish-speaking children from low socioeconomic status (SES) families. Both students were in a bilingual education reading program for children who were at risk for reading failure. The case of Marta and Sylvia is described in Exhibit 6.1.

Exhibit 6.1. How Low Expectations Can Lead to High Performance and High Expectations Can Lead to Declining Performance

Marta: Low Expectations

Marta's teacher initially predicted she would be in the lowest 5 of 29 students, primarily because of her attitude, low effort, inattention, and careless work. However, because the lack of effort bothered the teacher, she kept Marta after school and told her she needed to improve her behavior and attitude and needed to be more careful and neat, and met with Marta's mother and told her the same thing and that Marta needed more practice at home.

Marta made slight improvement by making more of an effort, resulting in the teacher revising her prediction upward. After a month break in school, Marta began to do much better, with the most observable changes in her attitude and behavior. She was more task-oriented and seemed more confident. When Marta had setbacks, the teacher viewed them as temporary (unstable), and thus not serious. By February, she referred to Marta as a *wonder child*; by April, Marta could do anything.

Marta succeeded because the teacher took positive and decisive steps toward changing her behavior early in year, instead of using actions that would lead to the self-fulfilling prophecy expectation effect.

Sylvia: High Expectations

Sylvia's teacher had high expectations for her achievement in first-grade reading. Early in first grade, the teacher referred to Sylvia as a *whippy kid* because her hand was frequently up, she usually answered correctly, and she did not forget homework or lose her syllable cards. The teacher was very satisfied with Sylvia's progress and had high expectations for first grade.

By December, the teacher said Sylvia was out of it most of the time and not was not progressing as previously. She did not finish seatwork assignments that were piling up and hindering her progress. Sylvia was a slow worker and when left to work alone, she rarely finished any assignment, resulting in a drop in the teacher's expectation. Sylvia's uncompleted work increased while her phonic skills fell below first-grade norms; she was now described as one of the *unsuccessful* readers.

(Continues)

As the year progressed, the children got longer assignments and were expected to complete more, with Sylvia's uncompleted work increasing. Because the teacher assumed Sylvia was working at her limit, she did not see a need to intervene. Goldenberg suggested the teacher consider:

- reducing her workload and telling her exactly how far she was expected to get in completing an assignment;
- giving her an amount that seems reasonable and hold her accountable, gradually increasing the work.

Several weeks later, the teacher reported Sylvia was finishing everything, with time on-task increasing to between 65% and 70% of time. Sylvia began to proudly announce how much she finished each day. In addition, the teacher's aid had expected Sylvia to finish her work before she was allowed to color an activity she enjoyed.

Goldenberg concluded that the teacher's initial high expectations had led her to assume Sylvia would do well on her own without explicit monitoring and/or action.

Source of Teacher Expectations

It is important for teachers to be aware of the potential sources that could affect their interaction with students and their teaching practices. What factors influence the expectations teachers form about students? Sources of expectations identified by Braun (1976) are shown in Fig. 6.1.

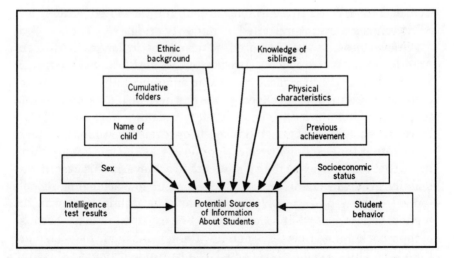

FIG. 6.1. Source of expectations. From "Teacher expectations: Sociopsychological Dynamics," by C. Braun, 1976. *Review of Educational Research, 46,* 185–213. Copyright © 1976 by the American Educational Research Association. Reprinted by permission.

It should be emphasized that the sources are potential ones. As stated earlier, awareness of differences does not automatically lead to self-fulfilling prophecies.

REFLECTION.   Which of these student characteristics will be more likely to influence you? What will you need to guard against? A self-evaluation of these potential sources of expectations can help you become more aware of biases that may lead to differential practices.

Beliefs about the nature of intelligence are a powerful source of teacher and school expectations. Two conceptions of intelligence—entity and incremental (Elliott & Dweck, 1988)—were presented in chapter 3. If teachers view intelligence as an entity, fixed and stable, they are likely to see students as *smart* or *dumb* and teach them according to the label. However, if teachers believe that intelligence is composed of many dimensions, is incremental, and that learning strategies can be taught, they will be more concerned with how much they can teach students.

How influential is SES and ethnicity on forming expectations? Social class and ethnicity were singled out as the two most observable characteristics that are likely to influence teacher beliefs (Baron, Tom, & Cooper, 1985). These two variables are often interrelated because low SES groups are overrepresented by minority groups.

A now-classic study compared achievement in low SES African-American and White schools (Brookover, Beady, Flood, Schweitzer, & Wisenbaker, 1979). The most important differences affecting achievement were; (a) the level of expectations teachers held for students, and (b) teacher commitment to ensuring that academics were learned. The more successful teachers established floor levels for student achievement rather than ceiling levels. A *floor level* was the minimal requirement that teachers expected all students to achieve; in this case, it was usually grade level. In contrast, teachers in low-achieving schools tended to have *ceiling-level* expectations. The ceiling level was the highest estimate of what students could be expected to learn because of their background (low SES) and no attempt was made to teach more than this. Thus, a ceiling level acted as a cap on learning, as shown in Fig. 6.2. Teachers in high-achieving schools who had floor-level requirements were largely successful at attaining the academic expectations.

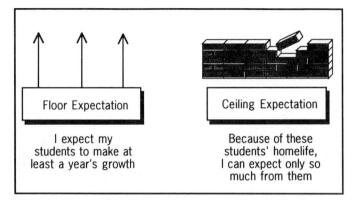

FIG. 6.2 Floor and ceiling effects.

Negative teaching practices in some high poverty classrooms were found by Shields (1995). Shields observed that a small percentage of teachers believed students from certain cultural or economic groups possessed significant limitations that could not be overcome and this affected how they taught. One example of a negative practice occurred in a first-grade reading class where half the students were Hispanic and half were White. The *low* reading group, composed of Hispanic students, was turned over to an aide for instruction instead of being taught by the regular teacher. Negative practices such as this were thought to be based on negative stereotypes about ethnic or socioeconomic background of students and what they could accomplish and affected teaching practices.

Brookover et al. (1979) concluded that, although a student body composed of minority or low SES students may predispose teachers and principals to accept low levels of achievement, this can be overcome through developing a positive academic climate.

How Do Teachers Communicate Expectations to Students?

Expectations are communicated to students by a variety of teaching practices. Table 6.1 presents a list of differential expectations as summarized by Good and Weinstein (1986). Selected classroom practices are described in greater detail.

Questioning Strategies. Teachers may use different questioning strategies for students thought to be low ability compared

TABLE 6.1

General Dimensions of Teachers' Communication of Differential Expectations
and Selected Examples

Dimensions	Students Believed to Be MORE Capable Have:	Students Believed to Be LESS Capable Have:
Task environment Curriculum, procedures, task definition, pacing, qualities of environment	More opportunity to perform publicly on meaningful tasks	Less opportunity to perform publicly especially on meaningful tasks (supplying alternate endings to a story vs. learning to pronounce a word correctly).
	More opportunity to think.	Less opportunity to think, analyze (since much work is aimed at practice).
Grouping practices	More assignments that deal with comprehension, understanding (in higher ability groups).	Less choice on curriculum assignments—more opportunity to work on drill-like assignments.
Locus of responsibility for learning	More autonomy (more choice in assignments, fewer interruptions).	Less autonomy (frequent teacher monitoring of work, frequent interruptions).
Feedback and evaluation practices	More opportunity for self-evaluation.	Less opportunity for self-evaluation.
Motivational strategies	More honest/contingent feedback.	Less honest/more gratuitous/less contingent feedback.
Quality of teacher relationships	More respect for the learner as an individual with unique interests and needs.	Less respect for the learner as an individual with unique interests and needs.

Note. From "Teacher expectations: A framework for exploring classrooms," by T. L. Good & R. Weinstein, *Improving Teaching (1986 ASCD Yearbook)*. Edited by Karen K. Zumwalt, Copyright © (1986 Alexandria, VA: Association for Supervision and Curriculum Development. Reprinted by permission. All rights reserved.

with students thought to be high ability (e.g., Allington, 1980). Typically, low-ability students were called on less often and given less time to answer. Teachers were also more likely to give low-ability students the answers or call on another student rather than providing hints or rephrasing questions to help them improve their responses. These low-ability students were less likely to be asked higher level comprehension questions. Questioning practices such as these communicate to students that they are less capable; they also deprive the lower achieving students an opportunity to develop higher level comprehension skills.

Grouping Practices. The effects of grouping practices can occur in individual classrooms such as reading groups and at the school level where tracking by ability is in place. A student's group assignment is likely to be the first factor that conveys a teacher's expectation for student achievement (Weinstein, 1993). Those expectations will be communicated by the curriculum, text, and instructional practices selected or designed by the teacher. What is the evidence about the effects of grouping practices on student achievement?

Group placement can communicate expectations, both directly and indirectly, to students (Weinstein, 1993). A direct expectation is conveyed by reading group assignment, whether high-or low-ability group, when students are given different instruction. For example, Good and Marshall (1984) found that low-ability groups spent much of their time in repetitive drill with inadequate instruction. An indirect way to communication expectations is the use of labels such as *special readers*, signifying the low reading group.

When students are segregated into separate classes, as in ability grouping (tracking), there are more opportunities for undesirable self-fulfilling prophecy effects (Brophy, 1985). A number of instructional practices have been identified whereby high- and low-track classes received differential instruction. In all cases, low-track classes seemed to have less opportunities to learn than high-track classes. The following are examples of differential instruction:

- Teachers in low-track classes tended to be less clear about objectives, made less attempts to relate material to student interests and backgrounds, were less open to student input, and were not as clear in introducing material (Evertson, 1982).
- Low-track classes were taught less demanding topics and skills, especially those involving higher level thinking skills; had less experienced teachers; and had less active learning and more seatwork and worksheet activities in math and science (Oakes, 1985).

How are positive expectations conveyed in the classroom? Wheelock (1992) found a number of ways that teachers communicated positive expectations (Exhibit 6.2).

Exhibit 6.2. How Teachers Can Communicate High Expectations

Lessons can communicate high expectations if they:

- Build on and validate students' prior knowledge and experience
- Help students construct their own knowledge
- Communicate information in a variety of ways
- Engage in dialogue that evokes more than one-word answers
- Require thinking skills such as comparing, contrasting, and applying knowledge
- Incorporate students' own cultural backgrounds into learning
- Involve students through a variety of activities that engage different kinds of intelligence
- Involve all students whether or not they volunteer comments

A teacher communicates high expectations for students by:

- Introducing activities in which every individual becomes invested in the group effort
- Communicating that making mistakes is part of learning and that practice and concentration promote improvement
- Creating an environment of mutual trust and cooperation among students and between students and the teacher
- Arranging seating in such a way that no student is "invisible" to the teacher or others

Permanent classroom "decorations" can convey high expectations so that:

- Students understand that learning continues beyond the completion of a classroom assignment and that extra time is still learning time
- Students work in an environment that stresses their responsibility for their own learning
- Teachers are relieved of the necessity of repeating directions related to assignments, allowing them to remain engaged in coaching or dialogue with students

A teacher can communicate high expectations by:

- Allowing students plenty of time to answer questions
- Giving hints and working with students if the answer does not come quickly
- Creating a student–teacher partnership in the uncovering of knowledge
- Putting students in the role of the teacher

(Continued)

A classroom environment can communicate high expectations by:

- Letting students know that their schoolwork is preparing them for life, not just for the next grade
- Providing images and information that encourage students to stretch their aspirations to include the possibility of a wide range of future options
- Distributing legitimate recognition to as many students as possible in as many ways as possible
- Assigning projects that require extended effort
- Providing examples of high-quality work as models of what is expected from the class

Praise from teachers can reinforce high expectations when:

- Praise informs students about the value of their accomplishments and orients them toward a better appreciation of their thinking and problem-solving abilities
- Praise focuses on the specifics of the accomplishment
- Praise is authentic and leaves students convinced that the teacher has given thoughtful consideration to performance and means what she says

A classroom can create high expectations through:

- A set of explicit guidelines that emphasize the school, parents, and students working together as a team
- Parental involvement in monitoring and supporting their children's work
- Provisions for keeping parents informed of student progress through regular and frequent reports, not just at report card time
- Regular face-to-face meetings between parents

Source. From "Crossing the Tracks" by A. Wheelock, 1992, pp. 95–99. New York: New Press. Adapted with permission.

Student Awareness of Teacher Expectations

To what extent are students aware of differential expectations held by teachers? Weinstein (1993) reviewed research that examined students' perceptions of their treatment by teachers. She found that students, ranging from first grade through sixth grade, were aware that teachers treat students differently. Reports by students indicate they were aware that low achievers are likely to: (a) receive more negative feedback, (b) get more rules and teacher directions, (c) receive lower expectations, and (d) have fewer opportunities or choices.

A relationship was found between students' perceptions about the value of study strategies and their perceptions about what their teachers wanted them to learn (Nolen & Haladyna, 1990). The findings indicate that when students thought that their teacher wanted them to think independently and thoroughly master the material to be learned, they were more likely to have a have a learning goal orientation rather than a performance orientation and thus value using learning strategies. The authors concluded that teachers' expectations can influence students to use study strategies.

By the same token, teachers need to be aware of the subtle ways they lower achievement and achievement expectations when they think they are helping the student. A study of how teachers adapted instruction for at-risk students (learning disabled in this case) was conducted by Miller, Leinhardt, and Zigmond (1988). They discovered teaching practices that did not require even moderate engagement by students. To the contrary, the practices acted as deterrents to students' developing more adaptive strategies. The practices included:

- shuffling of information without really processing it (e.g., transferring information from the chalkboard to a notebook, to homework, or tests);
- teachers reading the text for students and extracting important information for students without requiring students to acquire information processing or reading comprehension skills;
- giving tests where 81% of the items came verbatim from a review sheet.

It is unrealistic for teachers not to be aware of student differences. The important principle is to teach in ways that will help all students develop their abilities.

Suggestions for Developing Appropriate Expectations

First, reduce the use of labels for individual students and groups. Labels such as *low ability, slow, deprived, poor,* or *learning disabled* imply fixed abilities. Instead of concentrating on a student's low ability, concentrate on what the student needs to learn. A positive expectation is, "Shanna may be a poor reader, but I will teach Shanna how to find a main idea and to recall prior knowledge." Teaching implications for expectations are listed in Strategy 6.1. In Exhibit 6.3, Isennagle (1993) described how he set expectations for his

Strategy 6.1. Teaching Implications for Expectations

The most important consideration is to establish high, realistic expectations. The following recommendations are based on Brophy (1983) and Good and Brophy (1997):

- Once expectations for students are established, maintain flexibility by noting and taking into account when their performance is improving or declining (recall Marta and Sylvia).
- Set standards at floor levels, not ceiling. As the class progresses, focus on how far they can go, not on limits that were established in the beginning.
- When giving individual students feedback,
  - Use individual comparison standards, not standards that compare their performance with other students.
  - Respond to success and failure with attributional feedback that gives the student information about why they were successful and how they can improve.
- Reteach another way when students have not understood a lesson. Continuing to teach the same way is not likely to lead to progress.
- Focus on assisting students to achieve as much as they can.

Exhibit 6.3. Setting Expectations for an Elementary Urban Classroom

In setting up a structure for my class, I work to establish both an intangible framework of mindset and spirit as well as a tangible structure of set routines, customs, and classroom practices.... Each student's heart must be caught up in the passion and enjoyment of learning and reading. This attitude is a mindset that must be nurtured daily. Time for this cultivating of spirit is set into every day's lesson plans. It is imperative that I teach each student that they can learn, regardless of whatever they believe hinders them.... Teaching students to know they can learn requires that I couple an academic sense of identity with a sense of mission. This begins the first moment I meet my pupils.

Welcome, graduating class of the year 2001. Yes, you are all learners, discoverers, and future high school and college graduates. In June 2001, you will no longer be in second grade but you will be going to college. Why? Because I have some of America's finest, some of the brightest students in the nation. Not one of you cannot learn. Don't play games with me, your parents, or yourselves and pretend you can't because I know and you know that you can. You will graduate from college and do something special for the world. Each of you will make me famous. Why? Because of the great things that each and every one of you will do.
Source. A. Isennagle, 1993, pp. 373–374.

elementary urban classroom. In the next section, teacher efficacy is concerned with how expectations translate into teacher confidence and practice about various types of teaching assignments.

TEACHER EFFICACY

Teacher efficacy is "the extent to which teachers believe that they have the capacity to affect student performance" (Ashton, 1984, p. 28). Two Rand Corporation studies first introduced teacher efficacy by having teachers rate themselves on the following two questions (Armour et al., 1976; Berman, McLaughlin, Bass, Pauly, & Zellman, 1977):

1. "When it comes right down to it, a teacher can't do much because a student's motivation and performance depends on his or her home environment."
2. "If I really try hard, I can get through to even the most difficult or unmotivated students."

Based on the Rand studies, the authors concluded that a teacher's sense of efficacy was one of the best predictors of increased student achievement and the extent of teacher change. Ashton and Webb (1986) continued self-efficacy research, focusing particularly on teachers' confidence about teaching low-achieving students.

Similar to self-efficacy, teacher efficacy has two components (Ashton & Webb, 1986). The first is general teaching efficacy or beliefs about what teachers, in general, can accomplish despite obstacles. This refers to beliefs about the teachability of students or subjects and is reflected in the first question cited previously. Personal teaching efficacy is a judgment about the extent the teacher, personally, can affect student learning. This is reflected by the second question. Teachers reflecting high and low efficacy have been identified at all levels of schooling: high school and middle school (Ashton & Webb, 1986; Warren & Payne, 1997), special education (Podell & Soodak, 1993), preservice teachers (Hoy & Woolfolk, 1990), and college developmental math (Klein, 1996). Teaching beliefs and practices that differentiate high- and low-efficacy teachers, effects on student achievement and motivation, influences on efficacy, and factors that increase efficacy are described in the remainder of this chapter.

Beliefs and Practices Related to Teacher Efficacy

How do teachers with a high sense of efficacy differ from those with low efficacy? They differ in their beliefs about students' capabilities, their capability to teach them, and in how they teach. A summary of teacher attitudes is shown in Table 6.2 (Ashton, 1984).

REFLECTION. The attitudes shown in Table 6.2 form a useful checklist to self-evaluate your own teaching beliefs. Think about each in your classroom.

Beliefs Related to Teacher Efficacy. As in teacher expectations, a belief about the nature of intelligence strongly differentiates high-and low-efficacy teachers. The following two statements recorded by Ashton and Webb (1986) illustrate this difference:

Teacher A, Low Sense of Efficacy: "I don't know if they [low-achieving students] will ever get it [basic skills] no matter how hard you work them. Partially [that's due to] immaturity and lack of motivation. I'm sure some of it has to do with their mental ability and capacity. I'm sure of that."
Teacher B, High Sense of Efficacy: "I don't believe it's right to give up on anybody. I guess that's why I keep trying. A student can fail every day in the week [but] I'm not going to accept it....Most students start doing some [work] and they ... see results. They're not going to be math wizards, but they're going to be able to do something before they leave this class" (Ashton & Webb, 1986, p. 86).

One of the biggest deterrents to high efficacy is the belief that intelligence is a fixed, stable ability (Ashton, 1984; Klein, 1996). Teachers with a high level of personal teaching efficacy, like Teacher B, are more likely to believe that all students can learn and to feel responsible for their learning than are teachers with low efficacy, like Teacher A. Teachers who have low efficacy are likely to believe that it is hopeless to attempt to teach students believed to have low intelligence.

Although little research has examined the relationship between teacher efficacy and student culture, student ethnicity may be a factor that influences efficacy. One study compared preservice and

TABLE 6.2
Eight Attitudes That Distinguish High- From Low-Efficacy Teachers

Teacher Attitude	High Efficacy	Low Efficacy
A sense of personal accomplishment	Feel their work with students is important and meaningful; that they have a positive impact on student learning.	Feel frustrated and discouraged about teaching.
Positive expectations for student behavior and achievement	Expect students to progress and, for the most part, find students fulfill their expectations.	Expect students to fail and react negatively to their teaching effort and to misbehavior.
Personal responsibility for student learning	Believe it's their responsibility to see their students learn and when student experience failure, look to their own performance for ways they might be more helpful.	Place responsibility for learning on students and, when students fail, look for explanations in terms of family background, motivation, or attitude.
Strategies for achieving objectives	Plan for student learning, set goals for themselves and for their students, and identify strategies to achieve them.	Lack specific goals for their students, uncertain about what they want their students to achieve, and do not plan strategies according to goals.
Positive affect	Feel good about teaching, themselves, and their students	Frustrated with teaching and often express discouragement and negative feelings about their work with students.
Sense of control	Confident they can influence student learning.	Experience a sense of futility in working with students.
Sense of common teacher–student goals; democratic decision making	Feel they are involved in a joint venture with students to achieve goals they have in common. Involve students in decision making and strategies for achieving goals.	Feel they are pitted in a struggle with students with goals and strategies in opposition to theirs. Impose decisions regarding goals and learning strategies on students without involving them in process.

Note. From "Teacher Efficacy: A Motivational Paradigm for Effective Teacher Education," by P. Ashton, *Journal of Teacher Education, 35,* 28–30. Copyright © 1994 by Sage Publications. Adapted by permission.

inservice teachers on their efficacy for teaching African-American students (Pang & Sablan, 1995). Overall, the teachers did not feel confident in their ability to teach African-American children, with preservice teachers reporting stronger efficacy than in-service teachers. An important finding is that the predominately White sample had limited knowledge of African-American students and their culture. The authors believe this is a factor that contributed to low efficacy.

Contrasting examples reported by Rosenholtz (1989) illustrate how teacher beliefs about student motivation influence their teaching practices:

Teacher A: I think the caliber of [the third grade] students generally has been the same [over the years]. Of course, there have been some students who didn't progress. Some students didn't progress because they didn't want to improve. That's their own decision. You can't do much about them; you can't really help them" (p. 117).

Teacher B: "I guess I pressure my [first grade] children a lot in the beginning. They find out that this is what she wants. She wants me to read. She wants me to like reading. She wants me to think school is fun. I want to do a good job. I think I do. I've had students say 'I can read all through the years.' ... Its important for me to do this for *all my* students. Some first graders are not ready for this yet. I try to keep the environment hopeful, give them special help, and they will come around. If they have special learning problems, I always try to help" (p. 118).

Teachers also may have a tendency for self-worth protection (chap. 3). When a teacher attributes a student's low achievement to lack of ability or low stable effort, the teacher protects him or herself from feeling responsible for the student's learning. Attributing poor achievement to a student's lack of ability or unwillingness to work, as Teacher A did, may lead teachers to use failure-avoiding strategies to protect their self-worth (Rosenholtz, 1989). These self-protective strategies may include accepting normally unacceptable work and then not persisting in instruction for these students. The critical difference is that Teacher A uses student motivation to justify students' poor performance, whereas Teacher B consciously cultivates student motivation.

Teaching Practices Related to Teacher Efficacy.   What specific teaching behaviors differentiate between high- and low-efficacy teachers? High-and low-efficacy teachers were found to differ in how they interact with students and in how they teach. High-efficacy teachers:

- tend to hold students accountable for their performance (e.g., insist that students attempt challenging questions and problems; Ashton & Webb, 1986);
- spend more time on academic learning in contrast to low-efficacy teachers, who spend more time on nonacademic pastimes (Gibson & Dembo, 1984);
- strive for higher goals for their students and set goals that are overall more ambitious than those with low efficacy (Allinder, 1995);
- develop supportive trusting relationships with students. Both practicing and preservice teachers reported themselves as more trusting of students, more able to give up their absolute control, and more willing to share responsibility with students for solving classroom problems (Ashton & Webb, 1986; Hoy & Woolfolk, 1990).
- work to build friendly relationships with low achievers and hold higher expectations for them (Ashton, 1984; Klein, 1996);
- are less likely to refer low SES students to special education (Podell & Soodak, 1993); and
- more confident in working with parents (Hoover-Dempsey, Bassler, & Brissie, 1987).

Finally, and most important, high-efficacy teachers are more likely to innovate and change their teaching practice. Sparks (1988) reported that high efficacy leads to a greater willingness to try new methods, see the importance of training in new practices, and use these new practices in the classroom. A consistent finding is that high-efficacy teachers are more likely to implement cooperative learning than are low-efficacy teachers (Ghaith & Yaghi, 1997). After teachers received training on the STAD model of cooperative learning, high-efficacy teachers indicated a greater willingness to implement it in their classrooms. They considered STAD as more congruent with how they currently teach and as less difficult to implement than did low-efficacy teachers. In another study, the teachers who implemented cooperative learning in their classroom expressed greater efficacy in promoting the learning of slow students compared with teachers who used traditional methods (Shachar & Shmuelevitz, 1997).

Teacher Efficacy and Student Self-Efficacy

Is student self-efficacy related to teacher efficacy? Teacher efficacy was found to have a stronger impact on the self-efficacy of low-achieving students compared with high-achieving students (Ashton & Webb, 1986; Midgley, Feldlaufer, & Eccles, 1989). A low-efficacy teacher is especially detrimental to the motivation of low-achieving students. In contrast, students have a chance to increase their self-efficacy with a high-efficacy teacher (Midgley et al., 1989).

Midgley et al. studied the influence of teacher efficacy on student self-efficacy in math beginning the last year of elementary continuing through the first year of junior high school. Measurements taken in the spring of both years indicate that students who had higher efficacy teachers had higher expectancies for their own performance in math. Students who had low-efficacy teachers viewed math as more difficult. What if students moved from a high-efficacy teacher in elementary to a low-efficacy teacher in junior high? Compared with students with high-efficacy teachers, these students showed the most change. With a low-efficacy teacher, students declined in their expectancies and judgments of task performance while judgment of task difficulty showed an increase.

Influences on Teacher Efficacy

The relationship of teacher efficacy and student confidence in academic performance underscores the importance of teacher efficacy. Because teacher efficacy affects the instructional methods used by teachers, an important question is this: What influences efficacy and, especially, what increases it? These factors are described next.

School and Classroom Environmental Characteristics.
A supportive school climate is one factor that influences high teacher efficacy. The support of administrators and colleagues is important. One supportive school organization structure is interdisciplinary teams, with common planning times as found in many middle schools

(Warren & Payne, 1997). Teachers in this arrangement had higher personal efficacy than teachers who were in departmental arrangements. The authors concluded that the common planning time makes a difference in teachers' judgment about their competence because of the opportunity to collaborate and share problems and concerns with team members.

Another set of factors relates to the characteristics of the school and classroom environment. Ashton and Webb (1986) found that many teachers felt unprepared to teach students deemed at risk. In a study of secondary classrooms, the most important classroom variable affecting efficacy was the students' ability level and the extent to which the teacher felt prepared to teach the students (Raudenbush, Rowen, & Cheong, 1992). If teachers were able to keep students engaged in learning, however, the negative effects of tracking on efficacy disappeared.

Teacher Experience. It seems like an obvious assumption that more experienced teachers will have higher efficacy, but is this the case? Based on findings from research, the answer is yes and no. Teacher efficacy does tend to increase during preservice training and student teaching when new skills are being learned and practiced (Hoy & Woolfolk, 1990). A study by Benz, Bradley, Alderman, and Flowers (1992) compared preservice and experienced teachers on beliefs about their effectiveness in handling 15 teaching situations. Preservice teachers expressed higher efficacy about handling difficult motivation problems, whereas the experienced teachers expressed higher efficacy on planning and evaluating lessons. The authors speculated that for the motivational problems, the preservice teachers were either idealistic or had learned strategies that were not available to the experienced group. The experienced teachers had a more extensive knowledge base in planning and evaluation and this likely led to their higher efficacy.

Ghaith and Yaghi (1997) also found efficacy differences between experienced and less experienced teachers in the implementation of the STAD cooperative learning approach. One difference was how compatible STAD was with their current teaching approach. Less experienced and high-efficacy teachers perceived STAD to be more compatible with how they taught. The more experienced teachers tended to rate the STAD as more difficult and less compatible with their teaching approach.

Subject Matter Preparation. Subject matter preparation is another factor that influences how effective teachers judge themselves to be. One problematic area for many elementary teachers is the teaching of science. For example, Ramey-Gassert and Shroyer (1992) found that many elementary teachers reported they had inadequate backgrounds in science and consequently avoided teaching it when possible. Because of these findings, efforts are being made to enhance science teaching efficacy at both preservice and in-service levels.

How does knowing about the factors that influence efficacy help me as preservice or practicing teacher? It tells me that experience alone is not enough to develop a strong belief in my ability to promote academic learning. It tells me that if my subject area is one where I have doubts about my ability to teach it well, I should seek to continue develop my expertise in this area. The following section describes factors that enhance teacher efficacy.

Enhancement of Teacher Efficacy

What factors lead to development or increase of teaching efficacy? The same factors that increase student self-efficacy—competence feedback and vicarious experience through models—are likely to increase teacher efficacy.

Self-Efficacy Factors. The LINKS model (Alderman, 1990), introduced earlier, provides a sequence that teachers might use to enhance efficacy (see Fig. 4.1):

- Set goals that are proximal, realistic, and specific related to the development of new teaching strategies.
- When you have experienced initial success for students, identify what you did that contributed to the successful outcome. This attribution will lead to a stronger sense of efficacy. If you are not successful, return to proximal goals and begin again.

One critical component for enhancing efficacy is to maintain an ongoing assessment of student progress to provide evidence of improvement (McDaniel & Dibella-McCarthy, 1989). As in self-efficacy, simply learning new skills is not sufficient to increase efficacy; teachers must also recognize when their skills are improving.

Social Support.   Support from colleagues or supervisors was found to be important for developing efficacy for both preservice and in-service teachers. Preservice teachers who work in teams in field experiences and worked together to develop and present lessons were found to have higher efficacy (Cannon & Scharmann, 1996; Wilson, 1996). The positive effect of collaboration was stated by one preservice teacher: "When you are in a group of people you tend not to be afraid because you know you are all working together" (Cannon & Scharmann, 1996, p. 432).

Another area where social support contributed to a sense of efficacy was planning and evaluating interventions for students with behavior problems (Kruger, 1997). Teachers' perception that their skills and abilities were appreciated by coworkers was the most helpful social support. The author concluded that if teachers are reassured of their worth as professionals, they might feel more confident about working with children with behavior problems.

Support from knowledgeable colleagues was an important factor in increasing science teaching efficacy for elementary teachers (Ramey-Gassert, Shroyer, & Staver, 1996).

Ross (1995) concluded that preparation of beginning teachers and staff development for practicing teachers needs to explicitly address teaching efficacy in addition to the enhancement of teaching skills. A staff development program that addressed both teaching skills and efficacy resulted in increased feelings of confidence for the participants (Fritz, Miller-Heyl, Kreutzer, & MacPhee, 1995). Teachers who participated in the training increased their feelings of personal competence in meeting the needs of students and saw fewer barriers to learning.

What can you do to develop your own teaching efficacy? Strategies and a planning and evaluation guide based on self-efficacy principles are presented in Strategy 6.2.

COLLECTIVE TEACHER EFFICACY

Thus far, the discussion has centered on the individual sense of efficacy of teachers. An overriding influence on student educational achievement may be the perceived collective efficacy of teachers. Collective efficacy is the sum of all teachers' sense of efficacy and the sum of teachers' beliefs about their schools' capability to educate students (Bandura, 1993, 1997). Lee and Smith (1996) investigated

---

Strategy 6.2. Developing High Teaching Efficacy

- Have a learning goal orientation for yourself; that effort will pay off in increased skills. Acknowledge that setbacks or outright failure will be part of the learning process. Focus on your progress whether you are an experienced teacher implementing a new practice or a preservice teacher learning to teach. This will reduce discouragement.
- Collect data on student progress. As students gain in achievement, so should your efficacy increase.
- Look to effective teachers as models of practice and for support. Use peer observation with feedback.
- Collaborate with peers who are interested in improving student achievement.
- Take advantage of professional development opportunities with colleagues so continuing support is available.
- The following steps can be used as a Planning and Evaluation Guide:

Planning

1. What knowledge or teaching skills do you now possess that will be useful?
2. What new teaching skills will you need to develop?
3. What are questions, unknowns, issues, or concepts that you may not fully understand? What major decisions will you need to make?
4. What are possible barriers to implementation—personal and external?
5. What is a way you could try this on a small scale? What is your starting point?

Evaluation

1. Observation—who could observe you?
2. What student data will be important?
3. Self-evaluation—self-observation, keeping a journal,
4. My self-efficacy at this point for developing and implementing this strategy or project is

Low confidence   High confidence

0———-1————2————-3———-4———-5———-6———-7

---

how the organization of high school teachers' work affected adolescent achievement. Regardless of the type of organization and decision making in schools, they found that the overriding factor related to student achievement was the teachers' perception of collective responsibility for student learning. Teacher beliefs about limitations of students' ability to learn and their ability to teach them was stronger than reforms in organization that had been put in place (Fig. 6.3).

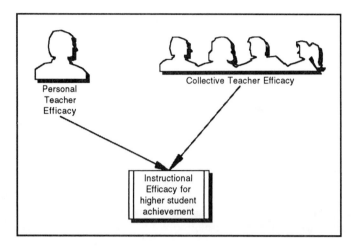

FIG. 6.3. Collective/personal efficacy.

Schools in which the staff collectively judge themselves as relatively powerless to get their students to achieve academic success are likely to convey a group sense of academic futility.... In contrast schools in which staff members collectively judge themselves highly capable of promoting academic success are likely to imbue their schools with a positive atmosphere of sociocognitive development. (Bandura, 1997, p. 248)

The high-achieving schools described by Brookover et al. (1979) can be considered examples of schools with a strong collective sense of efficacy.

REVIEW OF MAJOR POINTS

1. Teachers' beliefs in students' abilities to learn and their confidence in their ability to promote academic learning both affect how they teach. This, in turn, affects students' motivation and achievement.

2. There is a distinction between teacher expectations and teacher expectation effects. Teacher expectations are inferences teachers make about students' future achievements, whereas expectation effect is the actual effect on student outcome as a result of teacher actions. Sustaining effects—when a teacher's actions toward

a student stays the same even when the student is improving—are more prevalent in the classroom.

3. The fact that teachers have different expectations for students does not lead to a self-fulfilling prophecy. An expectation affects how teachers respond to the students; in turn, the students are more likely to behave in the expected manner.

4. Expectations are influenced by labels assigned to students, teacher beliefs about intelligence, and student characteristics such as SES and ethnicity. Expectations are communicated to students through teaching practices such as questioning strategies, grouping, curriculum and materials used, and the use of labels such as *low ability*.

5. Although a student body composed of minority or low SES students may predispose teachers and principals to accept low levels of achievement, this can be overcome through developing a positive academic climate, where expectations are set at floor level instead of ceiling levels, and students are taught in ways that help *all* of them develop their abilities.

6. Personal teaching efficacy is a form of self-efficacy that refers to how effective teachers judge themselves to be in a given teaching situation. A teacher's sense of efficacy was found to one of the best predictors of increase in student achievement, having stronger impact on the self-efficacy of low-achieving students compared with high-achieving students

7. Teachers with a high sense of efficacy are more likely to develop supportive, trusting relationships with students; share responsibility; strive for higher goals for their students; spend more time on academic learning; and innovate and change their teaching practices.

8. Teacher efficacy is influenced by support of the school climate, experience, and subject matter preparation.

9. Teacher efficacy is positively influenced by improvement of teaching skills, competence feedback, social support by colleagues and supervisors, collaborative working relationships, and directly addressing efficacy.

Motivational Toolbox

1. Important points to think about and lingering questions

2. Strategies I can use now

3. Strategies I want to develop in the future

CHAPTER 7

Promoting Optimal
Motivation and Engagement:
Social Context

One of the greatest tasks of teachers is to help students learn how to be recipients of care. Those who have not learned to do this by the time they have entered school are at great risk and their risk is not just academic.

—Noddings (1992, p. 108)

Classroom learning and motivation are inherently embedded in a social context (Corno & Rohrkemper, 1985). Classrooms are composed of a teacher and individual students who are likely to be diverse in many ways (e.g., ethnicity, gender, ability, SES, skills of self-regulation, goals, interests, and special needs). Instructional groups are of varying sizes: whole group, small groups ranging from informal to well-planned cooperative learning groups, partners on the computer, and teams on the playground. Additionally, informal interactions such as students talking to each other, teasing, name calling, and comparing work are ongoing. In all cases, teachers are continually interacting both with individuals and groups of students. What is the relationship between social context and optimal student motivation and engagement?

The social interactions influence motivation in a number of ways, both positive and negative. Social context has been found to influence classroom engagement, academic effort, and subsequent school success and failure at all levels of schooling. Social context was identified as a factor in the following situations:

- reduction of drop-out rate in secondary schools (Wehlage, Rutter, Smith, Lesko, & Fernandez, 1989);

- increased student engagement in secondary schools (Newmann, 1992);
- increased retention rates in college (Tinto, 1993);
- successful transition from elementary to middle school (Eccles & Midgley, 1989);
- level of engagement of urban middle and high school students (Goodenow, 1993);
- a key classroom dimension among successful elementary teachers of culturally diverse children (e.g., African-American children [Ladson-Billings, 1994; Latino children [Rueda & Moll, 1994]).

If optimum motivation is to happen, a major priority is to build a classroom climate where students support each other for learning and not only want to achieve, but also care about their classments' achievement.

The following sections of this chapter explain the nature and importance of psychological membership or belonging for cognitive engagement, identify factors that build or hinder membership, and present environmental variables that can be altered by teachers to build a positive social context.

SENSE OF MEMBERSHIP OR BELONGING

Wehlage et al. (1989) asserted that a sense of school membership is the foundation on which educational engagement is built. What is school membership? Psychologically, *membership* is described by Goodenow (1993) as the "extent to which students feel personally accepted, respected, included, and supported by others in school environment" (p. 80). A sense of school membership is based on the satisfaction of three basic human needs: autonomy, competence, and belonging or relatedness (Connell & Wellborn, 1991). When students experience a sense of belongingness in a school context, they are more likely to adopt goals valued by the school. In contrast, a context that does not allow for satisfaction of these three needs will diminish motivation and lead to alienation and poor performance (Ryan & Stiller, 1991). To the extent that students feel disconnected to school, they are likely to reject school goals. For example, Steele (1992) proposed that one reason for the lower achievement of African

Americans is that identification with school is missing. A low sense of school belonging and low school motivation was found among urban adolescents (Goodenow & Grady, 1993). What factors seem to be necessary for students to identify with schools and be willing to adopt the goals of school and work toward them?

Social Bonds

Wehlage et al. (1989) studied 14 schools that were successful with at-risk students. A common factor among all schools was the *social bonds* that connected students to the school. Four factors were identified that establish social bonds to the school:

- Attachment. Students are socially bonded to the extent that they have social and emotional ties to adults and peers in the school. This attachment is reciprocal: "The school/teacher cares about me and I care about my actions." Therefore, students have a vested interest in meeting expectations of others and abiding by the norms of behavior expected in the school.
- Commitment. Social bonds are formed by commitment—a conscious decision by students about what they have to do to achieve the school's goals (e.g., working in classes where they have no real interest). If students do not have hope for the future, however, commitment is more unlikely.
- Involvement. Student involvement in school activities both academic and nonacademic increases the likelihood of bonding. If student are not active participants in school, they are more often disengaged as evidenced by their passivity.
- Belief. Students' belief that an education is important and their faith in the school to provide them with an education is asserted by Newmann (1992) to be the bedrock of membership. The first three factors are somewhat dependent on this one. This is also a reciprocal relationship, requiring that teachers also believe that students are competent to learn and achieve the goals of school.

Understanding the groups or categories by which students identify themselves (social identity) is important in building a climate for a sense of membership. The next section examines social identity and membership.

Social Identity and Membership

Students, adolescents in particular, define themselves by the groups with which they affiliate (Goodenow, 1992). This is the essence of social identity, an identity based on group membership. Students may experience a sense of membership or belonging at several levels: school, individual classroom, and subgroups (e.g., peer group, cultural or ethnic, athletic teams, religious affiliation). How does social identity affect a sense of belonging and engagement in school? Goodenow contended that the extent to which a group identifies with goals and values of school, and/or devalues academic effort and achievement, affects engagement for learning. In view of the culturally diverse population in schools, it is important to understand the role and influence of social identity on motivation and achievement. When social interactions are negative, school can be a stressor or a source of vulnerability for students (Clark, 1991). By the same token, social identity and support networks (including interracial friendships) can serve as protective mechanisms that contribute to student adjustment.

Peer Group Influence and Membership

Peer subgroup affiliation has a strong influence on a sense of school membership, either negative or positive. Peers may influence each other not to work hard to achieve or to work and achieve (Berndt & Keeth, 1992; Brown, 1993). An insightful view of social identity is reported by Farrell (1990), who interviewed urban students in a dropout-prevention program. The primary identity for these students was based on how others—family, friends, teachers, and other adults—responded to them. For example, although others might respond to the adolescent as a friend/peer, they made little response to the possible identity of these adolescents as a student or future worker. Adolescents in this program were less likely to think of student or potential worker as an identity for themselves. Because peers can encourage each other to view school experiences positively or negatively, a major task for teachers and parents is to understand the nature of peer relationships so this influence is directed toward engagement. How does negative peer influence work?

Negative Peer Influence. Peer influence plays a major role in the extent to which the peer group values or devalues academic effort and achievement (Goodenow, 1992). Farrell (1990) observed this negative peer influence at work in the dropout program where students got little support from their peers for liking classes. They hid their academic ability to keep from being ostracized by their friends. In fact, friends reinforced each other to avoid work and be disruptive.

Brown (1993) made a distinction between peer influence for academic achievement and academic excellence. He noted that, although there is positive academic peer pressure to graduate from high school, the pressure is more to get by academically rather than to excel. The emphasis is more toward getting good grades (performance goals) than on working hard and learning (learning goals). Brown concluded that the general peer norm is to strive for academic adequacy rather than academic excellence. Peer pressure seems to impose upper as well as lower limits on intellectual effort that students can put forth without fearing some sanctions. There is, however, a more direct anti-achievement at work in many school contexts.

Anti-Achievement. What is the nature of direct anti-achievement? Why are high-achieving students often the target of ridicule by peers, resulting in students either hiding their academic achievement or, in the words of Fordham and Ogbu (1986), "putting on the brakes" as far as effort is concerned? Brown (1993) identified several factors that lead to negative views of achievement:

- There is a brain–nerd connection or peer distinction between students who excel and those who do not. The stereotypic image of *brains* is a label often carrying with it negative characteristics such as nerd, brainiac, and geek—all implying social misfit.
- Because some students are excelling, teachers expect more from other students and they have to work harder.
- Pressure for academics is often overshadowed by pressure toward nonacademic activities such as social activities and part-time work. Pressure to keep up with status symbols valued by peer groups leads to part-time jobs to buy symbols like designer label athletic shoes. There is an inverse correlation between number of hours working and grade point average. The more hours worked (more than 15 hours per week is detrimental), the lower the GPA. In this way, peer pressure works indirectly by distracting students to other interests.

Adult Influence on Effort and Student Achievement.

Brown asserted that teachers and other adults have the potential to influence peer culture both positively and negatively. There are several ways that teachers and adults help teenagers justify limited effort toward achieving in school:

- Passive acceptance of the peer group structure. Teachers expect that students will behave in keeping with their peer group affiliations and make no attempt to intervene with the structure. In other words, teachers passively accept the brain–nerd differentiation.
- Favoritism toward athletes. Athletes often receive more esteem in school and are often seen by other students as receiving special treatment like more academic help from teachers.
- Peer group separation. " ... Tracking systems may drive a wedge between crowds that undermine achievement of lower-track students" (Brown, 1993, p. 87). Ability grouping forces isolation among students at different achievement levels, with each group forming its own peer culture. When students are grouped by ability tracks, low achievers are isolated from models of achievement motivation and more effective strategies.
- Blame or excuse the victim. Effort may be undermined when adults use stereotypical images to either excuse or blame students based on social identity categories and crowds to which they belong. For example, a teacher may excuse poor student test performance on the basis of family background. By the same token, a teacher may blame the family background for the performance. In either case, student achievement is undermined.

How can educators promote a positive peer culture? Brown recommended ways that educators can enhance rather than undermine the academic motivations of American adolescents.

1. Teachers increase awareness of adolescent social systems. Be aware of the peer group social structure that operates in a particular school, the norms that operate within each group, the relationship of one group to another, as well as the loyalty students display to their own group. It is important for teachers to appreciate the dynamics of the brain–nerd connection and the burden of "acting

White," as well as recognizing the hostility of groups to one another. At the same time, they must be careful not to reinforce stereotypes.

2. Avoid making achievement a game of winners and losers. Ability grouping and grading on a curve place students in competitive situations as winners or losers. Alternative grading systems are discussed in chapter 8.

3. Enhance the status of academic achievement. Brown believed this is the most powerful influence on student achievement. Because there is a positive relationship between student achievement and popularity, schools should give more public recognition to high achievement. Schools can recognize academic excellence in areas that are outside the core curriculum, such as trade fairs. Avoid sending mixed messages about the relative merit of academic and nonacademic achievement. This often happens when more prominence is given to the school's athletic achievements than to academic achievements.

REFLECTION. Think about the status of academic achievement in schools in your community. What is the status of academic achievement compared with the status of sports?

Cultural Identity and Membership

A sense of membership and cognitive engagement is affected in important ways by the sociocultural orientations that students bring to school (Newmann, 1992). Students who identify with the expectation that working hard in school and achieving will lead to occupational success are likely to invest themselves in the academic work of school. In contrast, students who have little hope that academic performance will lead to occupational success are less likely to invest themselves in school work. What are factors that affect identification with norms of schooling?

Based on his research into schooling, Ogbu (1987) differentiated between immigrant and nonimmigrant minorities regarding cultural differences, identity, and school learning. Voluntary or immigrant minorities are people who have come to this country voluntarily seeking a better life and were accepted as a member of this society (e.g., Asians such as Japanese and Koreans; Europeans such as Irish and Bosnians). Nonimmigrant or involuntary minorities are people who were originally brought to this country against their will through slavery or conquest (e.g., African Americans, Latinos, American Indians) and they were not fully accepted into mainstream society. Ogbu contended that voluntary minorities more readily accept the relationship among hard work, academic performance, and occupational success without seeing a conflict with their identity. The dilemma for minority students who are not members of the dominant culture is, "if I identify with and accept the academic goals of school, does this mean I lose my cultural identity?" How does this dilemma affect school motivation and learning?

For some minority students, school learning is equated with the learning of culture and language of the dominant culture, White Americans, and is seen as a loss of social identity with negative consequences. Fordham and Ogbu (1986) described this phenomena as "oppositional social identity." This occurs when involuntary minorities, such as African Americans and Latinos who have had a subordinate position in society, develop a sense of collective identity in opposition to the social identity of White Americans. For adolescents to behave in ways that are perceived as reflecting the values of the dominant culture is to act White" or act Anglo with negative consequences. These adolescents achieve group loyalty by defining certain attitudes and group behavior as White and unacceptable (e.g., speaking standard English, working hard for good grades). They use peer pressure to discourage one another from engaging in those activities. What are manifestations of this discouragement? Students in a high school in Washington, DC, interviewed by Fordham and Ogbu (1986) provide a vivid picture of how they reacted to peer pressures:

Max, a football player: Max is from a middle-class home. He is taking advanced courses because his parents make him. Although his parents try to pull him away from his friends, he holds onto them at the expense of his academic progress because they are important to him and his sense of identity. To be accepted, he limits his effort and performance.

Shelvy an underachieving female: Shelvy thinks, ideally, that everybody wants to be a brainiac, but fear that if they perform well in school that would bring some added responsibilities and problems. This began at the sixth grade for Shelvy. "It was me and these two girls, we used to hang together all the time. They used to say we was brainiacs, and no one really liked us … it's something you want to be, but you don't want your friends to know. Because once they find out you're a brainiac the first thing they say is, 'she thinks she's cute and she's smart. She thinks she's better than anyone else.' So what do most brainiacs do? They sit back and they know an answer and they won't answer it" (p. 191).

What are the strategies of high-achieving students who have learned to compete successfully in the dominant culture, whereas underachieving students such as Max and Shelvy have not? A primary strategy adopted by high-achieving students is accommodation without assimilation (Mehan, Villanueva, Hubbard, & Lintz, 1996; Ogbu, 1992). This happens when students maintain their cultural identifies while recognizing the necessity of academic achievement for their future success. Marta and Andrew are two students who exemplify forms of accommodating without assimilating (Mehan et al., 1996):

Marta, a Latino student: Marta affirms her cultural identity and also achieves academically. In the third grade, Marta pledged to become perfectly bilingual, maintaining her native Spanish while developing acceptable English and academic skills. She fulfilled this and entered college in 1992. Her parents respect her bicultural motives but, at same time, are pleased that she and her friends respect their background.

Andrew, an African-American student: Andrew recognizes that his teachers expect a certain way of talking and acting in school. To accommodate to the school and teachers' expectation for academics, he varies his speech behavior according to different social situations. In the neighborhood Andrew uses the style of his peers, whereas in school he tries to use the standard expected there.

Students like Marta and Andrew maintain duel identities—one in school and one in the neighborhood. Another strategy used by students who want to succeed is to camouflage or disguise their true academic identity by not letting their peers know they study; by acting like the class clown; or by participating in athletics, where it's okay to get A grades (Ogbu, 1992). The task for schools and teachers is to establish a climate that builds a sense of membership while valuing students' culture and social identity. What characteristics of school builds a sense of membership?

Conditions for Membership

Four broad conditions of school that set the stage for social bonding or membership were identified by Newmann (1992). These four conditions—clarity of purpose, fairness, personal support, and success—if in place, support a climate of caring.

• Clarity of purpose or agreement on goals is necessary for a sense of membership. Not only is agreement important, but students need to see there is a serious attempt to accomplish the goals. It is difficult for students to feel a sense of membership when the purpose is unclear or when the school seems to have a number of competing purposes.

• Fairness is necessary for a sense of membership. Students may believe they are treated unfairly in areas of discipline, opportunities, and rewards. Although discrimination may not be blatant, students of low SES may experience subtle inequity. Do all students have equal access to resources and the best teachers? Students of minority backgrounds may feel excluded from membership when teachers, curriculum, and extracurricular activities do not take into account their unique experience.

• Personal support from teachers and students is essential if students are to attempt challenges in learning. When chances for success are risky and uncertain, students need support of both peers and teachers.

• Successful experiences are necessary for students to experience a developing sense of competence. Newmann cautioned that a sense of membership will not be achieved by grade inflation or by reducing the rigor of academic demands.

A caring environment with these four components communicates that students are worthy and important members of school and that the school is serious about helping them develop competence. How can schools and teachers build this environment? Essential for optimum membership and engagement in the classroom is a classroom structure for autonomy and responsibility and a climate for social support.

A CLASSROOM ENVIRONMENT FOR OPTIMUM
MEMBERSHIP AND ENGAGEMENT

A sense of membership and engagement is most likely to be present when student needs for belonging/social connectedness, autonomy/self-direction, and competence are met (Battistich, Solomon, Kim, Watson, & Schaps, 1995; Solomon, Watson, Battistich, Schaps, & Delucchi, 1992). A caring community both conveys a set of values and helps establish the motivation to abide by them. It is characterized by mutual concern and respect among students who care about the welfare of others and give support as needed. Three areas essential for providing such a climate are: (a) a classroom structure for autonomy and responsibility, (b) social support through cooperative learning, and (c) teacher support. These areas all fall within the teachers' domain of responsibilities and are areas they can influence.

Classroom Structure for Autonomy
and Social Support

A number of studies have documented positive motivational effects when students have opportunities for some degree of autonomy or ownership in classroom learning. Establishing a structure that provides such opportunities requires an understanding of autonomy, classroom structure, and classroom management practices.

Classroom Autonomy.   What is autonomy or self-direction in a classroom? deCharms (1976, 1984) described the two ends of a continuum for autonomy as origin—pawn. To feel like an origin is to feel like one has the freedom and competence to make choices. To feel like a pawn is to feel controlled by external forces in the environment. deCharms pointed out that we cannot be origins in all situations; students have required courses and teachers have prescribed curriculums. Motivationally, the most important aspect is the extent to which one feels like an origin or pawn. Skinner (1995) stated that, "Although contexts don't 'give' children or adults control, they can provide opportunities for people to exercise control" (p. 54).

Classroom autonomy occurs when teachers communicate choice and allow room for student initiative, with students viewing learning activities as connected to their personal goals and values (Connell & Wellborn, 1991). However, the establishment of a climate that en-

sures psychological and physical safety while giving students opportunities for choice with responsibility is a major balancing act for the
teacher. Concerns expressed by teachers include: Will the classroom
environment turn into chaos when I give students choices? How
much can students be involved in decision making? What choices are
appropriate for students?

Teachers are rightfully concerned about how much choice to give
students. Although it may seem like a paradox, structure is the key
to providing opportunity for student choice (Skinner, 1995). Developing a student sense of autonomy does not mean that teachers give
up their legitimate power and responsibility or what Noblit (1993)
termed the *ethical use of power*. A classroom of optimal freedom is
not a laissez-faire classroom where there are no rules, nor is it even
a democratic one; instead, it is one where students are, in a sense,
grooved by teachers (deCharms, 1976). Opportunities are provided
for students to exercise control, but they are not given control. A
teacher's role is to set boundaries for work, social/behavioral expectations, and responsibility. Figure 7.1 illustrates a fragile balance.
Where does a teacher begin this difficult balancing act?

Viewing students' readiness for choice and self-direction from
their zone of proximal development (ZPD) will help teachers decide
how much structure students need and what they can do autono-
mously. The ZPD is the distance between what students can do on
their own and what they can do with expert assistance by more
capable peers or adults (Vygotsky, 1978). The task for the teacher is
to identify the students' starting level for self-direction, assist or
teach them strategies for self-direction at that level, and gradually

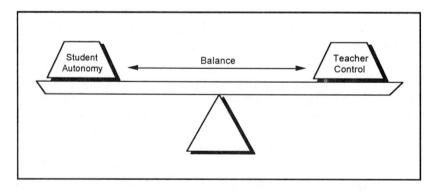

FIG 7.1. Balance between teacher control and student autonomy.

TABLE 7.1

Teacher Behaviors for Levels of Motivational Maturity

Level of Maturity	Teacher Behavior
Low maturity	Use structure including clear goals and directions with frequent monitoring and positive feedback with corrections.
Low–moderate	Model breaking tasks into subgoals followed by student practice. Continue monitoring but have students begin checking their own work.
High–moderate	Assist students as needed. Encourage student participation in setting goals, defining standards, evaluating their own work and behavior, and devising solutions.
High maturity	Little teacher guidance is needed with students able to judge when they need help; students set own goals and work through difficulties on their own.

Note. From "Motivation and Effective Teaching," by R. Ames and C. Ames, 1996. In J. L. Idol & B. F. Jones (Eds.), Educational Values and Cognitive Instruction: Implications for Reformation (pp. 247–261). Hillsdale, NJ: Lawrence Erlbaum Associates. Adapted by permission.

reduce the amount of monitoring and direction as students take on more responsibility (see Fig. 7.2). A beginning guide for assisting students is the four levels of motivational maturity—ranging from low to high—proposed by Ames and Ames (1991). For students at low maturity, the goal is to assist them to move toward high-motivational maturity (see the LINKS model in chap. 4).

Greater direction by the teacher is needed at lower levels of maturity. As students become more capable of guiding themselves, the teacher gradually removes the level of support. Teacher behaviors that provide assistance at each level of motivational maturity are shown in Table 7.1.

Although it might be expected that these levels correspond with age, high school teachers (and even college faculty) will find students at lower levels of motivational maturity who need more structure. At the same time, some younger students may be more mature and require less structure.

In summary, autonomy is not just a matter of open-ended choices for students. Choices are carefully planned by the teacher, based on students having the competency to understand and make choices. Decisions have to be made about what activities are appropriate and not appropriate for student choices or decision making. Pointers to keep in mind are shown in Strategy 7.1.

Strategy 7.1. Guidelines for Giving Choices

- Once the basic rules and procedures are established at the first of the year, it is possible to give students increased freedom within the limits of the classroom setting.
- Give carefully planned choices and then be sure that students have the competency to understand and make the choices. Choices do not have to be given every day.
- Make the choices meaningful and of equal value. Decision making does not mean giving students a choice between an easy or a difficult task. Giving students a choice between essay and true–false questions is not a viable choice because these have different purposes in learning and assessment.

REFLECTION. Think about your students and their learning tasks. What opportunities for choice can you offer students at their level of motivational maturity?

Classroom Management Practices. The establishment of a structure that supports student autonomy is carried out largely through the implementation of effective classroom management practices. This is a task that again calls for a balance between structure and autonomy. Ladson-Billings (1994) identified a commonality among successful teachers of African-American children as; "Psychological safety is a hallmark of each of these classrooms. The students feel comfortable and supported" (p. 73). Freiberg (1997) described such a classroom as one with "a sense of purpose, order, and predictability to the classroom organization allowing for greater creativity and active learning" (p. 3). Again, the issue for teachers, is balance between the creation of a classroom that provides opportunity for choice, but is free of behaviors that disrupt learning.

Research on classroom management practices indicate that more effective teachers focus on planning and preparation designed to provide optimum learning time and prevent problems (Emmer & Assiker, 1990). The first few weeks of a school year are the most important because this is a time when norms for academic and social behaviors are established that will extend throughout the year. Once rules are established at the first of the year, it is possible to give students increased freedom within the limits of the classroom setting, gradually "loosening the reins." Students may be involved, to the extent they have the capability, in establishing the rules. Rules common to many classrooms are:

Rule 1. Be polite and helpful.

Rule 2. Respect other people's property.

Rule 3. Listen quietly while others are speaking.

Rule 4. Respect and be polite to all people.

Rule 5. Obey all school rules. (Evertson, Emmer, Clements, & Worsham, 1997, p. 23)

The texts—*Classroom Management for Secondary Teachers* (Emmer, Evertson, Clements, & Worsham, 1997) and *Classroom Management for Elementary Teachers* (Evertson et al., 1997)—provide detailed guidance for establishing a positive classroom management system. Strategy 7.2 provides guidelines on establishing norms.

McCollum (1995) found evidence for the importance of classroom management for high levels of engagement in high-poverty classrooms. The majority of high-poverty classrooms had high levels of engagement characterized by (a) well-established, but flexible routines; (b) few disruptions; and (c) ongoing monitoring of student work. The importance of orderly behavior by students for an effective learning environment cannot be underestimated. This was found to be the most critical condition for whether teachers implemented new teaching practices (Newmann, Rutter, & Smith, 1989. Similarly, some teachers in an urban high school did not use instructional practices such as cooperative learning and whole-class discussion because of apprehension about possible student misbehavior (Alderman, 1996).

Strategy 7.2. Establish Norms

Establish norms for:

- Social support system and peer respect. Define respect for your classroom, along with examples of behavior that will not be tolerated. In the classroom described by Noblit (1993), "The worst infraction of all was to laugh if someone did not know the right answer to a question" (p. 30).
- Help seeking. Establish the custom that all students will be helpers and helpees at some point. Students should understand that help seeking when needed is an adaptive strategy, not cheating.
- Academic work. Discuss with students the meaning of student responsibility and the motivational effects of different attributions for success and failure.
- Accountability and monitoring. Explain how work will be monitored, how students can monitor, and the type of feedback students can expect.

Two extremes regarding order in classrooms were noted by McCollum (1995). Classrooms can be a somewhat happy place with few overt discipline problems but have little academic learning, or they can be highly orderly with no real engagement. Structure or order is often thought of as a detriment to student autonomy. However, optimal structure provides support for student autonomy because it offers students consistency in expectations, feedback, and consequences (Connell, 1990). By the same token, inconsistency results in a lack of autonomy support. Management perspectives of two effective teachers are shown in Exhibit 7.1.

Sources of Social Support

Social support involves interaction between teacher and students and between students. What elements of support are found in supportive classrooms? Classrooms characterized by cohesiveness, satisfaction, and goal direction were preferred by students and were associated with positive outcomes (Battistich et al., 1995). These researchers proposed that student social responsibility may contribute directly to student's academic competence. In this section, sources of social support—cooperative learning, help seeking, and teacher support—are described.

Exhibit 7.1. Teacher Examples of Classroom Management Perspectives

I know it seems old fashioned but I believe the students benefit from structure. I look them squarely in the eye at the beginning of the year and tell them you will read, and you will read soon. I tell my entire class we all have to know how to read and it's everybody's responsibility to make sure everyone learns to read well. (Ladson-Billings, 1994, p. 114)

As for order, Stephanie Terry's classroom was one of most orderly I have ever seen—I never once heard her raise her voice, never saw her shame a child ... order emerged out of curriculum she had created and the sense it gave students that what they were doing is important. "They've come to know that is the place where they do good work and they won't get much done—they won't get to do science, for example—if they don't get along, if everything is chaotic." The whole approach to classroom management couldn't help having an effect on social relations. One of first things I noticed was the consideration Stephanie's students had for one another.... The work the children did fostered a particular attitude toward self and a kind of cooperative interaction. She encouraged both individual responsibility and respect for others. (Rose, 1995, pp. 110–111)

Cooperative Learning

Epstein (1988) asserted that students' social and academic peer group relations are critical for developing character, personal ethics, and social values. A key factor in this are the grouping structures used in the classroom. Group structures affect how students interact, become friends, and influence each other in engagement in learning. Cooperative learning is a grouping structure that can be an important factor in building a classroom that supports a sense of membership. Cooperative learning was one of the elements in the Child Development Project (CDP), which had the goal of developing a classroom climate as a caring community (Solomon et al., 1992).

Cooperative, along with competitive and individualistic, learning is one of three types of goal structures that can operate in a classroom. The processes at work for each type of goal structure differentially affect student motivation (Slavin, 1995).

Students compete against each other for rewards and grades in a competitive structure. In a norm-based grading system (e.g., some form of grading on a curve), students' grades are determined by how they rank. This form of competition promotes negative motivational outcomes by emphasizing the importance of ability in performance, thus separating winners and losers (Ames & Ames, 1984). Students who win evaluate their ability as high and those who lose see their ability as low—conditions that foster a performance goal orientation.

The criteria for success in an individualistic goal structure are absolute standards. One student's effort has no effect on others' goal attainment. This structure fosters a learning goal orientation where effort is perceived as valued. The limitation of an individualistic structure is that it does not explicitly foster peer interaction for learning.

Cooperative learning structures are based on the premise that each student's efforts toward a common goal contributes to other students' learning (Johnson, Maruyama, Johnson, Nelson, & Skon, 1981). Students can attain personal goals only by helping their team members to attain the learning objectives. What is the contribution of cooperative learning groups to the sense of school membership and belonging and engagement? Cooperative learning has been found to be beneficial for diverse groups of students: low-achieving, minority, mainstreamed or included, as well as higher achieving students (Slavin, 1995). According to Berndt and Keefe (1992), cooperative learning contributes to a classroom environment that (a) encourages the formation of supportive friendships between classmates, (b) encourages students to act in helpful rather than competitive ways toward classmates, and (c) provides students time and opportunity to interact with each other.

Small-group learning teams were singled out as being particularly useful for strengthening in-school support systems for African-American students (Clark, 1991). Interracial friendships are enhanced when African-American and White students have the opportunity to work cooperatively on class assignments and to participate together in extracurricular activities.

Motivational Effects of Cooperative Learning. What are the motivational effects of cooperative learning? Research on cooperative methods indicate that they have positive effects on achievement and on student self-esteem and locus of control (Slavin, 1995). Slavin argued that the most important motivational outcome of cooperative learning is the effect on student self-esteem. Two components of self-esteem affected by cooperative learning are (a) a feeling of being liked by peers, and (b) a feeling of academic competence. The motivation of low-achieving students, in particular, can be enhanced or inhibited by the type of goal structure. If the structure is competitive, low-achieving students will perceive that they lack ability in comparison with their more successful classmates. Low achievers should experience greater success in cooperative classrooms because cooperative group structures tend to minimize the focus on ability (Ames & Ames, 1984). More important, cooperative goal structures can foster peer norms for higher achievement (Slavin, 1995).

Establishing Effective Groups. There are several types of cooperative learning structures (e.g., STAD, Jigsaw, Group Investigation). The key question for teachers, however, is what makes an effective group regardless of the type of structure? The most important factor is that groups operate effectively. A common thread for all structures is that each student has a responsibility for the attainment of the group goal. Tasks for learning are divided among students; they cooperate to be sure all students can fulfill their responsibility because the group's success depends on efforts of all group members who share the same reward (grade). Slavin contended that effective group learning depends on group rewards and individual accountability. A number of sources are available that provide specific guidelines for establishing effective cooperative learning (e.g., Cohen, 1994; Johnson, Johnson, & Holubec, 1995; Kagen, 1992; Slavin, 1995). The next section focuses on the composition of groups.

Composition of Groups. Group membership is an important factor in establishing a climate that fosters a sense of membership. As a general rule, cooperative learning groups are organized heterogeneously (mixed according to gender, ability, and ethnicity). The CDP project (Solomon et al., 1992) goes further. A goal of the project was to make sure that, by the end of year, students will have worked in groups with most, if not all, of their classmates. Similarly, Miller and Harrington (1992) suggested periodically rotating teams so students can have first-hand experience with as many of their classmates as possible. In the case of elementary classrooms, different teams can be used in different curriculum units. A question arises as to how to form groups when there are only a small number of minority students in the class. When this is the case, Miller and Harrington recommended that, rather than spreading the few minorities across as many teams as possible, it is better to have several heterogenous groups that are balanced according to cultural diversity, with the remaining groups homogenous. A cooperative learning group is depicted in Fig. 7.2.

What are potential problems in group composition? Cohen (1994) identified status as a potential motivational problem when groups are heterogeneously grouped according to ability. For example, stu-

FIG. 7.2. Cooperative teamwork.

dents known to be high or low achieving may be given higher or lower status by other students based on these ability expectations. In this case, students with low status may have less access to resources, less opportunity for talk, and may be ignored by other group members. Miller and Harrington (1992) explained the problems in terms of social identity. If a student focuses on his or her lack of academic skills, these skills may become less valued, resulting in the student's seeking to forge a different identity (e.g., tough) to restore his or her self-esteem. To reduce dominance by high-status students in the group, Cohen (1994) recommended training students in group participation norms; that is, actually having students practice the norms, not just telling students about these participation norms. Morris (as cited in Cohen, 1994) developed the following group participation norms to train students:

1. Say your own ideas.
2. Listen to others; give everyone a chance to talk.
3. Ask others for their ideas.
4. Give reasons for your ideas and discuss many different ideas. (Cohen, 1994, p. 53)

Additional guidelines and cautions in using cooperative groups are shown in Strategy 7.3.

Strategy 7.3. Guidelines For Using Cooperative Groups

- Do not assume students will have the social skills to work as an effective group. Teachers (to their dismay) occasionally think students such as those in college-prep classes will automatically have skills to work effectively as a group. When these students have been accustomed to performance goal classroom structures, they may believe that if team members learn more, their ability is diminished.
- Foster a learning goal orientation to help address student beliefs described previously.
- Distribute responsibility among group members. Make sure all group members are responsible for a task specific to the group goal.
- Have groups set team goals as a marker for progress and evaluate their goal accomplishment each session.

In summary, effective use of cooperative learning, in some form, is a key component in building a climate where peers support and help each other. In chapter 2, help seeking was described as an adaptive skill for coping with academic success and related to attributional beliefs. Help seeking should be seen as a normal social interaction in a classroom climate that supports a sense of membership. Nelson-Le Gall (1991, 1992) argued that, although whole class and individualistic structures impede help seeking, cooperative learning promotes it. An important role of the teacher is to establish norms for help seeking as an adaptive strategy. In cooperative learning, there are both help seekers and help givers. Classmates—a readily available source of help—may be ignored by a student seeking help because of explicit or implicit classroom norms that convey a message that cooperative work is a form of cheating. Cooperative learning, when well designed and implemented, helps students see help seeking as an adaptive strategy.

Teacher's Role in Social Support

How important is teacher support for establishing a climate for a sense of belonging and engagement? Personal support from teachers and students is the third condition listed by Newmann (1992) as setting the stage for social bonding. In his study of students in a dropout-prevention program, Farrell (1990) concluded that teacher–student bonding was an important factor affecting the purpose of school for these students. By this he meant there must be someone in students' lives who values them and education. For students where there was no student–teacher bonding, peer influence dominated and generally did not support learning.

Teachers play a critical role in creating a supportive classroom climate—a climate characterized by mutual concern and respect. Academic performance of minority students is enhanced when their teachers and other school personnel are seen as supportive and helpful (Clark, 1991). Teacher support is evidenced by (a) showing concern for all students, and (b) being interested in their ideas, experiences, and products (Solomon et al., 1992). Ladson-Billings (1994) described such teachers as believing that "students have to care not only about their own achievement but also about their classmates achievement" (p. 69).

What does this support look and sound like to students? The following are descriptions and examples gathered through classroom observations and interviews with teachers and students (Ladson–Billings, 1994; Nieto, 1992, 1994; Rose, 1995):

- In Calexia, caring had as much to do with faith and cognition as with feeling. All children whatever their background had the capacity to learn. And this belief brought with it a responsibility: It was the teacher's intellectual challenge to come to understand what must be done to tap that potential (Rose, 1995, p. 87).
- They're all great.... All my teachers were wonderful. Its [sic] just a feeling you have. You know they really care for you. You just know it. You can tell. Teachers who don't have you in any of their classes or haven't had you, they still know who you are (Nieto, 1994, p. 407).
- What students liked about an eighth-grade class: "The teacher listens to us, respects us, lets us express our opinion, looks us in the eye when she talks to us, speaks to us when she sees us in the halls or cafeteria" (Ladson-Billings, 1994, p. 68).

In these examples, concern and interest are tied to developing academic and social skills of all students. Simply giving students individual attention does not develop a supportive classroom environment. Page (1991) described how a teacher's attempts to attend to social needs in a low-track ninth-grade classroom backfired. This is illustrated by the following incidents in a classroom that alternated between order and chaos.

- A student who needed help blurted out, interrupting the discussion in progress. Meanwhile the teacher moved back and forth assisting four students individually for 15 to 30 seconds each. Although this appeared to provide encouragement, as recommended for supportive classrooms, the individual attention to the students was both unsolicited and distracting (refer to chap. 2, where unsolicited help by the teacher may be viewed as a low ability cue by the student).
- The teacher attempted to show interest by asking if an absent student was sick. This was interpreted by students as checking on the student's attendance by getting them to *rat out* him or her.

Page concluded that this class lacked cohesiveness. There were no shared norms for social interaction and support. Instead, each person tried to satisfy his or her individual needs, competing for the teacher's attention.

Support in Culturally Diverse Classrooms

It was noted earlier that one detriment to school membership is lack of identification with school by minority students. The social aspects of the classroom environment have been found to be more important to children of color than to mainstream children (Delpit, 1995). How is teacher support demonstrated in a culturally diverse classroom? The first step as a teacher is to have knowledge about students' culture (Ogbu, 1992; Villegas, 1991). Relevant knowledge helps teachers to (a) be sensitive to verbal and nonverbal signals from learners, (b) create a classroom climate that encourages students to express themselves, (c) be sensitive to themes of social relevance, and (d) help students recognize and accept that they can participate in two cultural frameworks for different purposes without losing their identity or being disloyal to their group.

In her profiles of successful teachers of African-American children, Ladson-Billings (1994) concluded that teachers worked to ensure each student of his or her individual importance. If students are of different cultural groups than the teacher, it is especially important for the teacher to work to develop commonalities with all students. For example, a White teacher from a different religion, with little in common with lower income African-American students, used the following techniques to draw students out, have them share their interests, and introduce them to new interests:

• She begins the year with an "interest questionnaire" that enables her to discover what students like to do outside of school, leisure-time activities, subjects they like and dislike. "I try to find out as much as I can about the students early in the year so I can plan instructional program that motivates them and meets their needs ... is also a great way to learn a little about their reading and writing levels." She also acknowledges their birthday (Ladson-Billings, 1994, p. 67).

Villegas (1991) pointed out that it is unrealistic for a teacher to have a thorough understanding of all cultural groups. The important factor is to know procedures for gaining information about all students, especially those of different cultures. Other ways to gain information are shown in Strategy 7.4.

Strategy 7.4. Learning About Students' Background

- Have students introduce themselves to you at the beginning of the year. This can be done through an interest questionnaire described earlier. Have students tell about what they like to do outside of school, their favorite/least favorite subjects, a successful experience they had in your subject, and their goals.
- Observe students in places other than the classroom (e.g., the playground, cafeteria, gymnasium, informal groups before school).
- Ask students questions about their cultural practices.
- Talk with parents as much as possible.
- Work with children to research various ethnic groups.
- Read about various ethnic groups.

Based on Ogbu (1992).

Student Perspective of Support

How do students describe teacher support? Dillon (1989) described a low-track, secondary English class in a rural area. Because their teacher "cared for them personally and cared about their performance and learning in class," the students cared more about their schoolwork. The successful minority students interviewed by Nieto (1994) described supportive teachers in various ways:

- Yolanda felt fortunate to have many teachers she felt understood and supported her in ways such as commenting on her bilingual ability, being a member in a folkloric Mexican dance group, or simply talking with her and other students about their lives. She added: "I really got along with the teachers a lot.... They were always calling my mom, like I did a great job. Or they would start talking to me.... And they were always congratulating me" (pp. 406–407).
- Vanessa. "[Most teachers] are really caring and supportive and are willing to share their lives and are willing to listen to mine. They don't just want to talk about what they're teaching you; they also want to know you" (p. 407).

Foster (1987) reported an African-American student's description of a good teacher as:

We had fun in her class but she was mean. I can remember she used to say, "Tell me what's in the story, Wayne." She pushed, she used to

get on me and push me to know. She made us learn. We had to get in
the books. There was this tall guy and he tried to take her on, but she
was in charge of the class and she didn't let anyone run her. I still have
this book we used in her class. (p. 68)

Nieto concluded that the most common characteristic expressed
by these students was a teacher who had affirmed them in language,
culture, or concerns. This type of teacher called on students' linguistic
and cultural knowledge, but not in a superficial way and students
were aware of the distinction between these.

Building a sense of membership so that all students experience a
sense of belonging are dependent on the conditions identified by
Newmann (1992): (a) agreement on the goals of education, (b) fairness and equal opportunity, (c) personal support from teachers and
peers, and (d) valid successful experiences. In the final analysis,
Delpit (1995) asserted that teachers have to accept students of
diverse cultures, and also accept the responsibility to teach them.

MAJOR POINTS FOR REVIEW

1. Social context influences classroom engagement, academic
effort, and subsequent school success and failure at all levels of
schooling. A sense of school membership is an important foundation
for educational engagement because students who experience a
sense of belongingness are more likely to adopt goals valued by the
school. The basis for a sense of school membership is social bonds
that connect students to the school. Four factors that establish social
bonds to the school are: attachment, commitment, involvement in
both academic and nonacademic school activities, and students'
belief that an education is important, with faith that the school will
provide them with an education.

2. A sense of belonging and engagement in school is affected by
social identity—an identity based on group membership. The extent
to which a group identifies with goals and values of school and/or
devalues academic effort and achievement affects engagement for
learning. The peer group plays a major role in the extent to which
academic effort and achievement are valued or devalued. Factors
that lead to negative views of achievement include stereotypic images such as brain–nerd connection, pressure toward nonacademic

activities such as social activities and part-time work, teacher passive acceptance of the peer group structure, favoritism toward athletes, and peer group separation.

3. The role of cultural identity in motivation is explained by Ogbu's differentiation between immigrant and nonimmigrant minorities regarding cultural differences, identity, and school learning. Voluntary minorities more readily accept the relationship among hard work, academic performance, and occupational success without seeing a conflict with their identity. Involuntary minorities who have experienced a subordinated position in this culture may fear that identification with the academic goals of school means loss of cultural identity. Students may develop the strategy of oppositional social identity to protect their cultural identity. A primary strategy adopted by high-achieving students who have learned to compete successfully in the dominant culture is accommodation without assimilation—maintaining their cultural identifies, but recognizing the necessity of academic achievement for their future success.

4. The task for schools and teachers is to establish a climate that builds a sense of membership while valuing students' culture and social identity. Four broad conditions of school that set the stage for a sense of membership are clarity of purpose, fairness, personal support, and success. Three areas essential for establishing a classroom for optimum membership and engagement are: classroom structure for autonomy and responsibility, cooperative learning, and teacher support.

5. Classroom autonomy occurs when teachers allow student initiative and choice, and students view learning activities as connected to their personal goals and values. Two ends of a continuum for autonomy are characterized as: origin, the perception that one has the freedom and competence to make choices; and pawn, the perception of being controlled by external forces. A major issue for teachers is to establish a balance between the creation of a classroom that provides opportunity for choice but is free of behaviors that disrupt learning. A teacher's role is to set boundaries for work, social/behavioral expectations, and responsibility. Choices are carefully planned by the teacher based on students having the competency to understand and make the choices.

6. A classroom environment that supports autonomy is built through effective classroom management principles from the begin-

ning of the year. Classrooms that have high levels of engagement (including high-poverty classrooms) are characterized by well-established, but flexible routines, few disruptions, and ongoing monitoring of student work.

7. Classrooms that provide social support are characterized by cohesiveness, satisfaction, and goal direction. Sources of social support include cooperative learning, help seeking, and teacher support.

8. Three types of goal structures operate in a classroom: cooperative, competitive, and individualistic learning, with each type differentially affecting student motivation. Cooperative learning has been found to be beneficial for diverse groups of students including low-achieving, minority, mainstreamed or included, as well as higher achieving students. Cooperative goal structures can foster peer norms for higher achievement.

9. Cooperative learning groups are organized heterogeneously (mixed according to gender, ability, and ethnicity). Effective groups provide social support and foster engagement: Each student has a responsibility for the attainment of the group goal, tasks for learning are divided among students, and group rewards are used with individual accountability. Help seeking should be seen as a normal social interaction in a classroom climate that supports a sense of membership.

10. Teacher support is evidenced by showing concern for all students, and being interested in their ideas, experiences, and products. In a culturally diverse classroom, teacher support is demonstrated by teachers having knowledge about students' culture and working to ensure each student of his or her individual importance. Because it is unrealistic for a teacher to have a thorough understanding of all cultural groups, the important factor is to know procedures for gaining information about all students, especially those of different cultures.

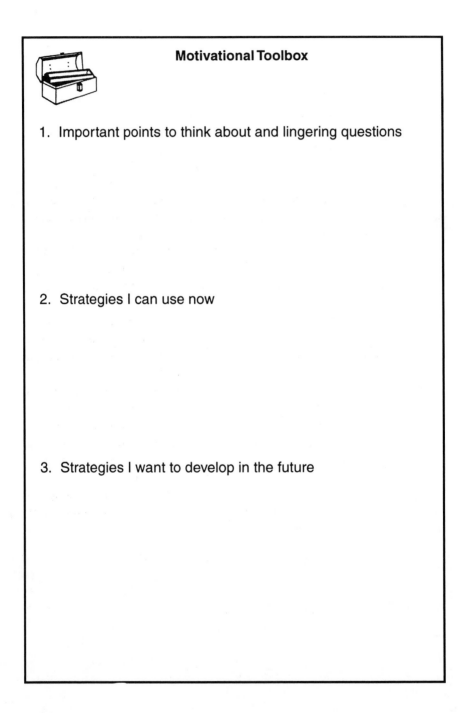

Motivational Toolbox

1. Important points to think about and lingering questions

2. Strategies I can use now

3. Strategies I want to develop in the future

CHAPTER 8

Tasks, Recognition, and Evaluation for Optimal Engagement and Motivation

Meaningful cognitive demands of formal education cannot be mastered through passive listening and reading, nor through being entertained, they require an engaged student.

—Newmann (1992, p. 14)

A classroom where students are engaged or involved does not just happen. The previous chapter established the importance of the social context for fostering student engagement. This chapter focuses on the motivational characteristics of three instructional variables that foster student involvement in learning: (a) learning tasks and activities, (b) incentives and recognition that promote and recognize student engagement, and (c) motivational effects of evaluation. These three variables form the core of classroom instruction affecting students' beliefs about their own ability, their willingness to apply effort, their goals, and consequently, their engagement in learning. How these variables are used determine the extent to which the classroom supports a learning or performance orientation.

CLASSROOM TASK MOTIVATION

This section examines the nature of task characteristics as they affect student motivation and engagement. Tasks and activities are the primary instructional variables that engage students in learning. "Tasks influence learners by directing their attention to the particular aspects of content and by specifying ways of processing information" (Doyle, 1983, p. 161). Motivation for instruction de-

199

mands that teachers not only "bring the task to the students," but also "bring students to the task" (Blumenfeld, Mergendollar, & Puro, 1992). This means specific task characteristics will attract student attention and interest. By the same token, teachers need to use strategies to promote student effort and/or the use of higher levels of thinking. This reciprocal relationship is shown in Fig. 8. 1.

Task Features and Types

What features or types of tasks are likely to get best efforts and highest engagement from students? Newmann (1992) described engaging tasks as "meaningful, valuable, significant and worthy of effort." Descriptors used to describe tasks that are motivating are: *authentic work or tasks* (e.g., Darling-Hammond, Ancess, & Falk, 1995; Newmann, Secada, & Wehlage, 1995), *active in-depth learning* (Darling-Hammond, 1997), and *thoughtful tasks* (Blumenfeld, 1992). A common feature of these tasks is the focus on higher order thinking, such as analysis and integration of knowledge, production of solutions or products, and connection to the world beyond school.

An example of a complex task requiring higher order thinking is reported by Newmann, Secada, and Wehlage (1995). In a social

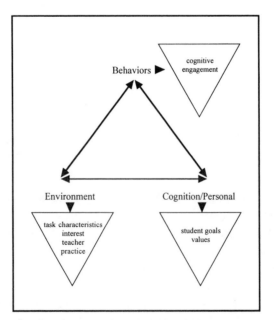

FIG. 8.1. Tasks in reciprocal relationships.

studies lesson, eighth-grade students were asked to consider the impact on the community of workers being laid off from work. The lesson began with the teacher helping the students to define terms related to the issue (e.g., *layoff, unemployment rate, local economy*). The teacher then presented information about the economy of their community and others of similar size but with different types of business and employment. In small groups, the students were asked to use the information they had been given and answer this question: What generalizations can you state about each of the local economies? Groups developed and reported their generalizations. After class discussion, a final generalization was developed by the class. To accomplish the task, students had to use the higher order thinking skills of analysis, development of hypotheses and generalizations, and comparison and contrast. What are the motivational aspects of tasks of this nature?

Task Complexity and Student Cognitive Engagement

One assumption is that high-level, challenging tasks, such as the social studies lesson, will have a positive influence on motivation and lead to greater student engagement. From a social-cognitive perspective, however, the role of task influence on motivation is more complicated because student perception of the task plays a mediating role. Although challenging tasks can increase student motivation, it is not an automatic occurrence (Blumenfeld, 1992). An important element for consideration is the interaction of task complexity with the types of information processing required of the student.

Doyle (1983) suggested that classroom tasks vary according to the type of mental operation needed. Some types of learning activities require a low level of cognitive processing, whereas others require a high level. Memory tasks (e.g., spelling) that simply ask students to reproduce information they have learned require only low levels of processing, with low risks for students. Challenging or complex tasks—where students are expected to apply information or draw inferences (e.g., evaluating portfolio entries or solving word problems in math)—require a high level of cognitive processing. When tasks are more open ended and challenging, they are more risky for the student and motivation may decrease. Blumenfeld (1992) proposed reasons that high-level challenging tasks, by themselves, may not lead to greater engagement by students:

- As the task becomes more difficult, either in the content or form it is to take, students may be unwilling to expend the effort necessary to accomplish it as intended.
- If students lack background knowledge of the content or an understanding of how to complete the task, cognitive engagement for complex tasks may decrease.
- As the amount of work increases in lengthy tasks, such as long-term projects, students may become discouraged and just concentrate on finishing the task.

To reduce the risks, students may try to negotiate with the teacher to simplify the assignment and/or the evaluation. If students are only held accountable for completing work and not for the content and understanding, a high-level task can be turned into a low-level task, lowering the level of cognitive processing. The dilemma for a teacher is that risk can lower motivation for the student, but lowering the risk for the student can lower the level of learning. Being aware of these points can help teachers better plan challenging tasks.

Social Organization and Task Engagement

The social context of the classroom also affects student task engagement. Cooperative learning was introduced in chapter 7 as a means of fostering students' sense of membership and belonging. The proportion of engaged time students spend on academic tasks is also impacted by cooperative learning; cooperative learning groups have a higher proportion of engaged time than do students not in cooperative groups (Slavin, 1995). This was confirmed by Moriarity, Douglas, Punch, and Hattie (1995) who studied the effects of classroom environment on motivation. Students in the cooperative learning environment had a higher degree of purposeful activity and task-related interaction. In the competitive environment, students not only had more off-task behavior but it increased over time.

In summary, successful groups promote student interactions that increase cognitive processing, higher order thinking, and integration of information (Blumenfeld, Marx, Soloway, & Krajcik, 1996). If groups do not work well together, however, student engagement declines (Blumenfeld, 1992). As emphasized in chapter 7, it is not just the use of cooperative learning, but how effectively the groups work that positively contributes to student engagement. For group work to foster cognitive engagement, students have to learn to share ideas, learn to disagree, and resolve differences in perspectives (Blumenfeld et al., 1996).

What teaching practices increase student engagement in tasks? The following section provides direction in this area.

Teacher Practices That Increase Student Task Engagement

> ... tasks do not exist independently from teachers. In order for high-level tasks to work, teachers need to insure that students engage cognitively with them. (Blumenfeld, 1992, p. 97)

Instructional practices related to student engagement were observed in several studies (Blumenfeld, 1992; Blumenfeld et al., 1992; Meece, 1991; Meece, Blumenfeld, & Puro, 1989). Although higher engagement was more likely in classrooms rated as having a high-learning goal orientation by students, this was not sufficient (see chap. 3 for learning orientation). These studies provided insight into practices that differentiated between teachers who were able to sustain high-level tasks and those who were less effective in the high-learning classrooms. Practices that made a difference were evident in whole-class, small-group, and hands-on tasks (Blumenfeld, 1992). Teacher practices in classrooms related to high levels of student engagement were summarized by Blumenfeld.

• Opportunities to learn. Teachers offered their students opportunities to learn by their choice of topics, activities, and type of task product. They provided meaningful topics and problems.

• Instruction. Teachers used a variety of high-quality instructional techniques, including the use of concrete illustrations, analogies, connecting of new concepts to students' prior knowledge, and requiring student application of the concepts.

• Press. Teachers pressed (pushed) students to think by requiring them to explain and justify answers; teachers reframed questions and broke tasks into smaller parts when students failed to comprehend. They monitored for comprehension rather than for correctness of procedures, encouraging answers from all students with techniques like asking for votes or asking students to compare responses.

• Support. Teachers used scaffolding to lead students gradually toward comprehension by providing samples for students to use, modeling the thinking processes and strategies needed instead of giving answers, breaking the task down into manageable steps, and encouraging collaboration among students and independence from the teacher.

• Evaluation. Teachers emphasized comprehension and mastery of content, showing less concern with just finishing tasks or having the right response. They allowed students who had not achieved a satisfactory level to rework assignments or retake a quiz.

What do such strategies look like in a classroom? Two teachers were selected by Blumenfeld (1992) to contrast how the use of the strategies made a difference in student engagement in their classes. The teachers, A and B, were similar in a number of areas: both assigned tasks that required thought, problem solving, and complex procedures; both integrated previous lessons; and both required a product that involved developing a design from a variety of materials. Although students in both classes reported a high learning goal motivation orientation, students in Teacher B's class reported lower levels of active learning or engagement. One key difference was less press and support for thought by Teacher B. Although the students in this class were attentive, Teacher B did not require widespread responding, which is necessary for cognitive engagement. Exhibit 8.1 shows a contrast of the practices of the two teachers, and Strategy 8.1 provides guidelines for increasing task motivation.

Exhibit 8.1. Contrast Between Teacher A and B

Teacher B often makes connections among key concepts himself, rather than asking students to do so. During discussion and recitation, he probes or asks students to elaborate less often than does Teacher A and frequently expands on a students' answers himself rather than asking them to think through the issue. He does not break down the problem or actually hold students account-able for planning and explaining their plans. His monitoring more often focuses on procedural than conceptual issues and he does not often engage in extended dialogue with the students to help them problem solve or clarify their thinking. Instead he often just says, "Try again." Finally, students are not held accountable for understanding, by having to write down or share conclusions with the group. Essentially, students in Mr. B's class could be highly involved in the task and quite motivated to learn, but would not necessarily have to think in-depth about what happened. One way to characterize the difference is that Mrs. A "brings the lesson to the students" via the opportunities for thought her practices afford, and she "brings the students to the lessons" via her practices that press for and support active learning. Mr. B. brings the "lesson to the students," but he less effectively "brings students to the lesson." (Blumenfeld, 1992, p. 97)

Strategy 8.1. Increasing Task Motivation

1.   Establish a mastery or learning climate and structure for the classroom. A mastery classroom includes the following components (Meece, 1991):

- Opportunities for students to develop an increased sense of competence by using concrete examples as needed and relating these to students' personal experience.
- Some opportunity for self-directed learning.
- Peer cooperation and collaboration with guidance for effective cooperative work.
- Emphasis on the intrinsic value of learning by showing students its relevance outside of school.

2.   Break a long-term project into steps or phases. Be sure students see the goal of the final product and the steps for completion.

3.   Use a variety of types of tasks and task structures that are appropriate for the particular goal. These include whole class, small group or cooperative learning, demonstrations, simulations, technology, and projects. Variation in types of tasks help convey to students that there are many types of ability and intelligences.

4.   Make sure that students have the capabilities needed to complete a task. For long-term projects, students need the capabilities of long-term and proximal goal setting and self-monitoring. For groupwork, they need social skills to work together. To use information from the Internet, students need capabilities of organizing and integrating large amounts of information.

5.   Support students through the use of scaffolding by providing examples as needed and modeling thinking. At the same time, press students to explain and justify answers and elicit responses from all students.

Task Interest

A widely accepted premise by educators and students is that interest enhances motivation. Interest—whether text material or task activity—is important motivationally because it influences attention and persistence and, in the long run, acquisition of knowledge by students. Thus, *make it interesting* is often seen as the panacea for lack of engagement. As in other aspects of motivation, the role of interest is more complex. What do we know about its influence?

Personal and Situational Interest

Two types of interest—personal and situational—may be evident in classrooms (Hidi, 1990). Personal interest is the individual interest that a student brings to the classroom—an interest, such as space exploration, that is based on a deep level of knowledge. As such, it develops slowly over time and has a powerful effect on student learning and performance. For example, students who have a deep interest in space exploration are more likely to use complex reading comprehension strategies, such as elaboration, while reading about that topic than students who lack interest (Schiefele, 1991). In contrast, situational interest results from some instructional activity or text material used in the classroom. This interest might be stimulated by interesting text, a science experiment, a computer simulation, or a learning activity that is relevant to students' lives. It may or may not have long-term effects on learning. Although the two types are triggered by a different source, each influences the other. An interest evoked by a particular topic or learning activity may eventually become a personal interest.

Hidi (1990) and Mitchell (1993) asserted that situational interest is more important for the classroom because teachers have no influence on the personal interests students bring with them. The reliance on personal interest would require individualization for each and every student, which is too time-consuming for teachers (Hidi, 1990). Furthermore, some personal interests may not contribute to goals of learning. For example, drugs may be of high interest to a student who is into the drug culture, but neither contributes to engagement in classroom tasks nor enhances decision making about drugs.

An important aspect of situational interest for teachers is whether it is short term (catches student attention) or continues over time (holds student attention; Mitchell, 1993). Some features of lessons catch or trigger student interest but may not hold interest in the long run, whereas other's hold or ensure the continuation of interest over time. Mitchell (1993) differentiated between activities that caught or activities that held the interest of secondary mathematics students by having students list aspects of their classrooms that were interesting or boring and explain why. Students indicated that computers, groups, and puzzles stimulated (caught) their interest but did not hold it over time. Their interest was held by:

- learning activities in math that were meaningful (e.g., when math content was related to their real-life problems), and
- activities in which they felt they were active participants in learning (e.g., laboratory activities and projects in math where students actually did something).

What about the role of topic interest in writing? Hidi and Anderson (1992) concluded that high-interest topics alone do not lead to longer or better quality expository writing. Student preferences are important if they have the prior knowledge to begin writing.

Interest and Comprehension of Text

Much of the research on interest has focused on its relationship to reading comprehension. When reading, children and adults understand and remember information better from topics of high interest than from topics of low interest (Garner, Alexander, Gillingham, Kulikowich, & Brown, 1991). However, a distinction is made between *make it interesting* and *find an interest?* What is the significance of this distinction for text comprehension?

Make it interesting refers to the use of highly interesting but unimportant details placed in the text or added to a lecture to make it more interesting (Garner et al., 1991). *Find an interest* refers to identifying topics that are of interest to students and then finding text and other materials on these topics. Garner et al. reminded us that, although John Dewey (1913) strongly believed in the role of interest for learning, he cautioned against artificial means to induce interest (e.g., interesting facts that are irrelevant to the topic). Wade (1992) stated, "Vivid, personalized anecdotes and seductive details will usually be considered interesting. However, this is not a viable strategy for creating interest" (p. 272). In fact, research has confirmed that when seductive details are placed in text, students recall these details, but do not recall important generalizations (Garner et al., 1991; Wade, 1992).

Task Enrichment and Engagement

Will enrichment or embellishment of tasks lead to increased student interest and engagement in more traditional learning activities? Embellishments asserted to make tasks more attractive and enjoyable for students include student control, curiosity, and personalization (Brophy, 1987; Lepper & Cardova, 1992; Malone & Lepper, 1987).

• *Choice or control*. Higher engagement is more likely when students feel a sense of ownership or some control in their learning educationally sound choices (Malone & Lepper, 1987). Types of choice include: elementary students choosing the books they read for pleasure (Gambrell & Morrow, 1996), students self-evaluating their work (Turner & Meyer, 1995), students in cooperative learning groups dividing tasks among themselves for a major assignment, and a student deciding how much practice will be needed to learn the words missed on a spelling test. In all cases, students must have the competencies to make the choices and assume responsibility for the choices (deCharms, 1976).

• *Curiosity.* Activities that appeal to students' curiosity are likely to attract students' interest (Lepper & Hodell, 1989). Curiosity can be provoked by providing students with information that is surprising or inconsistent with their prior knowledge (Brophy, 1987). An example is found in Kay Toliver's (1993) math classes. Ms. Toliver often uses literature to introduce mathematical topics to gain students' interest. In one example, she uses a "Dr. Seuss" story about a mysterious substance— "oobleck"— to introduce a lesson on complex fractions. "After reading a short excerpt from the story with my students, I introduce the idea of a complex substance; from there, I introduce the concept of complex fractions as it relates to the story line" (p. 42).

• *Contextualization and personalization.* Tasks are likely to be appealing to students when they are more personal or presented in a naturalistic context (Cardova & Lepper, 1996). This also makes abstract concepts more concrete for learners. For example, when Ms. Hudson, a high school English teacher, begins the study of "Romeo and Juliet" by showing the movie before reading the play, the play is less abstract and more meaningful for students.

Although embellishments can increase task interest and attractiveness, they are not a panacea for student engagement. Lepper and Cardova (1992) expressed concern that:

> a number of the activities we observed children using in schools appeared to have purchased motivation at the expense of learning. These were activities that children found interesting and exciting, but from which they seemed to learn little, except how to "win" the game. (p. 192)

A research study was designed to determine if the embellishment of computer-based learning to make it more fun would increase the motivation and learning of students (Cardova & Lepper, 1996).

Learning activities were embellished by contextualization, personalization, and choice. In the embellishment conditions, students rated initial motivation higher than did students in the control group; they reported being more willing to spend extra time in the learning activity, experiencing greater enjoyment, and using complex cognitive operations. However, there was no difference between the groups in long-term intrinsic motivation.

Based on findings from research on embellishing tasks, the researchers concluded that embellishments have beneficial effects on motivation when certain principles are adhered to (Cardova & Lepper, 1996; Lepper & Cardova, 1992).

- Embellishments do not automatically enhance intrinsic motivation. They must be carefully planned to ensure they support learning, not undermine it.
- Embed the embellishments in the learning activities so as not to distract students from the important objectives.
- The most important principle is a *match* between the actions required for learning and the actions required for enjoyment. For example, the goals of winning the game and the goals of learning the material should be congruent.
- As a final caution, the novelty of the embellishments may wear off and eventually lose their impact on motivation.

Strategies for increasing interest are described in Strategy 8.2.

Strategy 8.2. Strategies for Increasing Task Interest

- Identify topics that are of interest to students and then provide material on high-interest topics. Caution: It is difficult, if not impossible, for teachers to cater to the personal interest of every child.
- Design tasks that create bridges between classroom activities and the culture of students and their concerns outside of school.
- Help students with attention and metacognition (see chap. 5) so they can selectively read for main ideas as well as for interesting details (Garner, Brown, Sanders, & Menke, 1992).
- Stimulate task interest or appreciation by telling students how important the skills and information are for everyday life and for being a successful student.
- Make abstract content more personal, concrete, or familiar to students. Use pictures, demonstrations, and hands-on activities as needed.

Interest and Cultural Relevance

In chapter 7, teachers' knowledge of students' culture was identified as important for building a supportive social climate. Knowledge of cultural factors also contributes to task interest and engagement. The motivational role of culture is seen by Rueda and Moll (1994) as similar to a bridge between the student and classroom tasks and activities. Rueda and Moll described a classroom literacy project with junior high school students in predominantly working-class, Latino neighborhoods. Teachers were concerned about the quantity and quality of student writing. During the project, writing assignments shifted from low-level activities, where students responded to worksheets and teacher questions, to activities that emphasized writing for communication. The assignments involved students writing about issues of significance to them in their community (e.g., immigration, gang life, bilingualism). According to the researchers, the shift to culturally relevant topics had immediate effects on student writing production. The amount of text written by students increased as did their coherence and organization.

The connection of instruction to students' background was also found to be associated with student engagement in high-poverty classrooms (Shields, 1995). In math, reading, and writing, teachers who connected these subjects to the student backgrounds had more students actively engaged in learning. The authors equated meaning in learning to having a sense of connection between home and school.

Students and Task Engagement

Although meaningful learning tasks and activities, in and of themselves, can increase or decrease student motivation, teachers cannot rely solely on task characteristics to attract and hold student engagement. For example, Lee and Anderson (1993) studied task engagement of four students in a science curriculum geared toward meaningful learning using scientific concepts—learning that required effort. The curriculum and teaching approaches worked for two students who believed the activities to be worth their time, but did not work for two other students who came to class with personal agendas that kept them from attaining the meaningful learning goals. The authors concluded that task engagement is a reflection of the interplay among the tasks and the curriculum, the teacher, and the motivation the students bring to the classroom.

Therefore, if high-level, challenging tasks are to have positive motivational effects, teacher must always be aware of more than just the complexity or level of cognitive processing required by the activities they select or design. What are other factors that affect engagement? The next section looks at different incentives or rewards commonly used by teachers to support engagement.

INTRINSIC AND EXTRINSIC INCENTIVES AND ACADEMIC ENGAGEMENT

Intrinsic and *extrinsic* are perhaps the two most familiar concepts used to describe motivated behavior. *Intrinsic motivation* is typically defined as students engaging in actions for their own sake and without coercion such as pleasure, learning, satisfaction, interest, and challenge. *Extrinsic motivation* occurs when students engage in activities to attain rewards, such as praise, grades, special privileges, and certificates or material rewards (e.g., money, pizzas). Although teachers may highly desire students who are intrinsically motivated for academic work, Brophy (1983) pointed out that many tasks required in school are not intrinsically motivating to students. To counteract this, many teachers rely heavily on extrinsic incentives including praise, tokens, smiley faces, and special recognition such as "student of the month." Are extrinsic incentives the answer? Is this an either/or issue?

The Relationship Between Extrinsic and Intrinsic Motivation

The answers to these questions lie in the relationship between intrinsic and extrinsic motivation. Although intrinsic and extrinsic motivation have often been viewed as polar opposites, current views of motivation acknowledge that these two sources of motivation represent a continuum from most extrinsic to least extrinsic, not opposing forms of motivation (Deci & Ryan, 1991; Rigby, Deci, Patrick, & Ryan, 1992). The continuum represents the extent to which students are controlled by the reward and determine their own actions. Based on this model, the more students determine their action, the more intrinsic their motivation. The four phases are:

1. *External regulation*—Students's behavior is externally controlled by rewards or punishment. *Example*: A student completes her homework for teacher praise or to avoid staying after school.

2. *Introjected regulation*—Students follow rules because they should, but do not accept the rule internally. *Example*: A student does her homework because that is what good students are supposed to do.

3. *Identified regulation*—Students accept a regulation because it is personally important for goal attainment. *Example*: A student works hard to improve word-processing skills because she believes it will help her be a better writer.

4. *Integrated regulation*—Students integrate and internalize different values and roles and are self-determined. *Example*: An adolescent values being a good athlete and a good student—these values could conflict. Being a student and an athlete is compatible with the student's self-identity and long-term goals.

The shift from extrinsic to intrinsic motivation is illustrated by an answer written by a high school senior in response to an essay question (see Exhibit 8.2). As this student illustrates, individuals may also pursue tasks for both intrinsic and extrinsic reasons. A runner may run for the challenge and satisfaction experienced and also to attain a scholarship for college. Both types of motivation can be present at any given time and their strengths may vary from situation to situation.

Exhibit 8.2. Shift From Extrinsic to More Intrinsic Motivation

The shift from extrinsic to intrinsic motivation is illustrated in the following answer written by a high school senior in response to an essay question:

When I came to [high school] I started jogging for several reasons: 1) I was told to; 2) it was a challenge; 3) I figured I needed the exercise. For these reasons, I jogged periodically in my sophomore and junior years and I'm sure that the activity benefitted me to some extent. My jogging this year, however, has been quite different in the source of motivation and the end rewards. Because of the research I did on aerobics I began to see jogging & fitness not as just activity but as a whole philosophy. I now feel that fitness is a necessary part of my life. As you once said, jogging can be more than pure physical activity, it can also be a source of aesthetic pleasure and accomplishment. For me jogging has been the latter.

Classroom Motivation: Extrinsic and Intrinsic

A primary concern for educators is how to balance the use of extrinsic incentives as needed to promote student task engagement while establishing a climate that also fosters intrinsic motivation. Stipek (1996) concluded that the elimination of extrinsic incentives is neither desirable nor realistic in today's classrooms. One drawback to the use of rewards is that, often, only a few students get all the rewards. Honor rolls by default are based on grades that may reflect the achievement level of the students when they entered the school, not improvement (Maehr, Midgley, & Urdan, 1992). At the same time, Corno and Rohrkemper (1985) asserted that intrinsic motivation to learn is a necessary but insufficient component for academic achievement. If rewards are used appropriately, intrinsic and extrinsic will be complementary components of motivation.

Effects of Extrinsic Rewards

The effect of extrinsic rewards on intrinsic motivation has been the subject of many research studies. The prototype for this research was a study that identified an intrinsically motivating activity, established different reward conditions for the activity, and assessed the extent of the activity following the reward (Lepper, Greene, & Nisbitt, 1973). Drawing with felt pens was identified as an intrinsic activity for some children in a preschool classroom. These children were placed in one of three conditions: (a) the children were told they would be rewarded with a "Good Player" certificate for playing with felt pens, (b) children were given an unexpected reward after they completed the activity, and (c) children neither expected nor received a reward for participation. Two weeks later, the children were observed during free play to determine the amount of drawing activity with the felt pens. The group in the expected reward condition spent less time in drawing activities than did either of the other two groups. These findings were interpreted to indicate that the more conspicuous the reward is, the more likely the person will attribute his actions to the reward, thus becoming more dependent on the extrinsic incentive.

Although such early research findings were interpreted to mean that extrinsic rewards given for an already intrinsically motivating activity had an undermining effect on intrinsic motivation in ages ranging from preschool to college students (e.g., Lepper & Greene,

1975), the effects of rewards on intrinsic motivation have been found to be much more complex. In some circumstances rewards enhance intrinsic activity, whereas in others they have negative effects (Cameron & Pierce, 1994). The effects of rewards under different conditions are discussed in the following sections.

Controlling and Informational Aspects of Rewards.   According to Deci and Ryan (1985), rewards affect motivation through informational or controlling aspects. When students' participation in an activity becomes a means to receive a reward, the effect of the reward is explained as controlling. The controlling effect is more likely to occur when students are rewarded with no accompanying information about developing competence in the activity or when the teacher highlights the connection between performing the activity and receiving the reward (e.g., "remember, if you don't do your homework, you won't get your homework points"). Rewards can have a positive effect when students are given information that the reward signifies their developing competence (e.g., "The homework part of your grade gives you the practice you need to be able to do the problems on your own"). This is similar to antecedent attributions.

Rewards, Task Contingencies, and Goals.   The effects of rewards on student motivation and performance will have differential effects according to the type of contingency or condition established for receiving the reward (Deci & Ryan, 1985) For classroom learning, students might be rewarded either for task completion or task outcome. Which do you think will have a more positive effect on student motivation and performance? Schunk (1983b) found that rewards contingent on the quality of the task outcome had positive effects on the level of task performance, self-efficacy judgments, and skill development of children. The positive effects were not found when children were rewarded only for task participation or task completion. Schunk explained that the differences in the effects of the two types of rewards occurred because task-contingent children were rewarded for progress, conveying the message that a sense of efficacy can be developed through effort. When rewards are given only for student participation, the importance of progress or improvement is not emphasized (Fig. 8.2).

FIG. 8.2. Certificate to recognize improvement.

The combination of task–outcome rewards and proximal goals were also found to have a positive effect on student self-efficacy (Schunk, 1984a). In this situation, rewards were thought to influence student goal commitment. According to Ford (1995), a desired reward undermines intrinsic motivation only if it creates an unintended goal conflict, (i.e., when the reward is more conspicuous than the original goal). The conspicuous reward distracts the person's attention from the original goal to the reward (e.g., "I get points for good grades, which I can use to buy something at the school store, so I want to get more points"). The reward system overshadows the students' satisfaction in their learning accomplishments or progress. However, rewards can facilitate motivation when a person has no goals or is avoiding a goal.

Verbal Praise.   Intrinsic interest can be enhanced by the use of verbal praise and positive feedback (Cameron & Pierce, 1994). Brophy (1981) concluded that, on the whole, teachers do not rely on praise for specific motivation and consequently do not systematically use it. In addition, praise is not distributed evenly, with outgoing, confident students receiving the most praise. Student reactions to praise tend to change as they grow older. Miller and Hom (1997) compared the reactions of students in Grades 4, 6, and 8 to vignettes where students received varying amounts of praise, blame, and rewards. A notable finding was that the eighth graders valued ability over rewards and praise. The authors concluded that praise may be interpreted as low ability by students.

What characteristics contribute to the effectiveness of praise? O'Leary and O'Leary (1977) identified three qualities that contribute to the effectiveness of praise:

1. Contingency. As with other types of rewards, praise must be given contingent on the performance of the student. Brophy (1981) concluded that the majority of praise given in classrooms does not function well because it is not contingent on performance.

2. Specificity. Praise should indicate the specific performance that is being recognized. This corresponds closely with guidelines for attributional feedback; specify the actions of the student (ability, effort, or strategies) that led to the performance.

3. Sincerity/variety/credibility. The praise should sound sincere to the individual receiving it. This is not likely to occur if a teacher makes a comment like *super job* for all types of performance. Using the same phrase repeatedly for any performance will, over time, erode the impact of praise and leave it meaningless for students.

In addition, praise can be overused by nonselectively praising all student work and responses, so that praise becomes meaningless in terms of influencing student motivation (Brophy, 1981). Lists such as "86 Words of Encouragement" are frequently circulated among teachers. Few of the of the phrases meet the criteria for effective praise (e.g., *that's great, outstanding*). Differences in effective and ineffective praise are presented in Table 8.1 (Brophy, 1981).

TABLE 8.1

Guidelines for Effective Praise

Effective Praise	*Ineffective Praise*
1. Is delivered contingently	1. Is delivered randomly or unsystematically
2. Specifies the particulars of the accomplishment	2. Is restricted to global positive reactions
3. Shows spontaneity, variety, and other signs of credibility; suggests clear attention to the students' accomplishment	3. Shows a bland uniformity, which suggests a conditioned response made with minimal attention
4. Rewards attainment of specified performance criteria (which can include effort criteria, however)	4. Rewards mere participation without consideration of performance processes or outcomes

TABLE 8.1 (Continued)

Effective Praise	*Ineffective Praise*
5. Provides information to students about their competence or the value of their accomplishments	5. Provides no information at all or gives students information about their status
6. Orients students toward better appreciation of their own task-related behavior and thinking about problem solving	6. Orients students toward comparing themselves with others and thinking about competing
7. Uses students' own prior accomplishments as the context for describing present accomplishments	7. Uses the accomplishments of peers as the context for describing students' present accomplishments
8. Is given in recognition of noteworthy effort or success at difficult (for *this* student) tasks	8. Is given without regard to the effort expended or the meaning of the accomplishment (for *this* student)
9. Attributes success to effort and ability, implying that similar successes can be expected in the future	9. Attributes success to ability alone or to external factors such as luck or easy task
10. Fosters endogenous attributions (students believe they expend effort on the task because they enjoy the task and/or want to develop task-relevant skills)	10. Fosters exogenous attributions (students believe that they expend effort on the task for external reasons—to please the teacher, win a competition or reward)
11. Focuses students' attention on their own task-relevant behaviors	11. Focuses students' attention on the teacher as an external authority figure who is manipulating them
12. Fosters appreciation of and desirable attributions about task-relevant behavior after the process is completed	12. Intrudes into the ongoing process, distracting attention from task-relevant behavior

Note. From "Teacher Praise: A Functional Analysis," by J. Brophy, 1981. In *Review of Educational Research, 51*(1), pp. 5–32. Copyright © 1981 by the American Educational Research Association. Reprinted by permission of the publisher.

The undermining effects of extrinsic rewards does not mean that extrinsic rewards should never be used (Ford, 1992). A summary of the effects of extrinsic rewards on intrinsic motivation follows (Cameron & Pierce, 1994; Ford, 1995):

- Verbal praise and positive feedback, when used appropriately, enhance students' intrinsic interest.
- Rewards have a negative impact on intrinsic motivation when they are given simply for engaging in a task or in an attempt to control the behavior of the person without consideration of any standard of performance.

- When the reward received is greater than initially expected, a person is more likely to view him or herself as performing for the reward.
- When students attribute the task outcome to their improving competency, a reward is more likely to enhance intrinsic motivation rather than undermine it.
- When high intrinsic motivation is already present, be cautious about introducing extrinsic rewards because they may dampen the intrinsic motivation.

Finally, Hennessey (1995) found that rewards did not have an undermining effect on intrinsic motivation when extrinsic factors were present if children are *immunized* or trained to focus on intrinsic factors. An implication for teachers is to build in discussions with students on intrinsic motivation factors as a means of immunizing students from the detrimental effects of rewards.

Guidelines for Using Incentives

The preceding discussion reveals that the use of extrinsic rewards is a complicated issue that can have unexpected or undesirable results if the possible consequences are not understood. Because rewards are used so extensively in many schools, the findings about the detrimental effects of rewards must appear confusing to teachers and parents. Guidelines for extrinsic rewards are shown in Strategy 8.3.

Limitations of Intrinsic Motivation

Is intrinsic motivation the solution for increasing student engagement? One perspective is that intrinsic motivation to learn is a necessary, but insufficient, component for academic achievement in classrooms; that is, one can enjoy learning or have an interest in a subject, but lack the strategies necessary for continuing motivation (Corno & Rohrkemper, 1985). Damon (1995) went further in expressing a concern that the benefits of intrinsic motivation have been oversold. One concern is that many learning activities required by the curriculum and viewed as necessary by the teacher may not be seen as interesting or necessary by students (Bandura, 1986; Brophy, 1983). It was noted previously that challenging, thoughtful tasks, which should be intrinsically motivating in and of themselves, may not lead to engagement (Blumenfeld, 1992). Nisen (1992) asserted that, just as students can come to rely on extrinsic rewards for

Strategy 8.3. Guidelines for Extrinsic Rewards

Sufficient Rewards. Avoid *scarcity of rewards,* where only a few students get all of the rewards, recognition, or approval (Covington, 1992). Do the same students continue to receive recognition in award assemblies, whereas rewards are virtually nonexistent for students who are low achievers? Awards such as "student of the month" or "teacher of the month" may place individuals in competition or may turn into, "Whose turn is it now?" The next guideline offers one solution.

Reward for Improvement. Rewards should recognize development of student competencies and progress. When giving rewards, keep the focus on improvement rather than ability. For example, rather than always giving awards only to those who make the honor roll or the highest grade (as is frequently the case), establish a reward system whereby students are routinely recognized for a "personal best" or individual improvement.

Getting Started. Extrinsic rewards can be used to get children started in an activity where there may not be much initial interest. If extrinsic rewards can be used to start children reading or playing an instrument, they may begin to experience new sources of motivation and enjoyment from the activity (Lepper, 1988). For example, a high school physical education department focused on fitness in which the primary activity was jogging. The teachers decided on ribbons to recognize accomplishments: a one-mile ribbon and then cumulative awards for 5, 15, and 25 miles. After the minimum (floor level) was attained, the additional awards were dependent on the students' goals and effort. Students' comments on their accomplishments included, "I'm so proud of myself." This is a clear example of an award that signified accomplishment. Some students continued to exceed the minimum, but never came for additional ribbons.

Fade Out Extrinsic Rewards. When extrinsic rewards are used, gradually diminish them, shifting the focus to a more intrinsic one where possible. This often happens when students gain competence in an area and the increased ability becomes more satisfying than the reward (Lepper, 1988; see Exhibit 8.1).

Public Rewards. One must be careful when using public recognition as a reward. The widespread use of charts reporting student accomplishments was noted by Ames and Ames (1991) in elementary classrooms. A teacher reported placing a chart that listed all students' names in the back of the room. Stars were placed by the names each time they got a perfect score. However, the teachers reported that the charts were checked by only the two students with the most stars. The chart was likely a demotivator for the other students. All students who meet the desired criteria, such as passing a state required proficiency test, could be given recognition.

Combine Rewards With Other Motivational Strategies. Rewards have been combined with other motivational strategies such as goal setting. Ruth (1996) combined contingency contracts with goal setting for students with behavioral and emotional difficulties. The combination of rewards and goals provided maximum success for the students.

motivation, they may also rely on immediate interest or personal desire for motivation. This handicaps learners when they are learning material that is necessary, but of no personal interest to them. In this situation, it was found that rewards helped students persist when they were assigned boring, difficult tasks. This is in contrast to students who had an intrinsic interest in a topic, but quit as soon as they lost interest. Wehlage et al., (1989) concluded that sustained effort in academic learning can be generated by both intrinsic and extrinsic incentives.

REFLECTION.   Examine the use of rewards in your classroom. Is there opportunity for all students to achieve legitimate recognition in some way? Does your reward system recognize developing competence and skills?

EVALUATION, GRADING PRACTICES, AND OPTIMAL MOTIVATION

School and classroom evaluation practices can have both positive and negative effects on student motivation and engagement. Crooks (1988) reviewed research on the influence of evaluation practices on students and concluded that evaluation influences motivation in the following areas:

- monitoring progress and developing skills of self-evaluation;
- students' motivation to study the subject and their perceptions of their capabilities in the subject;
- students' choice of (and development of) learning strategies;
- students' continuing motivation;
- student's self-perceptions, such as their self-efficacy as learners.

Given that motivation is affected by evaluation, the first question is, how do different types of assessment systems affect motivation?

Criterion and Norm-Referenced Assessment

Criterion and norm-referenced assessment were introduced in chapter 3 in the context of social and individual comparison. In criterion-referenced assessment, criteria for the grades are established in advance. The grades are then determined on the basis of students' attainment of the specific skills regardless of other students' performance. A norm-referenced assessment system assigns grades to students based on how their performance stands in relation to that of their classmates (Airasian, 1996). Grading systems that rank students in some way are using norm-referenced assessment. Such a system has no clearly defined standard; the most extreme example is "grading on the curve." In other words, a criterion-referenced system shows real achievement, whereas a norm-referenced system does not indicate any specific knowledge or skill attainment (Wiggins, 1993). When a teacher says, "Regina made the highest grade on the test," this does not indicate how much she learned; it only suggests how her performance compares to others.

Which system is most likely to yield the greatest motivation—competing against an accepted standard or competing against others? A grading system that makes a student's grade dependent on the performance of others places the emphasis on an ability or performance goal focus rather than on a mastery or learning goal focus (Mac Iver, 1993). In contrast, competing against a defined standard allows students to monitor their progress toward achieving the standard, which should shift their emphasis to improving their previous performance not scoring higher than classmates.

Level of Standards

What level of standards has the most positive influence on student motivation? "Clear and worthy standards, combined with the measuring of incremental progress always provide incentives to the learner, even when the gap between present performance and the standard is great" (Wiggins 1993, p. 153). The effect of evaluation standards on student effort was part of a large-scale study by Natriello and Dornbush (1984). Not surprisingly, the findings indicate that higher standards led to greater student effort and the likelihood of their attending class (similarly, difficult goals lead to greater productivity than easy goals; chap. 4). However, if students believed that the standards were unattainable, they were more likely to become disengaged from learning. Furthermore, students' effort were affected by the extent to which they believed the evaluation of their work accurately reflected the level of their performance. If students believed the evaluation was faulty in some way, they were less likely to think the task deserved their effort.

Motivational Variables Considered
by Teachers in Grading

What motivational variables do teachers consider when arriving at grades and on what criteria are these judgments made? In one study, teachers responded to classroom grading scenarios by indicating how they would evaluate the student and why they made the decision (Brookhart, 1993). Brookhart concluded that the meaning of a grade for teachers was closely related to the idea of student work. When describing grades or grading, teachers frequently used phrases or terms like *the work (s)he did* and *perform* or *performance*, denoting something students did or accomplished. Teachers reported that they considered effort as well as achievement when assigning grades.

What student behaviors do teachers consider as effort? Among the behaviors noted in the Natriello and Dornbush study (1984) were (a) the number of assignments completed, (b) the number of assignments turned in on time, (c) the extra amount of time spent to master particular tasks, and to some degree, (d) the extent to which a student strived to be an overachiever.

How do teachers use other variables such as student ability levels, effort, and attitude to adjust student achievement scores? A case study of the grading practices of 15 high school teachers found that 13 of the 15 teachers gave significant weight to effort and motivation as a grading variable, although they stated that they strived not to use student attitudes in grades (Stiggins, Frisbie, & Griswold, 1989). The teachers were divided in terms of how they included ability into the grading decisions. Half of the teachers stated they used different grading procedures for high- and low-ability students. For example, teachers graded high-ability students solely on achievement, whereas low-ability students were graded on achievement and effort.

There are no easy answers to the use of factors such as effort and ability. From this evidence, considerations to keep in mind when using effort as a criteria for grading are:

- There is not a *right way* to use effort as part of the grading criteria. The important consideration is to understand effort as a motivational factor and how the evaluation system can recognize and foster it.
- Operationalize effort—that is, specify what effort is and how it is taken into account in evaluation (see Strategy 2.7).

- When students have an opportunity to improve a project or paper, effort is built into the task.

REFLECTION.   Think about how you include or will include effort in your grading system. Do you include effort and do you think it is effective for promoting student motivation and learning?

Evaluation and Feedback

When evaluating student performance, what type of feedback to the student is most likely to foster motivation? This is one area where incentive and evaluation intersect. Feedback is an outcome of evaluation but can act as an incentive as well, depending on the type. Wiggins (1993) asserted that feedback should provide user-friendly information about how students are doing and how they might improve, not just comments of praise and blame. When evaluating a paper, for example, the best feedback is a comment to help a student understand why the paper worked or why a mistake is a mistake.

How much feedback is needed? Four levels of feedback—from little or none to gradually more explicit amounts of feedback—were proposed by Schutz and Weinstein (1990). The following levels follow Wiggin's suggestion that feedback be user friendly:

Level 1: Simple Knowledge of Results. This first level only tells the students that they are correct or incorrect or how many points they have lost or attained. No other information is provided to the student.

Level 2: Knowledge of Results + Identification of the Error. At the second level, students are given information about why the response is correct or incorrect. Such feedback might say, "You gave a good example, but did not fully explain the concept."

Level 3: Knowledge of Results + Identification of the Error + Discussion of the Best Answer. This level provides the student with the standards that would constitute the best answer. The instructor might say, "Reports that meet the top criterion will clearly integrate examples and concepts."

Level 4: Knowledge of Results + Identification of the Error + Discussion of the Best Answer + Discussion of Strategies to Avoid the Problem in the Future. At this level, the feedback is extensive.

Students are given information that includes effective strategies to help them self-monitor. For example, the instructor might suggest, "review guidelines for the project."

These levels of feedback enable a teacher to give students the type of feedback that is needed for the expected level of performance. Level 4 feedback might be most appropriate when beginning complex tasks. After students know the criteria, Level 1 feedback may be sufficient.

An Evaluation System Based on Motivation Principles: Incentives-Based Improvement Program

What would an evaluation program be like that is based on specific motivational principles? Mac Iver (1993) developed such a program based on goal-setting theory (Locke & Latham, 1984; see chap. 4) and achievement goal theory (Ames, 1992; see chap. 3). Mac Iver argued that these principles can be used to diagnose major weaknesses in traditional evaluation and recognition practices and provide a basis for an improvement system. A traditional norm-referenced system has the following characteristics that influence motivation:

- Success is defined in competition with others, making the goals unreachable for many students.
- When students' best efforts go unnoticed and unrewarded, their commitment to the goal of academic success is likely to be lessened.
- Focusing on ability by rewarding comparative achievements rather than individual improvement highlights ability differences among pupils, does not reward strategic effort, and does not encourage students to see beginning mistakes as a normal part of learning new skills.

To overcome these detriments to motivation, Mac Iver designed a system where goals would be specific and challenging, but reachable. This would encourage a *mastery-focused orientation* because it would deemphasize the importance of normative standards. It would also create a classroom environment where students of differing abilities have fairly equal opportunities for success. Equally important would be a climate where no students (including high-ability students) are likely to consistently experience success without strategic effort. An improvement point scoring system devised for cooperative learning (Slavin, 1990) was modified as the basis for an individual evaluation and recognition program.

The Incentives for Improvement program was implemented by volunteer teachers in 23 middle school classrooms in inner-city Baltimore schools (Mac Iver, 1993). Three major components were involved:

- *Rounds of quizzes.* Students were given a base score that was the average percent correct on recent quizzes. The specific goal for students on a quiz was to increase their own base scores by more than nine points. Each round consisted of three quizzes.
- *Improvement points.* Improvement points were awarded according to the extent that students met their specific goal. This meant students also received clear feedback concerning their goal attainment. Scoring is shown in Table 8.2.
- *Recognition.* Official recognition was provided for all students who raised their performance level throughout the year in the form of "Rising Star" or "Milestone" rewards. The types of recognition included certificates and other small rewards to provide variety (e.g., a pencil with a "milestone award" imprint or an "I am a rising star" button).

TABLE 8.2

How to Earn Improvement Points

If You ...	You Earn
Beat your base score by more than 9 points	30 Improvement Points
Beat your base score by 5 to 9 points	20 Improvement Points
Score within 4 points of your base score	10 Improvement Points
Get a perfect paper	30 Improvement Points
Score within 5 points of a perfect paper	20 Improvement Points

Note. From "Giving Their Best: Grading and Recognition Practices That Motivate Students to Work Hard," by D. J. MacIver & D. J. Reuman, 1993/1994. In *American Educator, 17*(4), 27. Reprinted with permission from the Winter 1993/1994 issue of the *American Educator*, the quarterly journal of the American Federation of Teachers.

There were positive effects for students in the Incentives for Improvement program in several areas. Compared with students not in the program, they: (a) had significantly higher fourth-quarter grades in target courses, (b) earned higher final grades than students in matched nonparticipating classes, and (c) were more likely to pass. Those students who were most at risk (those with low general averages from the previous year) especially benefited; 12% more of the students who were in experimental classes passed than did students in control classes. These students reported expending more effort (e.g., studying harder for quizzes and tests and working closer to their potential) than did students in control classes.

Mac Iver concluded that by giving students a proximal, concrete goal to strive for on every graded assignment, project, test, or quiz, the program may motivate more students to perform up to their potential with beneficial effects on their grades. The program also affects teacher practices. When teachers closely monitor student progress in a regular and systematic way, they are more aware of the accomplishments of low-performing students, which can in turn lead to increased teacher efficacy and motivation.

CONCLUSION

Dimensions of classroom instruction—tasks, incentives, evaluation, and autonomy (chap. 7)— are asserted by Ames (1992) to be essential for a classroom structure that supports a learning goal orientation for students. This chapter explored these dimensions as they affect motivation and engagement of students. Taken altogether, these components place the emphasis on effort instead of ability. Then within the structure, the crucial role of the teacher is to teach the personal qualities of self-regulation. The key component in building a classroom structure for optimal student motivation and engagement is, in the long run, the teacher's own instructional efficacy. The integration of these components is shown in Fig. 8.3. This will be a major step in building a classroom for motivational equality.

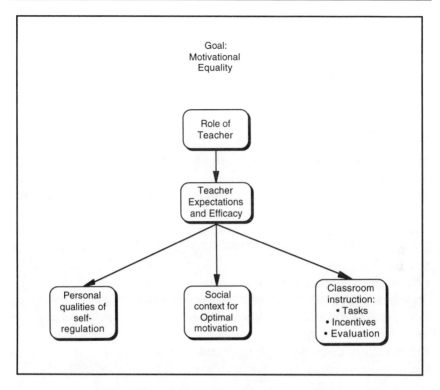

FIG. 8.3. Components for motivational equality.

REVIEW OF MAJOR POINTS

1. Task and activities that engage students in learning are described as meaningful, authentic, challenging, and thoughtful, all requiring higher level thinking. The interaction of task complexity and information processing is required of students. More challenging tasks may not lead to greater engagement by students by themselves. The dilemma for a teacher is that risk can lower motivation for the student, but lowering the risk for the student can lower the level of learning.

2. Teaching practices that increase student task engagement are opportunities to learn, a variety of high-quality instructional techniques, press (push) students for thinking that requires them to

explain and justify answers, scaffolding to lead students gradually toward comprehension, and evaluation that emphasizes comprehension and mastery of content. Effective group work fosters cognitive engagement when students learn to share ideas, disagree, and resolve differences in perspectives.

3.   Task interest is important motivationally because it influences attention and persistence and also the acquisition of knowledge by students. Two types of interest are personal interest: the individual interest that a student brings to the classroom and situational interest, which results from some instructional activity or text material used in the classroom. Situational interest is more important for the classroom and may be short term (catch student attention) or continue over time (hold student attention). For reading from texts, seductive details added to text to make it interesting are more often recalled by students than important generalizations. Find an interest refers to identifying topics that are of interest to students, then finding text and other materials on these topics.

4.   Tasks can be enriched to increase student interest and engagement by opportunity for student sense of choice and ownership—activities that provoke curiosity and personalization of learning. Cultural knowledge acts as a bridge between the student and interest in classroom tasks and activities. Teachers' knowledge of students' culture is important for contributing to task interest and engagement.

5.   Extrinsic and intrinsic motivation represent a continuum from most extrinsic to least extrinsic, not two different types of motivation. In some circumstances, extrinsic rewards undermine or reduce intrinsic motivation; in other circumstances, they enhance intrinsic motivation. Rewards affect motivation through informational or controlling aspects. Rewards contingent on the quality of the task outcome rather than task completion are more likely to have positive effects on the level of task performance and motivational factors. Rewards have a negative impact on intrinsic motivation when they are given simply for engaging in a task without consideration of any standard of performance.

6.   Verbal praise and positive feedback can enhance students' intrinsic interest under certain conditions. Praise is more effective when it is

contingent on performance, indicates the specific performance that is being recognized, and is sincere to the individual receiving it.

7. Guidelines for use of extrinsic rewards include: recognize a variety of competencies, avoid the *scarcity of rewards* problem where only a few students get all of the recognition; focus the rewards on improvement rather than on ability; and use this only to get individuals started in a activity then gradually diminish usage, shifting the focus to a more intrinsic one where possible.

8. Intrinsic motivation may be viewed a necessary but insufficient component for academic engagement. Learning activities that are viewed as necessary by the teacher and required by the curriculum may not be seen as interesting or necessary by students. Similar to relying on extrinsic rewards for motivation, students may also rely on immediate interest or personal desire for motivation and are handicapped when learning material, which is necessary but of no personal interest to them.

9. Evaluation influences motivation by helping students monitor progress, influencing students' motivation to study and the choice of learning strategies, and influencing students' continuing motivation and self-efficacy as learners.

10. The criteria for evaluation influence student motivation. Criterion-referenced assessment is determined on the basis of students' attainment of preset criteria. Norm-referenced assessment system assigns grades to students based on how their performance compares to that of their classmates. Criterion-referenced assessment is more likely to promote learning goals. The level of standards for evaluation influences student motivation with higher standards more likely to be associated with greater effort by students. Effort is often used by teachers to determine student grades.

11. Depending on how it is given, feedback is both an outcome of evaluation and an incentive. Motivational feedback should provide user-friendly information about how students are doing and how they might improve, not just comments of praise and blame. Four levels of feedback—from little or none to explicit amounts—may be needed by students. An evaluation program that focused on goals, effort, and improvement was devised by Mac Iver to increase student motivation. The program based on these components resulted in improved grades and more students passing their work.

Motivational Toolbox

1. Important points to think about and lingering questions

2. Strategies I can use now

3. Strategies I want to develop in the future

CHAPTER 9

Implementing Motivation Strategies in the Classroom

A major goal of formal education should be to equip students with the intellectual tools, self-beliefs, and self-regulatory capabilities to educate themselves throughout their lifetime.

—Bandura (1993, p. 136)

An overview of motivation problems/challenges and possibilities for addressing the problems was presented in chapter 1. A primary assertion was that motivation has to be explicitly addressed as part of classroom instruction. This chapter (a) discusses concerns and issues that are often expressed by preservice and practicing teachers about the implementation of motivation strategies, (b) presents steps for planning and implementing motivational strategies, and (c) gives brief descriptions of programs that offer possibilities for fostering positive motivation and achievement.

POSSIBLE CONCERNS AND ISSUES

There are general issues that must be thought about and resolved or they may become barriers to implementation of motivation strategies in the classroom. What barriers do you envision when thinking about the implementation of a motivational plan of action? Think about the following issues.

1. *How much do you really want to improve motivation?* You make think this question is unnecessary. As teachers, although we value student motivational qualities such as effort and self-control, we may not think it is our job to teach them. We often focus on these qualities

only from a negative viewpoint; "Students don't try, they can't concentrate" (Sockett, 1988). The flip side is, "What am I going to do about improving these student attitudes and behaviors in my classroom?" This aspect is often neglected or it is assumed that these qualities are unteachable. In this book, we have seen that teachers can influence many factors that affect motivation. For example, students can be taught tools like self-instruction to improve their concentration.

2. *The students in my classroom come from many cultures. I'm afraid of imposing motivational qualities because they might be contradictory to their culture.* Motivational qualities such as beliefs about the value of formal education, school achievement, good behavior, and parent involvement are neutral or similar and are valued across different cultures (Goldenberg & Gallimore, 1995; Sockett, 1988). For example, Goldenberg and Gallimore found that immigrant Latino parents were similar to U.S. residents regarding the importance of education as a ladder of social and occupational mobility. Similarly, the family patterns of high-achieving African-American students valued academic pursuits and established achievement norms for their children (Clark, 1983).

If these common goals among different cultures are not acknowledged, disparities between home values and school practice are more likely (Goldenberg, 1994). For example, Goldenberg reported that a parent complained that teachers perceived that children from immigrant Latino backgrounds were deprived. To compensate for this perception, teachers let students play all day instead of teaching them. This was contrary to the achievement goals that parents had for their children.

A most important factor in teaching diverse student populations is to learn about their families' cultural values. Teachers can then build on commonalities between school and families while acknowledging and honoring the cultural differences.

3. *I'm a high school teacher and my students come from middle school without goals and study strategies but I have to teach my curriculum. I don't have time to teach motivation and strategies.* This relates to the issue stated in the first question. In the short term, it may seem that valuable time would be taken from content. However, if the absence of qualities such as goals and study strategies interfere with students' academic progress, what is our option but to teach

students the tools they need. Programs that infused academic goals with student tools for success are described in the last section of this chapter.

IMPLEMENTING MOTIVATIONAL STRATEGIES OR PROGRAMS

As stated in chapter 1, it is important for teachers to actively plan for optimal motivation and engagement, not just react to problems. With a plan based on applicable knowledge, teachers are in a position to revise and refine it as needed.

Teacher Motivation

The successful implementation of motivation strategies depends a great deal on the teacher's motivation. Motivational characteristics of teacher efficacy, goal setting, risk taking, volition, and persistence are especially important for carrying out a plan of action. The following are essential aspects of motivation for a plan to be successful:

- Set your goals—distal and proximal.
- Research your environment, identify potential obstacles or difficulties.
- Take moderate risks. Reflect on the self-worth motive in terms of your own risk-taking and self-protective strategies.
- Establish a monitoring/feedback mechanism for yourself.
- Get feedback and support from peers, administrators, and parents.
- Go back to Square 1 if necessary and revise.
- Above all, be persistent.

Beginning of the Year and Setting Expectations

The beginning of the year is a time to set the framework for a motivation climate for all students. The basic framework for optimal motivation and engagement is established at this time: a climate that supports a sense of membership, task components that foster engagement, and the incentive and grading system. This is the time to discuss adaptive motivation processes with students, attributions for success and failure, the meaning of effort in your class, views of intelligence, and the importance of learning strategies. These may be conveyed in class discussions, use of posters with key reminders, or a more elaborated manual. Exhibit 9.1 presents a template for a STEPS manual for success that I developed for my classes.

Exhibit 9.1. Template for a Student Motivation Manual

Overview of Expectations	Expectations for the course and the importance of becoming an effective student and why we want students to excel.
Need for Strategy Instruction	Our awareness of student need for motivation and learning strategies and our commitment helps students learn and/or refine learning strategies.
Profiles of Successful and Unsuccessful Students	Learning strategy and motivational profiles (based on composites) of successful, unsuccessful, and improving students.
Motivation Strategies Needed by Students	Attitudes, motivation, and strategies that will enhance students chance of success in the course. Examples are: high expectations, goals, effort, learning goal focus, seeking help when needed, time management, and volitional strategies.
Learning Strategies Needed by Students	A beginning list of strategies: use of text aids, elaboration, organization such as graphic organizers, importance of learning for understanding, and application.
Supplements Included	Guidelines for attention and concentration, notetaking, and effective participation in small groups. Forms for goal setting, time management log, and record keeping.

The content depends on courses and age of students. Posters can be used for younger students.
From Alderman (unpublished).

A Problem-Solving Approach

A problem-solving approach can help you devise a sequence of steps that becomes more manageable. The IDEAL problem-solving model (Bransford & Stein, 1994) serves as a useful process for reflecting on your practice and when planning and implementing a motivational plan. The process includes the following phases: (a) identifying a problem, (b) defining a problem, (c) evaluating alternatives, and (d) looking back or evaluating the plan.

1. *Identifying a problem.* Identifying and defining the motivational problems or challenges is the first step. Examine your current practice. What motivational problems exist in your school or classroom? What do you want to improve? What do you want and expect students to accomplish? What motivational tools will they need? Deliberately gathering information about student motivation will often enlighten you about motivation problems and potentials that you may have previously overlooked. Information about student motivation comes from both formal and informal discussions and written assignments. Strategy 9.1 presents ideas for gathering information about student perceptions of motivation and their strategies.

Strategy 9.1. Gathering Motivational Information by Verbal Reports

- Ms. Hudson began the school year by having students write about one achievement they had experienced. She then typed up the stories without names and passed them back to the students for discussion. An activity like this not only gives information, but gets students thinking about their achievement motivation and goals.
- Conduct group discussions on how students define *success* and how they know they are successful. This provides insights about the extent to which students have performance and learning goal orientations. Discussion of success also gives indications of whether students define success in comparison with others or to their own accomplishments.
- Have students predict their performance on exams and tell how they studied. Then, they can compare their prediction with their actual grade and tell how they will study next time (see Exhibit 2.1).
- At the beginning of the year, ask students to write about "What makes you feel successful, in math, writing, etc." and "Describe one successful experience in science or art."

An obvious starting point is to gather information about students' attributional beliefs. The results may surprise you. For example, third-grade teachers classified their students' perception of attributional beliefs according to ability level (Carr & Kurtz-Costes, 1994). The teachers judged high-ability students to have more positive attributions than low-ability students. However, ability level can be misleading. Some low achievers may possess a positive but inaccurate view of their abilities, whereas some higher ability students may attribute their performance primarily to external factors. Strategy 2.1 suggested ways to gather information about students' attributions for success and failure.

2. *Defining the problem and goal*. At the beginning, your goals may be both long and short term, group and individual. A long-term goal for the class might be, "I want to develop a classroom climate to support and foster self-regulation so that my students can become independent learners and develop a core of resiliency." A short-term goal for an individual may simply be, "I want to get Tyrone to complete his assignments."

3. *Choosing goals and strategies*. The problem you have identified will guide strategy selection. One major consideration is the extent you can or will change a basic teaching format. Implementation of strategies such as attributional feedback does not require changes in your basic instructional approaches. Strategies to get Tyrone to complete his assignments are not likely to require changes in a basic approach to teaching. The goal to establish a climate to support and foster self-regulation will require more comprehensive changes in your classroom. One guideline for beginning intervention strategies is to take a "small but beautiful" approach (Pressley et al., 1989). This means try the plan or strategies on a small scale and then monitor the effects. For example,

- follow the steps of the LINKS model (chap. 4) with a student like Tyrone who is not completing his assignments or a student who is displaying signs of learned helplessness. Keep track of the results.
- give attributional feedback to students about the possible reasons for success and failure.
- examine the recognition or reward system that you use for the class. If the same few students are receiving the recognition, expand the types of competencies that receive recognition.

4. *Monitoring and evaluating the plan*. The next step (and a very important one) is monitoring and evaluating the effects of the plan of action. The following are possible sources of feedback:

- *Student data*. What student data are important? For example, did Tyrone's assignment-completion record increase after you used the LINKS model to help him complete assignments? What is Tyrone's assessment of his progress? After you revised the recognition criteria, did a wider range of students receive recognition?
- *Observation*. Who can observe your classroom and provide useful feedback about what you are doing? Possible sources are a peer teacher or an administrator.
- *Self-evaluation*. Keep a journal or log describing the effects of the intervention and your own reactions to the strategy or plan. This can also be a source of self-efficacy as you note progress.
- *Examine the effects and revise as needed*. These sources will provide you with information for revising as needed.

POSSIBILITIES FOR MOTIVATIONAL EQUALITY

The problem of motivational inequality was introduced in chapter 1. To reiterate, *motivational equality* means students have optimum motivation for intellectual development. Numerous strategies for assisting students in developing adaptive attitudes and strategies have been presented in prior chapters. In this section, four comprehensive programs that have confronted barriers to achievement and provided possibilities for motivational equality are briefly described. These programs are:

- The Benchmark program for poor readers;
- "Consistency Management," a classroom management program to develop student self-discipline;
- Practical Intelligence for Schools (PIFS) helps students develop tools for self-management; and
- Advancement Via Individual Determination (AVID), a program that places previously low-achieving students in college-prep classes and provides the support for them to succeed.

These four programs were selected because they are comprehensive, include motivational components, and have evidence of success in challenging educational situations.

Benchmark

Benchmark, a school for poor readers, has the premise that every student is teachable (Gaskins, 1994; Gaskins & Elliot, 1991). Students enter the program at ages 7 to 10, essentially as nonreaders. Twenty years of research-based curriculum development has gone into the program designed to guide students to be goal-oriented, planful, strategic, and self-assessing. Seventeen core cognitive strategies were selected by faculty as needed by all students. The self-regulatory strategies include learning and metacognitive strategies, as well as organization, effort, and self-control.

The strategies are taught within each content area. A minicourse, "Psych 101: A Course for Learning About Learning," is embedded in each content course. The first topic in the minicourse is belief about intelligence, with the emphasis on intelligence as incremental. Students are taught that they have control over how *smart* they are (see chap. 3 for an incremental-entity view of intelligence in motivation). After 4 days, this topic is followed by the study of effort, focusing on the meaning and types of effort. Students are then taught metacognitive control strategies in four categories: control of person, control of task, control of environment, and control of strategies. Note the similarity to the volitional control strategies described in chapter 5.

Ongoing evaluation of the program at Benchmark revealed that middle school students made progress during the 3-year project as measured by academic assessment measures and teacher reports (Gaskins, 1994). Teacher anecdotal reports indicate that students used a variety of awareness and control strategies. The curriculum and teaching strategies of this program continue to undergo revision. Detailed descriptions of the curriculum and lessons can be found in *Implementing Cognitive Strategies Across the School* (Gaskins & Elliot, 1991).

Consistency Management

Consistency management is a classroom management approach designed initially for inner-city elementary schools, but is now implemented in upper grades as well (Freiberg, 1993; Freiberg, Stein, & Huang, 1995). The program emphasizes student ownership and responsibility, where teachers and students work together to create communities to support self-discipline. Students take responsibility for the organization and daily operations of the classroom with 30 or more jobs open to all students. One job is classroom manager, whose duties range from passing out papers to assisting substitute teachers, coordinating paper flow and attendance, and collecting and returning papers. Another is the absentee manager, who prepares a packet of assignments when a student is absent.

Parent support and involvement occur in several ways. In one way, parents talk to classes about how workplace rules relate to classroom rules. Parent and community involvement workshops are conducted on "How to help your child be successful in school."

The program has an incentive component for both students and teachers. Small nonmonetary incentives are awarded to individuals or classes that achieve goals set by the class. Teachers who demonstrated exemplary and consistent work attendance were recognized as well.

Schools who implemented the program were compared with similar schools that did not have the program. The comparisons indicate that schools with the consistency management program had greater achievement over 4 years than did the comparison schools. Students were more involved in classwork and more task oriented than in comparison schools. The number of student referrals to the office for disciplinary procedures decreased dramatically over a four-year period. In addition, teacher absences also decreased over this period.

Practical Intelligence for School (PIFS)

This program (Gardner, Kerchevksy, Sternberg, & Okagaki, 1994) is based on Gardner's (1983) theory of multiple intelligences and Sternberg's (1985) triarchic theory of practical intelligence. Multiple intelligence theory includes seven types of intelligences. The triarchic theory identified components that are involved in intelligent acts. Both theories have the premise that stimulation is necessary for the development of intelligence. The PIF's curriculum was based on this premise and was designed to enable students to take responsibility for their own learning. The focus was on three areas: managing yourself, managing tasks, and cooperating with others. Examples of topics and skills in these three areas are:

- Managing yourself: understand the kinds of intelligence, understand test scores, know how you work best, show what you learned, collect thoughts, and set goals
- Managing tasks: learn processes to help you solve problems, break habits, get organized, get the assignment in on time, understand questions, and find the main idea
- Cooperating with others: learn what to say, put yourself in another's place, solve problems in communication, and see school as a social system.

The topics in the curriculum were taught to seventh graders of three mixed-ability groups in two schools in a middle-income suburb. In one school, a stand-alone curriculum was implemented. In the second school, the curriculum was infused within subject areas. Students who experienced the PIFS curriculum were compared with students in control groups who did not experience the curriculum. Students who experienced the stand-alone curriculum had higher scores on the motivation and study strategy inventories than students in the control groups. Although students in the second school did not differ on the pre- and posttest inventory, the researchers explained that the differences in the schools were due to the trainers for the program, not the curriculum. In the more successful school, the trainers were more demanding. The curriculum developers are now working on a program that has aspects of both the stand-alone and infused curriculum.

Advancement Via Individual Determination (AVID)

A student from the AVID program, Lilla, was introduced in chapter 5. AVID is an *untracking* program that places previously low-achieving students (primarily from low-income, minority backgrounds) in the same college prep programs as high-achieving students (Mehan, Villanueva, Hubbard, & Lintz, 1996). The program began with one teacher who was determined that students would not automatically be placed in a remedial track based on their background (Ruenzel, 1997). The students were typically passive learners who did not know what serious study entailed. Although they had goals to attend college, they had no idea of the type of preparation and steps needed to be ready.

AVID students receive explicit instruction in the informal curriculum of school (Mehan et al., 1996). The instructional features include:

- Study and test-taking skills. The centerpiece of the program is a special method of notetaking for compiling main ideas, abstracting key concepts, and identifying questions that guide analysis. Test taking, including preparation for the SAT, is taught in all classes.
- Step-by-step planning and preparation for college entry. Students are coached about the complicated process of entering college. They learn how to write their statement of purpose, fill out applications, and apply for financial aid. This is similar to the PLAN program described in chapter 5.
- Conflict resolution for interacting with teachers. In this component, students are taught social skills such as how to talk to teachers and ask for help.
- Teacher advocates. The teachers in AVID act as advocates on behalf of students in both academic and personal matters.

A recent study found that the number of AVID graduates who attend college is greater than the national average (Mehan et al., 1996). For example, 55% of the African-American students who participated in the program for at least 3 years attend college, compared with 33% nationally. Forty-three percent of the Hispanic students attend college, compared with 20% nationally.

POSSIBILITIES AND HOPE

We began this exploration into motivation by delineating problems and challenges. It was asserted that the knowledge base offers possibilities for teachers to help students reach their potential. All four programs described here have provided possibilities for students developing their potential. They also provided possibilities for how schools and teachers can make a difference. The programs all developed explicit curriculums for their target population. The development of personal competencies that can help students be academically successful was not left to chance or as an implicit by-product of schooling. All four programs required investment in the professional preparation of teachers.

Yes, there are motivational problems and challenges in schools. However, there are also many possibilities for addressing the problems. The important question is one posed by Asa Hilliard (1991); "Do we have the will to educate all students?" If we do not take the challenge now, when will we? We cannot solve problems overnight, but teachers and students together can begin the journey toward a future with hope. The expectation for this journey is *progress not miracles.*

Glossary

Attribution: The perceived causes of success and failure.

Autonomy: The need to see one's actions as internally initiated.

Big-fish-little-pond-effect (BFLPE): The effect of using group comparisons on one's perception of ability.

Ceiling expectation: The assumption that student background sets a ceiling level of attainment.

Distal goals: Goals far removed in time.

Ego-involvement: Evaluate ability in comparison with others.

Entity view of intelligence: Belief that intelligence is global and fixed.

Extrinsic motivation: Motivation from sources outside an individual.

Failure-avoiding strategies: Strategies used to protect self-worth from view that one is not smart.

Floor expectation: The minimum level that all students are expected to achieve.

General teaching efficacy: Belief about the extent to which teachers in general can be effective with different students.

Helplessness (also *learned helplessness*): Belief that one is powerless to affect a given situation.

Incremental view of intelligence: Belief that intelligence is malleable; as one learns more, intelligence is increased.

Individual comparison: Comparison of one's performance to previous performances.

Instrumental activity: Explicit activity to attain a goal.

Intrinsic motivation: The source of motivation is internal to the person.

Learning goal: Focus on learning or mastery; see also *task involvement* and *mastery goal*.

Level of aspiration: The goals to which one aspires with reference to the level of difficulty.

Maladaptive motivation patterns: Negative attributions and self-defeating behaviors.

Mastery goal: See *learning goal*.

Metacognition: Awareness of one's knowledge, strategy use, and the use of self-corrective activities.

Oppositional social identity: The rejection of values of the dominant culture for fear of losing identity.

Origin: Tendency to be the cause of one's actions; related to autonomy.

Pawn: Feeling of powerlessness or subject to control by external sources.

Performance goal: Focus on looking smart and proving ability.

Personal teaching efficacy: Belief about how much a teacher personally can affect learning.

Possible selves: The positive and negative selves one envisions for the future.

Proximal goal: A nearby or short-term goal.

Resiliency: The ability to bounce back in adverse circumstances.

Scaffold: The assistance provided by an expert peer or an adult.

Self-efficacy: Belief about one's capabilities to perform the actions necessary to accomplish a task.

Self-fulfilling prophecy: An expectation that comes true because of actions based on an erroneous expectation.

Self-handicapping: Deliberate strategies such as not trying to maintain a positive self-image.

Self-instruction: Verbal or covert instruction to control one's actions.

Self-monitoring: Observation and evaluation of progress.

Self-regulation: Degree to which individuals are active participants in their own learning.

Self-worth: Need for students to maintain a positive image of their competence.

Social comparison: Using performance of others as the standard for comparison.

Sustaining expectation effect: Responding to students in the same way although their behavior is changing, resulting in maintaining the behavior.

Task involvement: Goal orientation for increasing learning or understanding.

Volition: Strength of will; strategies to persist despite obstacles.

REFERENCES

Abi-Nader, J. (1987). "A house for my mother": An ethnography of motivational strategies in a successful college preparatory program for Hispanic high school students. *Dissertation Abstracts International, 48*(2), AAT87/1558.

Abi-Nader, J. (1990). "A house for my mother": Motivating Hispanic high school students. *Anthropology and Education Quarterly, 21*, 41–58.

Abi-Nader, J. (1991). Creating a vision of the future. *Phi Delta Kappan, 72*, 546–549.

Airasian, P. W. (1996). *Assessment in the classroom*. New York: McGraw-Hill.

Alderman, M. K. (1985). Achievement motivation and the preservice teacher. In M. K. Alderman & M. W. Cohen (Eds.), *Motivation theory and practice for preservice teachers* (pp. 37–51). Washington, DC: ERIC Clearinghouse on Teacher Education.

Alderman, M. K. (1990). Motivation for at-risk students. *Educational Leadership, 48*, 27–30.

Alderman, M. K. (1996, April). *Two sides of the coin, motivation problems and needs in an urban high school and the knowledge base from research: Does it match?* Paper presented at the annual meeting of the American Educational Research Association, New York.

Alderman, M. K., Klein, R., Seeley, S., & Sanders, M. (1993). Preservice teachers as learners in formation: Metacognitive self-portraits. *Reading Research and Instruction, 32*, 38–54.

Allinder, R. M. (1995). An examination of the relationship between teacher efficacy and curriculum-based measurement and student achievement. *Remedial and Special Education, 16*(4), 247–254.

Allington, R. (1980). Teacher interruption behaviors during primary grade oral reading. *Journal of Educational Psychology, 72*, 371–377.

Alloy, L. B., Abramson, L. Y., Peterson, C., & Seligman, M. E. (1984). Attributional style and the generality of learned helplessness. *Journal of Personality and Social Psychology, 46*(3), 681–687.

Ames, C. (1992). Classrooms: Goals, structures, and student motivation. *Journal of Educational Psychology, 84*(3), 261–271.

Ames, C., & Ames, R. (1984). Goals, structure, and motivation. *The Elementary School Journal, 85*(1), 39–52.

Ames, C., & Archer, J. (1988). Achievement goals in the classroom: Students' learning strategies and motivational processes. *Journal of Educational Psychology, 80*, 260–267.

Ames, R., & Ames, C. (1991). Motivation and effective teaching. In J. L. Idol & B. F. Jones (Eds.), *Educational values and cognitive instruction: Implications for reformation* (pp. 247–261). Hillsdale, NJ: Lawrence Erlbaum Associates.

Ames, R., & Lau, S. (1982). An attributional analysis of student help seeking in academic settings. *Journal of Educational Psychology, 74*, 414–423.

Andrews, G. R., & Debus, R. (1978). Persistence and the causal perception of failure: Modifying cognitive attributions. *Journal of Educational Psychology, 70*(2), 154–166.

Argyris, C., & Schon, D. (1974). *Theory in practice: Increasing professional effectiveness*. San Francisco: Jossey-Bass.

Armour, D., Conry-Oseguera, P., Cox, P., King, N., McDonnell, L., Pascal, A., Pauly, E., & Zellman, G. (1976). *Analysis of the school preferred reading program in selected Los Angeles minority schools* (Report No. R-2007-LAUSD). Santa Monica, CA: The Rand Corporation.

Ashton, P. (1984). Teacher efficacy: A motivational paradigm for effective teacher education. *Journal of Teacher Education, 35*(5), 28–32.

Ashton, P. T., & Webb, R. B. (1986). *Making a difference: Teachers' sense of efficacy and student achievement*. New York: Longman.

Bandura, A. (1986). *Social foundations of thought and action*. Englewood Cliffs, NJ: Prentice-Hall.

Bandura, A. (1993). Perceived self-efficacy in cognitive development and functioning. *Educational Psychologist, 28*(2), 117–148.

Bandura, A. (1997). *Self-efficacy: The exercise of control*. New York: Freeman.

Bandura, A., & Cervone, D. (1983). Self-evaluative and self-efficacy mechanisms governing the motivational effects of goal systems. *Journal of Personality and Social Psychology, 45*, 1017–1028.

Bandura, A., & Cervone, D. (1986). Differential engagement of self-reactive influences in cognitive motivation. *Organizational Behavior and Human Decision Processes, 38*, 92–113.

Bandura, A., & Schunk, D. H. (1981). Cultivating competence, self-efficacy, and intrinsic interest through proximal motivation. *Journal of Personality and Social Psychology, 41*, 586–598.

Baron, R. M., Tom, D. Y. H., & Cooper, H. M. (1985). Social class, race, and teacher expectations. In J. B. Dusek (Ed.), *Teacher expectations* (pp. 251–269). Hillsdale, NJ: Lawrence Erlbaum Associates.

Battistich, V., Solomon, D., Kim, D., Watson, M., & Schaps, E. (1995). Schools as communities, poverty levels of student populations, and student attitudes, motives, and performances: A multilevel analysis. *American Educational Research Journal, 32*(2), 627–658.

Bell, C. M., & Kanevsky, L. (1996, April). *Promoting positive achievement motivation in a regular grade 2 classroom*. Paper presented at the annual meeting of the American Educational Research Association, New York City.

Bempechat, J., Nakkula, M. J., Wu, J. T., & Ginsberg, H. P. (1996). Attributions as predictors of mathematics achievement: A comparative study. *Journal of Research and Development, 29*(2), 53–59.

Benard, B. (1993). Fostering resiliency in kids. *Educational Leadership, 49*(3), 44–47.

Benson, R. (1988). Helping pupils overcome homework distractions. *The Clearing House, 61,* 370–372.

Benz, C., Bradley, L., Alderman, M., & Flowers, M. (1992). Personal teaching efficacy: Developmental relationships in education. *Journal of Educational Research, 85*(5), 274–286.

Bergin, D. (1989). Student goals for out-of-school learning activities. *Journal of Adolescent Research, 4,* 92–109.

Berman, P., McLaughlin, M. W., Bass, G., Pauly, E., & Zellman, G. (1977). *Federal programs supporting educational change: Vol. VII. Factors affecting implementation and continuation.* Santa Monica, CA: The Rand Corporation.

Berndt, T. J., & Keefe, K. (1992). Friends' influence adolescents' perceptions of themselves at school. In D. H. Schunk & J. L. Meece (Eds.), *Student perceptions in the classroom* (pp. 51–68). Hillsdale, NJ: Lawrence Erlbaum Associates.

Blumenfeld, P. C. (1992). The task and the teacher: Enhancing student thoughtfulness in science. In J. Brophy (Ed.), *Advances in research on teaching* (pp. 81–114). Greenwich, CT: JAI Press.

Blumenfeld, P. C., Marx, R. W., Soloway, E., & Krajcik, J. (1996). Learning with peers: From small group cooperation to collaborative communities. *Educational Researcher, 25*(8), 37–40.

Blumenfeld, P. C., Mergendoller, J. R., & Puro, P. (1992). Translating motivation into thoughtfulness. In H. H. Marshall (Ed.), *Redefining school learning* (pp. 207–239). Norwood, NJ: Ablex.

Borkowski, J. G. (1988). Understanding inefficient learning: Attributional beliefs and the training of memory and comprehension strategies. In M. M. Gruneberg, P. E. Morris, & R. N. Sykes (Eds.), *Practical aspects of memory* (pp. 287–293). New York: Wiley.

Borkowski, J. G., & Muthukrishna, N. (1992). Moving metacognition into the classroom: "Working models" and effective strategy teaching. In M. Pressley, K. R. Harris, & J. T. Gutherie (Eds.), *Promoting academic literacy: Cognitive research and instructional innovation* (pp. 477–501). Orlando, FL: Academic Press.

Borkowski, J. G., & Thorpe, P. K. (1994). Self-regulation and motivation: A lifetime perspective on underachievement. In B. J. Zimmerman & D. H. Schunk (Eds.), *Self-regulation of learning and performance* (pp. 45–74). Hillsdale, NJ: Lawrence Erlbaum Associates.

Borkowski, J. G., Weyhing, R. S., & Carr, M. (1988). Effects of attributional retraining on strategy-based reading comprehension in learning-disabled students. *Journal of Educational Psychology, 80*(1), 46–53.

Bransford, J., & Stein, B. S. (1994). *The ideal problem solver: A guide for improving thinking, learning, and creativity* (2nd ed.). New York: Freeman.

Braun, C. (1976). Teacher expectations: Sociopsychological dynamics. *Review of Educational Research, 46*, 185–213.

Britton, B. K., & Tessor, A. (1991). Effects of time management practices on college grades. *Journal of Educational Psychology, 83*, 405–410.

Brookhart, S. M. (1993). Teacher grading practices: Meaning and value. *Journal of Educational Measurement, 30*(2), 123–142.

Brookover, W., Beady, C., Flood, P., Schweitzer, J., & Wisenbaker, J. (1979). *School social systems and student achievement: Schools can make a difference.* New York: Bergin.

Brophy, J., & Kher, N. (1986). Teacher or social cues as a mechanism for developing student motivation to learn. In R. Feldman (Ed.), *Social psychology applied to education* (pp. 257–288). New York: Cambridge.

Brophy, J. E. (1981). Teacher praise: A functional analysis. *Review of Educational Research, 51*, 5–32.

Brophy, J. E. (1983). Conceptualizing student motivation. *Educational Psychologist, 18*, 200–215.

Brophy, J. E. (1985). Teacher–student interaction. In J. B. Dusek (Ed.), *Teacher expectancies* (pp. 303–328). Hillsdale, NJ: Lawrence Erlbaum Associates.

Brophy, J. E. (1987). Socializing student motivation to learn. In M. L. Maehr & D. Klieber (Eds.), *Advances in motivation and achievement: Enhancing motivation* (pp. 181–210). Greenwich, CT: JAI Press.

Brown, B. B. (1993). School culture, social politics, and the academic motivation of U.S. students. In T. M. Tomlinson (Ed.), *Motivating students to learn* (pp. 63–98). Berkeley, CA: McCutchan.

Brown, J., & Weiner, B. (1984). Affective consequences of ability versus effort ascriptions: Controversies, resolutions, and quandaries. *Journal of Educational Psychology, 76*(1), 146–158.

Brown, S. M., & Wahlberg, H. J. (1993). Motivational effects on test scores of elementary students. *Journal of Educational Research, 86*(3), 133–136.

Butkowsky, I. S., & Willows, D. M. (1980). Cognitive-motivational characteristics of children varying in reading ability: Evidence for learned helplessness in poor readers. *Journal of Educational Psychology, 72*(3), 408–422.

Butler, R., & Neuman, O. (1995). Effects of task and ego achievement goals on help-seeking behaviors and attitudes. *Journal of Educational Psychology, 87*(2), 261–271.

Butler, R., & Orion, R. (1990). When pupils do not understand the determinants of their success and failure in school: Relations between internal, teacher and unknown perceptions of school achievement. *British Journal of Educational Psychology, 60*, 63–75.

Cameron, J., & Pierce, W. D. (1994). Reinforcement, reward, and intrinsic motivation: A meta-analysis. *Review of Educational Research, 64*, 363–424.

Cannon, J. R., & Scharmann, L. C. (1996). Influence of a cooperative early field experience on preservice elementary teachers' science self-efficacy. *Science Education, 80*(4), 419–436.

Cardova, D. J., & Lepper, M. R. (1996). Intrinsic motivation and the process of learning: Beneficial effects of contextualization, personalization, and choice. *Journal of Educational Psychology, 88*(4), 715–730.

Carr, M., & Kurtz-Costes, B. E. (1994). Is being smart everything? The influence of student achievement on teachers' perceptions. *British Journal of Educational Psychology, 64*, 263–276.

Carroll, L. (1963). *Alice's adventures in Wonderland*. New York: Macmillan.

Claiborn, W. (1969). Expectancy effects in the classroom: A failure to replicate. *Journal of Educational Psychology, 60*, 377–383.

Clark, M. L. (1991). Social identity, peer relations, and academic competence of African American adolescents. *Education and Urban Society, 24*(1), 41–52.

Clark, R. (1983). *Family life and school achievement*. Chicago: University of Chicago Press.

Clifford, M. M. (1986). The effects of ability, strategy, and effort attributions for educational, business, and athletic failure. *British Journal of Educational Psychology, 56*, 169–179.

Cohen, E. G. (1994). *Designing groupwork* (2nd ed.). New York: Teachers College Press.

Collier, G. (1994). *Social origins of mental ability*. New York: Wiley.

Connell, J. P. (1990). Context, self, and action: A motivational analysis of self-system processes across the life span. In D. Cicchetti & M. Beechly (Eds.), *The self in transition: Infancy and childhood*. Chicago: University of Chicago Press.

Connell, J. P., & Wellborn, J. G. (1991). Competence, autonomy, and relatedness: A motivational analysis of self-system processes. In M. R. Gunnar & L. A. Roufe (Eds.), *Self-processes and development*. Hillsdale, NJ: Lawrence Erlbaum Associates.

Cooper, H., & Good, T. L. (1983). *Pygmalion grows up: Studies in expectation communication process*. New York: Longman.

Corno, L. (1993). The best-laid plans: Modern conceptions of volition and educational research. *Educational Researcher, 22*(2), 4–22.

Corno, L. (1994). Student volition and education: Outcomes, influences, and practices. In B. J. Zimmerman & D. H. Schunk (Eds.), *Self-regulation of learning and performance* (pp. 229–254). Hillsdale, NJ: Lawrence Erlbaum Associates.

Corno, L., & Kanfer, R. (1993). The role of volition in learning and performance. In L. Darling-Hammond (Ed.), *Review of research in education* (pp. 3–43). Washington, DC: American Educational Research Association.

Corno, L., & Rohrkemper, M. (1985). The intrinisc motivation to learn in classrooms. In C. Ames & R. Ames (Eds.), *Research on motivation in education* (pp. 53–90). New York: Academic Press.

Covey, S. (1989). *The 7 habits of highly effective people*. New York: Simon & Schuster.

Covington, M. V. (1984). The self-worth theory of achievement motivation: Findings and implications. *The Elementary School Journal, 85*(1), 5–20.

Covington, M. V. (1992). *Making the grade: A self-worth perspective on motivation and school reform*. New York: Cambridge University Press.

Covington, M. V., & Beery, R. (1976). *Self-worth and school learning*. New York: Holt, Rinehart & Winston.

Covington, M. V., & Omelich, C. L. (1979). Effort: The double-edged sword. *Journal of Educational Psychology, 71*, 169–182.

Crooks, T. J. (1988). The impact of classroom evaluation practices on students. *Review of Educational Research, 58*(4), 438–481.

Csikszentmihalyi, M. (1990). *Flow: The psychology of optimal experience*. New York: Harper & Row.

Culler, R. E., & Holahan, C. J. (1980). Test anxiety and academic performance: The effects of study-related behaviors. *Journal of Educational Psychology, 72*, 16–20.

Damon, W. (1995). *Greater expectations*. New York: The Free Press.

Darling-Hammond, L. (1997). *The right to learn: A blueprint for creating schools that work*. San Francisco: Jossey-Bass.

Darling-Hammond, L., Ancess, J., & Falk, B. (1995). *Authentic assessment in action*. New York: Teachers College Press.

Day, J. D., Borkowski, J. G., Dietmeyer, D. L., Howsepian, B. A., & Saenz, D. S. (1992). Possible selves and academic achievement. In L. T. Winegar & J. Valsinar (Eds.), *Children's development within social context* (pp. 181–201). Hillsdale, NJ: Lawrence Erlbaum Associates.

Day, J. D., Borkowski, J. G., Punzo, D., & Howsepian, B. (1994). Enhancing possible selves in Mexican American students. *Motivation and Emotion, 18*(1), 79–103.

deCharms, R. (1976). *Enhancing motivation*. New York: Irvington/Wiley.

deCharms, R. (1984). Motivational enhancement in educational settings. In R. E. Ames & C. Ames (Eds.), *Research on motivation in education* (pp. 275–310). Orlando, FL: Academic Press.

Deci, E. L., & Ryan, R. M. (1985). *Intrinsic motivation and self-determination in motivation*. New York: Plenum.

Deci, E. L., & Ryan, R. M. (1991). A motivational approach to self: Integration in personality. In R. Dienstbier (Ed.), *Nebraska symposium on motivation* (pp. 237–288). Lincoln, NE: University of Nebraska Press.

Delpit, L. (1995). *Other people's children*. New York: The Free Press.

Dewey, J. (1913). *Interest and effort in education*. New York: Houghton-Mifflin.

Diener, C. I., & Dweck, C. S. (1978). An analysis of learned helplessness: Continuous changes in performance, strategy, and achievement cognitions following failure. *Journal of Personality and Social Psychology, 36*, 451–462.

Dillon, D. R. (1989). Showing them that I want them to learn and that I care about who they are: A microethnography of the social organization of a secondary low-track English-reading class. *American Educational Research Journal, 26*, 227–259.

Doverspike, J. (1973). Group and individual goals: Their development and utilization. *Educational Technology, 13*(2), 24–26.

Doyle, W. (1983). Academic work. *Review of Educational Research, 53*, 159–200.

Dweck, C. S. (1975). The role of expectations and attributions in the alleviation of learned helplessness. *Journal of Personality and Social Psychology, 31,* 674–685.

Dweck, C. S. (1986). Motivational processes affecting learning. *American Psychologist, 41*(10), 1040–1048.

Dweck, C. S. (1992). The study of goals in psychology. *Psychological Science, 3*(3), 165–167.

Dweck, C. S., & Goetz, T. E. (1978). Attributions and learned helplessness. In J. H. Harvey & W. Ickles (Eds.), *New directions in attribution research* (pp. 157–159). Hillsdale, NJ: Lawrence Erlbaum Associates.

Dweck, C. S., & Leggett, E. L. (1988). A social-cognitive approach to motivation and personality. *Psychological Review, 95,* 256–273.

Eccles, J., Wigfield, A., Harold, R. D., & Blumenfeld, P. (1993). Self and task performance during elementary school. *Child Development, 64,* 830–847.

Eccles, J. S., & Midgley, C. (1989). Stage-environment fit: Developmentally appropriate classrooms for young adolescents. In C. Ames & R. Ames (Eds.), *Research on motivation in education: Goals and cognitions* (pp. 139–186). San Diego: Academic Press.

Elliott, E. S., & Dweck, C. S. (1988). Goals: An approach to motivation and achievement. *Journal of Personality and Social Psychology, 54,* 5–12.

Ellison, L. (1992). Using multiple intelligences to set goals. *Educational Leadership, 50,* 69–72.

Emmer, E., Evertson, C., Clements, B., & Worsham, M. E. (1997). *Classroom management for secondary teachers* (4th ed.). Boston: Allyn & Bacon.

Emmer, E. T., & Assiker, A. (1990). School and classroom discipline programs: How well do they work? In O. Moles (Ed.), *Student discipline strategies: Research and practice* (pp. 129–165). Albany, NY: SUNY Press.

Epstein, J. L. (1988). Effective schools or effective students: Dealing with diversity. In R. Haskins & D. MacRae (Eds.), *Policies for America's public schools: Teachers, equity, and indicators* (pp. 89–126). Norwood, NJ: Ablex.

Evertson, C. (1982). Differences in instructional activities in higher- and lower-achieving junior high English and math classes. *Elementary School Journal, 82,* 329–350.

Evertson, C., Emmer, E., Clements, B., & Worsham, M. E. (1997). *Classroom management for elementary teachers* (4th ed.). Boston: Allyn & Bacon.

Eysenck, M. W. (1988). Anxiety and attention. *Anxiety Research, 1,* 9–15.

Farrell, E. (1990). *Hanging in and dropping out.* New York: Teachers College Press.

Farrell, E. (1994). *Self and school success.* New York: Teachers College Press.

Finn, J. D., Pannozzo, G. M., & Voekle, K. E. (1995). Disruptive and inattentive-withdrawn behavior and achievement among fourth graders. *Elementary School Journal, 95*(5), 421–434.

Flavell, J. H., Miller, P. H., & Miller, S. A. (1993). *Cognitive development* (3rd ed.). Englewood Cliffs, NJ: Prentice-Hall.

Ford, M. E. (1992). *Motivating humans: Goals, emotions, and personal agency beliefs.* Newbury Park, CA: Sage.

Ford, M. E. (1995). Motivation and competence development in special and remedial education. *Intervention in Schools and Clinics, 31*(2), 70–83.

Fordham, S., & Ogbu, J. U. (1986). Black students' school success: Coping with the "burden of 'acting white' ." *The Urban Review, 18*(3), 176–206.

Foster, M. (1987). "It's cooking now": An ethnographic study of a successful Black teacher in an urban community college. *Dissertation Abstracts International, 48* (7) (University Microfilms No. AA18722682).

Freiberg, H. J. (1993). School that fosters resilience in inner-city youth. *The Journal of Negro Education, 62*(3), 364–376.

Freiberg, H. J. (1997, March). *Consistency management and cooperative discipline: A longitudinal perspective*. Paper presented at the annual meeting of the American Educational Research Association, Chicago.

Freiberg, H. J., Stein, T. A., & Huang, S. (1995). Effects of a classroom management intervention on student achievement in inner-city elementary schools. *Educational Research and Evaluation, 1*(1), 36–66.

Frey, K. S., & Ruble, D. N. (1990). Strategies for comparative evaluation: Maintaining a sense of competence across the life span. In R. Kolligian & J. Sternberg (Eds.), *Competence considered* (pp. 167–189). New Haven, CT: Yale University Press.

Frieze, I. H. (1980). Beliefs about success and failure in the classroom. In J. H. McMillan (Ed.), *The social psychology of school learning* (pp. 39–78). New York: Academic Press.

Frieze, I. H., & Snyder, H. N. (1980). Children's beliefs about the causes of success and failure in school settings. *Journal of Educational Psychology, 72*(2), 186–196.

Fritz, J. J., Miller-Heyl, J., Kreutzer, J. C., & MacPhee, D. (1995). Fostering personal teaching efficacy through staff development and classroom activities. *Journal of Educational Research, 88*(4), 200–208.

Fulk, B. J., & Mastropieri, M. A. (1990). Training positive attitudes: "I tried hard and did well." *Intervention in School and Clinic, 26*(2), 79–83.

Gaa, J. P. (1973). Effects of individual goal-setting conferences on achievement, attitudes, and goal-setting behavior. *Journal of Experimental Education, 42*, 22–27.

Gaa, J. P. (1979). The effect of individual goal-setting conferences on academic achievement and modification of locus of control orientation. *Psychology in the Schools, 16*, 591–597.

Gambrell, L. B., & Morrow, L. M. (1996.). Creating motivation contexts for literacy learning. In L. Baker, P. Afflerbach, & D. Reinking (Eds.), *Developing engaged readers in home and school communities* (pp. 115–136). Hillsdale, NJ: Lawrence Erlbaum Associates.

Gardner, H. (1983). *Frames of mind. The theory of multiple intelligences*. New York: Basic Books.

Gardner, H., Kerchevksy, M., Sternberg, R. J., & Okagaki, L. (1994). Intelligence in context: Enhancing students' practical intelligence in school. In K. McGilly (Ed.), *Classroom lessons: Interpreting cognitive theory and classroom practices* (pp. 105–128). Cambridge, MA: MIT Press.

Garibaldi, A. M. (1993). Creating prescriptions for success in urban schools: Turning the corner on pathological explanations for academic failure. In T. M. Tomlinson (Ed.), *Motivating students to learn*. Berkeley, CA: McCutchan.

Garner, R., Alexander, P. A., Gillingham, M. G., Kulikowich, J. M., & Brown, R. (1991). Interest and learning from text. *American Educational Research Journal*, *28*(3), 643–659.

Garner, R., Brown, R., Sanders, S., & Menke, D. J. (1982). "Seduction details" and learning text. In K. A. Renniger, S. Hidi, & A. Krapp (Eds.), *The role of interest in learning and development* (pp. 239–254). Hillsdale, NJ: Lawrence Erlbaum Associates.

Gaskins, I. (1994). Classroom applications of cognitive science: Teaching poor readers how to learn, think, and problem solve. In K. McGilly (Ed.), *Classroom lessons: Interpreting cognitive theory and classroom practices* (pp. 129–154). Cambridge, MA: MIT Press.

Gaskins, I., & Elliot, T. (1991). *Implementing cognitive strategy instruction across the school*. Cambridge, MA: Brookline.

Ghaith, G., & Yaghi, H. (1997). Relationships among experience, teacher efficacy, and attitudes toward the implementation of instructional innovation. *Teaching and Teacher Education*, *13*, 451–458.

Gibson, J. D. (1998). *Enhancing motivation of African American adolescents*. Unpublished doctoral dissertation, University of Akron, OH.

Gibson, S., & Dembo, M. H. (1984). Teacher efficacy: A construct validation. *Journal of Educational Psychology*, *76*, 569–582.

Glasser, W. (1990). *Quality schools*. New York: Harper & Row.

Goldenberg, C. (1992). The limits of expectations: A case for case knowledge about teacher expectancy effects. *American Educational Research Journal*, *29*(3), 517–544.

Goldenberg, C. (1994). Promoting early literacy achievement among Spanish-speaking children: Lessons from two studies. In E. Heibert (Ed.), *Getting ready from the start: Effective early literacy interventions* (pp. 171–199). Boston: Allyn & Bacon.

Goldenberg, C., & Gallimore, R. (1995). Immigrant Latino parents' values and beliefs about their children's education: Continuities across cultures and generations. In M. L. Maehr & P. R. Pintrich (Eds.), *Advances in motivation and achievement* (pp. 183–228). Greenwich, CT: JAI Press.

Goldman, S. (1982). Knowledge systems for realistic goals. *Discourse Processes*, *5*, 279–303.

Good, T. L., & Brophy, J. E. (1994). *Looking in classrooms* (6th ed.). New York: Harper & Row.

Good, T. L., & Brophy, J. E. (1997). *Looking in classrooms* (7th ed.). New York: Harper & Row.

Good, T. L., & Marshall, S. (1984). Do students learn more in heterogenous or homogeneous achievement groups? In P. Peterson & L. Cherry-Wilkenson (Eds.), *Student diversity in the organization process* (pp. 15–38). New York: Academic Press.

Good, T. L., & Weinstein, R. (1986). Teacher expectations: A framework for exploring classrooms. In K. K. Zumwalt (Ed.), *Improving teaching (The 1986 ASCD Yearbook)*. Alexandria, VA: Association for Supervision and Curriculum Development.

Goodenow, C. (1992). Strengthening the links between educational psychology and the study of social contexts. *Educational Psychologist, 27*(2), 177–196.

Goodenow, C. (1993). The psychological sense of school membership among adolescents: Scale development and educational correlates. *Psychology in the Schools, 30,* 79–90.

Goodenow, C., & Grady, K. E. (1993). The relationship of school belonging and friends' values of academic motivation among urban adolescent students. *Journal of Experimental Education, 62*(1), 60–71.

Gordon, K., Padilla, A. M., Ford, M., & Thoresen, C. (1994, April). *Resilient students' beliefs about their schooling environment: A possible role in developing goals and motivation.* Paper presented at the American Educational Research Association, New Orleans.

Graham, S. (1984). Communicating sympathy and anger to black and white children: The cognitive (attributional) consequences of affective cues. *Journal of Personality and Social Psychology, 47,* 40–54.

Graham, S. (1989). Motivation in African Americans. In G. L. Berry & J. K. Asaman (Eds.), *Black students: Psychosocial issues and academic achievement* (pp. 40–68). Newbury Park, CA: Sage.

Graham, S. (1991). A review of attribution theory in achievement contexts. *Educational Psychology Review, 3*(1), 5–39.

Graham, S. (1994). Motivation in African Americans. *Review of Educational Research, 64*(1), 55–117.

Graham, S., & Barker, G. P. (1990). The down side of help: An attributional-developmental analysis of helping behavior as a low-ability cue. *Journal of Educational Psychology, 82*(1), 7–14.

Graham, S., & Golan, S. (1991). Motivational influences on cognition: Task involvement, ego involvement, and depth of information processing. *Journal of Educational Psychology, 83*(2), 187–194.

Graham, S., & Harris, K. R. (1994). The role and development of self-regulation in the writing process. In D. H. Schunk & B. J. Zimmerman (Eds.), *Self-regulation of learning and performance* (pp. 203–228). Hillsdale, NJ: Lawrence Erlbaum Associates.

Graham, S., & Harris, K. R. (1996). *Making the writing process work: Strategies for composition and self-regulation.* Cambridge, MA: Brookline.

Graham, S., Harris, K. R., & Reid, R. (1992). Developing self-regulated learners. *Focus on Exceptional Children, 24,* 1–16.

Graham, S., MacArthur, C., Schwartz, S., & Page-Voth, V. (1992). Improving the compositions of students with learning disabilities using a strategy involving product and process goal setting. *Exceptional Children, 58,* 322–334.

Graham, S., & Weiner, B. (1996). Theories and principles of motivation. In D. Berliner & R. Calfee (Eds.), *Handbook of educational psychology* (pp. 63–84). New York: Macmillan.

Greenspan, S., & Lodish, R. (1991). School literacy: The real ABCs. *Phi Delta Kappan, 72,* 300–308.

Gresham, F. M. (1984). Social skills and self-efficacy for exceptional children. *Exceptional Children, 51*(3), 253–261.

Gresham, F. M., Evans, S., & Elliott, S. N. (1988). Self-efficacy differences among mildly handicapped, gifted, and nonhandicapped students. *The Journal of Special Education, 22*(2), 231–240.

Guthrie, J. T., Van Meter, P., McCann, A. D., Wigfield, A., Bennett, L., Poundstone, C. C., Rice, M. E., Faibisch, F. M., Hunt, B., & Mitchell, A. M. (1996). Growth of literacy engagement: Changes, motivations and strategies during concept-oriented reading instruction. *Reading Research Quarterly, 31*, 306–332.

Hare, B. (1985). Stability and change in self-perception and achievement among black adolescents: A longitudinal study. *The Journal of Black Psychology, 11*, 29–42.

Harris, K. R. (1990). Developing self-regulated learners: The role of private speech and self-instructions. *Educational Psychologist, 25*(1), 35–49.

Harris, K. R., & Graham, S. (1985). Improving learning disabled students' composition skills: Self-control strategy training. *Learning Disability Quarterly, 8*, 27–36.

Harter, S. (1982). The perceived competence scale for children. *Child Development, 53*, 87–97.

Heider, F. (1958). *The psychology of interpersonal relationships*. New York: Wiley.

Hennessey, B. A. (1995). Social, environmental, and developmental issues and creativity. *Educational Psychology Review, 7*, 163–183.

Heyman, G. D., & Dweck, C. S. (1992). Achievement goals and intrinsic motivation: Their relation and their role in adaptive motivation. *Motivation and Emotion, 16*(3), 231–247.

Hidi, S. (1990). Interest and its contribution as a mental resource for learning. *Review of Educational Research, 60*, 549–571.

Hidi, S., & Anderson, V. (1992). Situational interest and its impact on reading and expository writing. In K. A. Renninger, S. Hidi, & A. Krapp (Eds.), *Role of interest in learning and development* (pp. 215–238). Hillsdale, NJ: Lawrence Erlbaum Associates.

Hill, K. T. (1984). Debilitating motivation and testing: A major educational problem possible solutions, and policy applications. In R. E. Ames & C. Ames (Ed.), *Research on motivation in education: Student motivation* (pp. 245–274). New York: Academic Press.

Hill, K. T., & Wigfield, A. (1984). Test anxiety: A major educational problem and what can be done about it. *Elementary School Journal, 85*(1), 105–126.

Hilliard, A. (1991). Do we have the will to educate all children? *Educational Leadership, 49*, 31–36.

Ho, R., & McMurtrie, J. (1991). Feedback and underachieveing children: Differential effects on causal attributions, success expectancies and learning processes. *Australian Journal of Psychology, 43*(2), 93–100.

Hodgkinson, H. (1993). American education: The good, the bad, and the task. *Kappan, 74*(8), 619–623.

Hoover-Dempsey, K. V., Bassler, O. C., & Brissie, J. S. (1987). Parent involvement: Contributions of teacher efficacy, school socioeconomic status, and other school characteristics. *American Educational Research Journal, 24,* 417–435.

Hoy, W. K., & Woolfolk, A. E. (1990). Socialization of student teachers. *American Educational Research Journal, 27*(2), 279–300.

Isennagle, A. (1993). A teacher reflects on his urban classroom. In R. Donmoyer & R. Kos (Eds.), *At-risk students* (pp. 369–380). New York: SUNY Press.

Johnson, D. W., Johnson, R. T., & Holobec, E. J. (1994). *Cooperation learning in the classroom.* Alexandria, VA: Association for Supervision and Curriculum Development.

Johnson, D. W., Maruyama, G., Johnson, R., Nelson, D., & Skon, L. (1981). Effects of cooperative, competitive, and individualistic goal structures on achievement: A meta-analysis. *Psychological Bulletin, 89,* 47–62.

Kagen, S. (1992). *Cooperative learning resources for teachers.* San Juan Capistrano, CA: Resources for Teachers.

Karabenick, S. A., & Knapp, J. R. (1991). Relationship of academic help seeking to the use of learning strategies and other instrumental achievement behavior of college students. *Journal of Educational Psychology, 83*(2), 221–230.

Klein, R. (1996). *Teacher efficacy and developmental math instructors at an urban university: An exploratory analysis of the relationships among personal factors, teacher behaviors, and perceptions of the environment.* Unpublished doctoral dissertation, University of Akron, Ohio.

Knapp, M. S., & Shields, P. M. (1990). Reconceiving academic instruction for the children of poverty. *Kappan, 71*(10), 752–758.

Kruger, L. J. (1997). Social support and self-efficacy in problem solving among teacher assistance teams and school staff. *Journal of Educational Research, 90,* 164–168.

Ladson-Billings, G. (1994). *The dreamkeepers: Successful teachers of African American children.* San Francisco: Jossey-Bass.

Lee, O., & Anderson, C. W. (1993). Task engagement and conceptual change in middle school science classrooms. *American Educational Research Journal, 30*(3), 585–610.

Lee, V. E., & Smith, J. B. (1996). Collective responsibility for learning and its effects on gains in achievement for early secondary school students. *American Journal of Education, 104,* 103–145.

Lepper, M., & Hodell, M. (1989). Intrinsic motivation in the classroom. In C. Ames & R. Ames (Eds.), *Research on motivation in education* (pp. 73–105). San Diego: Academic Press.

Lepper, M. R. (1988). Motivational consideration in the study of instruction. Cognition and Instruction, 5(4), 289–309.

Lepper, M. R., & Cardova, D. I. (1992). A desire to be taught: Instructional consequences of intrinsic motivation. *Motivation and Emotion, 16*(2), 187–208.

Lepper, M. R., & Greene, D. (1975). Turning work into play: Effects of adult surveillance and extrinsic rewards on children's intrinsic motivation. *Journal of Personality and Social Psychology, 31,* 479–486.

Lepper, M. R., Greene, D., & Nisbitt, R. E. (1973). Undermining children's intrinsic interest with extrinsic rewards: A test of the overjustification hypothesis. *Journal of Personality and Social Psychology, 28,* 129–137.

Licht, B. G. (1983). Cognitive-motivational factors that contribute to the achievement of learning-disabled children. *Journal of Learning Disabilities, 16,* 483–490.

Licht, B. G., & Dweck, C. S. (1984). Determinants of academic achievement: The interaction of children's achievement orientation with skill area. *Developmental Psychology, 20,* 628–636.

Licht, B. G., Strader, S., & Swenson, C. (1989). Children's achievement related beliefs: Effects of academic area, sex, and achievement level. *Journal of Educational Research, 82,* 253–260.

Locke, E. A., & Latham, G. P. (1984). *Goal setting: A motivational technique that works.* Englewood Cliffs, NJ: Prentice-Hall.

Locke, E. A., & Latham, G. P. (1990). *A theory of goal setting and task performance.* Englewood Cliffs, NJ: Prentice-Hall.

Locke, E. A., Shaw, K. N., Saari, L. M., & Latham, G. P. (1981). Goal setting and task performance: 1969–1980. *Psychological Bulletin, 90,* 125–152.

Mac Iver, D. J. (1993). Effects of improvement-focused student recognition on young adolescents' performance in the classroom. In M. L. Maehr & P. R. Pintrich (Eds.), *Advances in motivation and achievement* (pp. 191–216). Greenwich, CT: JAI Press.

Mac Iver, D. J., & Reuman, D. A. (1993/1994). Giving their best: Grading and recognition practices that motivate students to work hard. *American Educator, 17*(4), 24–31.

Mac Iver, D. J., Stipek, D. J., & Daniels, D. H. (1991). Explaining within-semester changes in student effort in junior high school and senior high school courses. *Journal of Educational Psychology, 83*(2), 201–211.

Maehr, M. L., Midgley, C., & Urdan, T. C. (1992). School leader as motivator. *Educational Administration Quarterly, 28,* 410–429.

Maeroff, G. J. (1988). Withered hopes, stillborn dreams: The dismal panorama of urban schools. *Kappan, 69*(9), 632–638.

Malone, T. W., & Lepper, M. R. (1987). Making learning fun: A taxonomy of intrinsic motivation for learning. In R. E. Snow & M. J. Farr (Eds.), *Aptitude, learning, and instruction: Vol. 3. Conative and affective process analyses* (pp. 223–253). Hillsdale, NJ: Lawrence Erlbaum Associates.

Manning, B. (1988). Application of cognitive behavior modification: First and third graders self-management of classroom behaviors. *American Educational Research Journal, 25*(2), 193–212.

Manning, B. (1991). *Cognitive self-instruction for classroom processes.* Albany, NY: SUNY Press.

Marcus, H., & Nurius, P. (1986). Possible selves. *American Psychologist, 41*(9), 954–969.

Marsh, H. W. (1987). The big-fish-little-pond effect on academic self-concept. *Journal of Educational Psychology, 79*(3), 280–295.

Marsh, H. W., Byrne, B. M., & Shavelson, R. (1988). A multifaceted academic self-concept: Its hierarchical structure and its relation to academic achievement. *Journal of Educational Psychology, 80*, 366–380.

Marsh, H. W., & Parker, J. (1984). Determinants of student self-concept: Is it better to be a relatively large fish in a small pond even if you don't swim well? *Journal of Personality and Social Psychology, 47*, 213–231.

Mathews, J. (1988). *Escalante the best teacher in America.* New York: Holt.

McCollum, H. (1995). Managing academic learning environments. In M. Knapp (Ed.), *Teaching for meaning in high-poverty classrooms* (pp. 11–32). New York: Teachers College Press.

McCready, L. (April, 1996*). Possible selves of African American adolescents.* Paper presented at the American Educational Research Association, New York.

McDaniel, E. A., & Dibella-McCarthy, H. (1989). Enhancing teacher efficacy in special education. *Teaching Exceptional Children, 21*(4), 34–40.

McDonough, M. L., Meyer, D. K., Stone, G. V. M., & Hamman, D. (1991, March). *Goal-setting and monitoring among first grade readers during seatwork: Process and differences in process among reading ability groups.* Paper presented at the annual meeting of the National Association of School Psychologists, Dallas, TX.

McInerney, D. M., Roche, L. A., McInerney, V., & Marsh, H. W. (1997). Cultural perspectives on school motivation: The relevance of goal theory. *American Educational Research Journal, 34*(1), 207–236.

Medway, F. J. (1979). Causal perception for school-related problems: Teacher perceptions and teacher feedback. *Journal of Educational Psychology, 71*(6), 809–818.

Meece, J. L. (1991). The classroom context and students' motivational goals. In M. L. Maehr & P. R. Pintrich (Eds.), *Advances in motivation and achievement* (pp. 261–285). Greenwich, CT: JAI Press.

Meece, J. L., Blumenfeld, P. C., & Hoyle, R. H. (1988). Students' goal orientations and cognitive engagement in classroom activities. *Journal of Educational Psychology, 80*(4), 514–523.

Meece, J. L., Blumenfeld, P. C., & Puro, P. (1989). A motivational analysis of elementary science learning environments. In M. Matyas, K. Tobin, & B. Fraser (Eds.), *Looking into windows: Qualitative research in science education.* Washington, DC: American Association for the Advancement of Science.

Meece, J. L., & Courtney, D. P. (1992). Gender differences in student perceptions. In D. L. Schunk & J. L. Meece (Eds.), *Student perceptions in the classroom* (pp. 209–228). Hillsdale, NJ: Lawrence Erlbaum Associates.

Meece, J. L., Eccles, J. S., & Wigfield, A. (1990). Predictors of math anxiety and its influences on young adolescents' course enrollment intentions and performance in mathematics. *Journal of Educational Psychology, 82*(1), 60–70.

Mehan, H., Villanueva, I., Hubbard, L., & Lintz, A. (1996). *Constructing school success.* New York: Cambridge University Press.

Meichenbaum, D. (1977). *Cognitive behavior modification.* New York: Plenum.

Mickelson, R. (1990). The attitude–achievement paradox among Black adolescents. *Sociology of Education, 63,* 44–61.

Midgley, C., Arunkumar, R., & Urdan, T. C. (1996). "If I don't do well tomorrow, there's a reason": Predictors of adolescents' use of academic self-handicapping strategies. *Journal of Educational Psychology, 88*(3), 423–434.

Midgley, C., Feldlaufer, H., & Eccles, J. S. (1989). Changes in teacher efficacy and students self- and task-related beliefs in mathematics during the transition to junior high school. *Journal of Educational Psychology, 81,* 247–258.

Miller, A. T., & Hom, H. L. (1997). Conceptions of ability and the interpretation of praise and blame. *The Journal of Experimental Education, 65,* 163–177.

Miller, N., & Harrington, H. H. (1992). Social categorization and intergroup acceptance: Principles for the design and development of cooperative learning teams. In R. Hertz-Lazarowitz (Ed.), *Interaction in cooperative groups* (pp. 203–227). New York: Cambridge University Press.

Miller, S. E., Leinhardt, G., & Zigmond, N. (1988). Influencing engagement through accommodation. *American Educational Research Journal, 25,* 465–487.

Miserandino, M. (1996). Children who do well in school: Individual differences in perceived competence and autonomy in above-average children. *Journal of Educational Psychology, 88*(2), 203–214.

Mitchell, M. (1993). Situational interest: Its multifaceted structure in the secondary school mathematics classroom. *Journal of Educational Psychology, 85,* 424–436.

Morgan, M. (1985). Self-monitoring of attained subgoals in private study. *Journal of Educational Psychology, 77,* 623–630.

Morgan, M. (1987). Self-monitoring and goal setting in private study. *Contemporary Educational Psychology, 12,* 1–6.

Moriarity, B., Douglas, G., Punch, K., & Hattie, J. (1995). Importance of self-efficacy as a mediating variable between learning environments and achievement. *British Journal of Educational Psychology, 65,* 73–84.

Natriello, G., & Dornbush, S. M. (1984). *Teacher evaluative standards and student effort.* New York: Longman.

Nelson-Le Gall, S. (1985). Help-seeking in learning. In E. Gordon (Ed.), *Review of research in education* (pp. 55–90). Washington, DC: American Educational Research Association.

Nelson-Le Gall, S. (1991). Classroom help-seeking. *Education and Urban Society, 24*(1), 27–40.

Nelson-Le Gall, S. (1992). Children's instrumental help-seeking: Its role in the social acquisition and the construction of knowledge. In R. Hertz-Lazarowitz & N. Miller (Eds.), *Interaction in cooperative groups* (pp. 49–68). New York: Cambridge University Press.

Nelson-Le Gall, S., & Jones, E. (1990). Cognitive-motivational influences on the task-related help-seeking behavior of black children. *Child Development, 61,* 581–589.

Newman, R. S. (1990). Children's help-seeking in the classroom: The role of motivation factors and attributions. *Journal of Educational Psychology*, *82*, 71–80.

Newman, R. S. (1991). Goals and self-regulated learning: What motivates children to seek academic help? In M. L. Maehr & P. R. Pintrich (Eds.), *Advances in motivation and achievement* (Vol. 7, pp. 151–183). Greenwich, CT: JAI Press.

Newmann, F. M. (1992). *Student engagement and achievement in American secondary schools*. New York: Teachers College Press.

Newmann, F. M., Rutter, R. A., & Smith, M. S. (1989, October). Organizational factors that affect school sense of efficacy, community, and expectations. *Sociology of Education, 62*, 221–238.

Newmann, F. M., Secada, W. G., & Wehlage, G. G. (1995). *A guide to authentic assessment: Vision, standards and scoring*. Madison, WI: Wisconsin Center for Educational Research.

Newmann, F. M., Wehlage, G. G., & Lamborn, S. D. (1992). The significance and sources of student engagement. In F. M. Newmann (Ed.), *Student engagement and achievement in American secondary schools* (pp. 11–39). New York: Teachers College Press.

Nicholls, J. G. (1978). The development of the concepts of effort and ability, perception of academic attainment, and the understanding that difficult tasks require more ability. *Child Development, 49*, 800–814.

Nicholls, J. G. (1979). Quality and inequality in intellectual development. *American Psychologist, 34*(11), 1071–1084.

Nicholls, J. G. (1983). Conceptions of ability and achievement motivation: A theory and its implications for education. In M. O. Stevenson, H. W. Stevenson, & S. G. Paris (Eds.), *Learning and motivation in the classroom* (pp. 211–237). Hillsdale, NJ: Lawrence Erlbaum Associates.

Nicholls, J. G. (1989). *The competitive ethos and democratic education*. Cambridge, MA: Harvard University Press.

Nicholls, J. G. (1990). What is ability and why are we mindful of it? A developmental perspective. In R. J. Sternberg & J. Kolligian (Eds.), *Competence considered* (pp. 11–40). New Haven, CT: Yale University Press.

Nicholls, J. G., & Miller, A. T. (1984). Development and its discontents: The differentiation of the concept of ability. In J. G. Nicholls (Ed.), *The development achievement motivation* (pp. 185–218). Greenwich, CT: JAI Press.

Nieto, S. (1992). *Affirming diversity*. New York: Longman.

Nieto, S. (1994). Lessons from students on creating a chance to dream. *Harvard Educational Review, 64*(4), 392–426.

Nisen, M. (1992). Beyond intrinsic motivation: Cultivating a "sense of the desirable." In F. K. Oser, A. Dick, & J. Patry (Eds.), *Effective and responsible teaching* (pp. 126–138). San Francisco: Jossey-Bass.

Noblit, G. W. (1993). Power and caring. *American Education Research Journal, 30*(1), 23–38.

Noddings, N. (1992). *The challenge to care in schools*. New York: Teachers College Press.

Nolen, S., & Haladyna, T. (1990). Motivation and studying in high school science. *Journal of Research on Science Teaching, 27*, 115–126.

Oakes, J. (1985). *Keeping track: How schools structure inequality*. New Haven, CT: Yale University Press.

Ogbu, J. U. (1987). Variability in minority school performance: A problem in search of an explanation. *Anthropology and Education Quarterly, 18*, 312–334.

Ogbu, J. U. (1992). Understanding cultural diversity and learning. *Educational Researcher, 21*(8), 5–14.

O'Leary, K., & O'Leary, S. (1977). *Classroom management: The successful use of behavior modification*. New York: Pergamon

Page, R. N. (1991). *Lower-track classrooms*. New York: Teachers College Press.

Pajares, F. (1996). Self-efficacy beliefs in academic settings. *Review of Educational Research, 66*(4), 543–578.

Pajares, F., & Johnson, M. J. (1994). Confidence and competence in writing: The role of self-efficacy, outcome expectancy, and apprehension. *Research in the Teaching of English, 28*(3), 313–331.

Pajares, F., & Miller, M. D. (1994). Role of self-efficacy and self-concept beliefs in mathematical problem solving: A path analysis. *Journal of Educational Psychology, 86*(2), 193–203.

Palmer, D. J. (1983). An attributional perspective on labeling. *Exceptional Children, 49*, 423–429.

Pang, V. O., & Sablan, V. (1995, April). *Teacher efficacy: Do teachers believe they can be successful with African American students*. Paper presented at the annual conference of the American Educational Research Association, San Francisco, CA.

Peak, L. (1993). Academic effort in international perspective. In T. M. Tomlinson (Ed.), *Motivating students to learn* (pp. 41–62). Berkeley, CA: McCutchan.

Pintrich, P. (1995). Understanding self-regulated learning. In P. Pintrich (Ed.), *Understanding self-regulated learning number 63* (pp. 3–12). San Francisco: Jossey-Bass.

Pintrich, P. R., & De Groot, E. V. (1990). Motivational and self-regulated learning components of classroom academic performance. *Journal of Educational Psychology, 82*, 32–40.

Pintrich, P. R., & Schrauben, B. (1992). Students' motivational beliefs and their cognitive engagement in classroom academic tasks. In D. H. Schunk & J. L. Meece (Eds.), *Student perceptions in the classroom* (pp. 149–183). Hillsdale, NJ: Lawrence Erlbaum Associates.

Podell, D., & Soodak, L. (1993). Teacher efficacy and bias in special education referrals. *Journal of Educational Research, 86*(4), 247–253.

Pressley, M., Johnson, C. J., Symons, S., McGoldrick, J. A., & Kurita, J. A. (1989). Strategies that improve children's memory and comprehension of text. *The Elementary School Journal, 90*(1), 3–32.

Pressley, M. F., & Levin, J. (1987). Elaborative learning strategies for the inefficient learner. In S. J. Ceci (Ed.), *Handbook of cognitive, social, and neuropsychological aspects of learning disabilities.* Hillsdale, NJ: Lawrence Erlbaum Associates.

Pressley, M., Woloshyn, V., & Associates (1995). *Cognitive strategy instruction* (2nd ed.). Cambridge, MA: Brookline Books.

Ramey-Gassert, L., & Shroyer, M. G. (1992). Enhancing science teaching self-efficacy in preservice elementary teachers. *Journal of Elementary Science Education, 4*(1), 26–34.

Ramey-Gassert, L., Shroyer, M. G., & Staver, J. R. (1996). A qualitative study of factors influencing science teaching self-efficacy of elementary teachers. *Science Education, 80*(3), 283–315.

Randhawa, B. S., Beamer, J. E., & Lundberg, I. (1993). Role of mathematics self-efficacy in the structural model of mathematics achievement. *Journal of Educational Psychology, 85*(1), 41–48.

Raudenbush, S. W., Rowan, B., & Cheong, Y. F. (1992). Contextual effects on the self-perceived efficacy of high school teachers. *Sociology of Education, 65*, 150–167.

Reid, M. K., & Borkowski, J. G. (1987). Causal attributions of hyperactive children: Implications for training strategies and self-control. *Journal of Educational Psychology, 79*, 296–307.

Reiher, R. H., & Dembo, M. H. (1984). Changing academic task persistence through a self-instructional attribution training program. *Contemporary Educational Psychology, 9*, 84–94.

Reynolds, M. C. (1994). Special education as a resilience-related venture. In M. C. Wang & E. W. Gordon (Eds.), *Educational resilience in inner-city America* (pp. 131–140). Hillsdale, NJ: Lawrence Erlbaum Associates.

Rigby, C. S., Deci, E. L., Patrick, B. C., & Ryan, R. M. (1992). Beyond the intrinsic-extrinsic dichotomy: Self-determination in motivation and learning. *Motivation and Emotion, 16*(3), 165–185.

Rohrkemper, M. (1985). Motivational coursework in teacher education. In M. K. Alderman & M. W. Cohen (Eds.), *Motivational theory and practice for preservice teachers (Teacher Education Monograph No. 4;* pp. 52–64). Washington, DC: ERIC Clearinghouse in Teacher Education.

Rohrkemper, M., & Corno, L. (1988). Success and failure on classroom tasks: Adaptive learning and classroom teaching. *Elementary School Journal, 88*, 297–312.

Rohrkemper, M. M. (1989). Self-regulated learning and academic achievement: A Vygotskian view. In B. J. Zimmerman & D. H. Schunk (Eds.), *Self-regulated learning and academic achievement: Theory, research, and practice* (pp. 143–167). New York: Springer-Verlag.

Rolison, M. A., & Medway, F. J. (1985). Teachers' expectations and attributions for student achievement: Effects of label, performance pattern, and special education intervention. *American Educational Research Journal, 22*(4), 561–573.

Rose, M. (1995). *Possible lives.* Boston: Houghton-Mifflin.

Rosenholtz, S. J. (1989). *Teachers' workplace: The social organization of schools.* New York: Longman.

Rosenthal, R., & Jacobson, L. (1968). *Pygmalion in the classroom: Teacher expectation and pupils' intellectual development*. New York: Holt, Rinehart & Winston.

Ross, J. S. (1995). Strategies for enhancing teachers' beliefs in their effectiveness: Research on a school improvement hypothesis. *Teachers College Record, 97*, 227–251.

Rueda, R., & Moll, L. C. (1994). A sociocultural perspective on motivation. In J. H. F. O'Neil & M. Drillings (Eds.), *Motivation: Theory and research* (pp. 117–140). Hillsdale, NJ: Lawrence Erlbaum Associates.

Ruenzel, D. (1997, February 5). AVID learners. *Education Week*, pp. 28–33.

Rust, C. (1992, January 26). Miss Bailey's lessons for life. *Houston Chronicle*, pp. 1G, 6G.

Ruth, W. J. (1996). Goal setting and behavior contracting for students with emotional and behavioral difficulties: Analysis of daily, weekly, and total goal attainment. *Psychology in the Schools, 23*(April), 153–158.

Ryan, R. M, & Stiller, J. (1991). The social contexts of internalization: Parent influences on autonomy, motivation, and learning. In M. L. Maehr & P. L. Pintrich (Eds.), *Advances in Motivation and achievement* (pp. 115–149). Greenwich, CT: JAI Press.

Sagotsky, G., Patterson, C. J., & Lepper, M. R. (1978). Training children's self-control: A field experiment in self-monitoring and goal-setting in the classroom. *Journal of Experimental Child Psychology, 25*, 242–253.

Schiefele, U. (1991). Interest and learning in motivation. *Educational Psychologist, 26*, 299–333.

Schraw, G., Horn, C., Thorndike-Christ, T., & Bruning, R. (1995). Academic goal orientations and student classroom achievement. *Contemporary Educational Psychology, 20*, 359–368.

Schunk, D. H. (1982). Effects of effort attributional feedback on children's perceived self-efficacy and achievement. *Journal of Educational Psychology, 74*, 548–556.

Schunk, D. H. (1983a). Goal difficulty and attainment information: Effects on children's achievement behaviors. *Human Learning, 2*, 107–117.

Schunk, D. H. (1983b). Reward contingencies and the development of children's skills and self-efficacy. *Journal of Educational Psychology, 75*, 511–518.

Schunk, D. H. (1984a). Enhancing self-efficacy and achievement through rewards and goals: Motivational and informational effects. *Journal of Education Research, 78*(1), 29–34.

Schunk, D. H. (1984b). Sequential attributional feedback and children's achievement behavior. *Journal of Educational Psychology, 76*, 1159–1169.

Schunk, D. H. (1985). Participation in goal setting: Effects on self-efficacy and skills of learning-disabled children. *The Journal of Special Education, 19*(3), 307–317.

Schunk, D. H. (1989). Self-efficacy and cognitive skill learning. In C. Ames & R. Ames (Eds.), *Research on motivation in education* (Vol. 3, pp. 13–44). San Diego: Academic Press.

Schunk, D. H. (1991a). Goal setting and self-evaluation: A social cognitive perspective on self-regulation. In M. L. Maehr & P. R. Pintrich (Eds.), *Advances in motivation and achievement* (pp. 85–114). Greenwich, CT: JAI Press.

Schunk, D. H. (1991b). Self-efficacy and academic motivation. *Educational Psychologist, 26,* 207–231.

Schunk, D. H., & Cox, P. D. (1986). Strategy training and attributional feedback with learning disabled students. *Journal of Educational Psychology, 78*(3), 201–209.

Schunk, D. H., & Hanson, A. R. (1985). Peer models: Influence on children. *Journal of Educational Psychology, 77,* 313–322.

Schunk, D. H., Hanson, A. R., & Cox, P. D. (1987). Peer model attributes and children's achievement behaviors. *Journal of Educational Psychology, 79,* 54–61.

Schutz, P. A. (1989). *An interactive process ontology for the self-regulating aspects of knowing, learning and emoting: The relationship between goals and feedback in learning.* Unpublished doctoral dissertation, The University of Texas at Austin.

Schutz, P. A. (1991). Goals in self-directed behavior. *Educational Psychologist, 2*(1), 55–67.

Schutz, P. A. (1994). Goals as the transactive point between motivation and cognition. In P. R. Pintrich, D. R. Brown, & C. E. Weinstein (Eds.), *Student motivation, cognition, and learning* (pp. 135–156). Hillsdale, NJ: Lawrence Erlbaum Associates.

Schutz, P. A., & Weinstein, C. E. (1990). Using test feedback to facilitate the learning process. *Classroom Companion, 6*(2), 73–74.

Seligman, M. E. P., & Maier, S. F. (1967). Failure to escape traumatic shock. *Journal of Experimental Psychology, 74,* 1–9.

Shachar, H., & Shmuelevitz, H. (1997). Implementing cooperative learning, teacher collaboration and teachers' sense of efficacy in heterogeneous junior high schools. *Contemporary Educational Psychology, 22,* 53–72.

Shelton, T. L., Anastopoulos, A. D., & Linden, J. D. (1985). An attribution training program with learning disabled children. *Journal of Learning Disabilities, 18,* 261–265.

Shields, P. M. (1995). Engaging children of diverse backgrounds. In M. Knapp (Ed.), *Teaching for meaning in high-poverty classrooms* (pp. 33–46). New York: Teachers College Press.

Simmons, W., & Grady, M. (1990). *Black male achievement: From peril to promise.* (Report of the Superintendent's Advisory Committee on black male achievement). Prince Georges County, MD: Prince Georges County Schools.

Sizer, T. R. (1986, September). Rebuilding: First steps by the coalition of essential schools. *Phi Delta Kappan, 67,* 38–42.

Skinner, E. A. (1995). *Perceived control, motivation, and coping.* Thousand Oaks, CA: Sage.

Slavin, R. E. (1990). *Cooperative learning: Theory, research, and practice.* Englewood Cliffs, NJ: Prentice-Hall.

Slavin, R. E. (1995). *Cooperative learning* (2nd ed.). Boston: Allyn & Bacon.

Smolen, L., Newman, C., Walthen, T., & Lee, D. (1995). Developing student self-assessment strategies. *TESOL, 5*, 22–26.

Sockett, H. (1988). Education and will: Aspects of personal capability. *American Journal of Education, 96*, 95–214.

Solmon, M. A. (1996). Impact of motivational climate on students' behaviors and perceptions in a physical education setting. *Journal of Educational Psychology, 88*(4), 731–738.

Solomon, D., Watson, M., Battistich, V., Schaps, E., & Delucchi, K. (1992). Creating a caring community: Educational practices that promote children's social development. In F. K. Oser, A. Dick, & J. Luc-Patry (Eds.), *Effective and responsible teaching* (pp. 383–396). San Francisco: Jossey-Bass.

Sparks, G. (1988). Teachers' attitudes toward change and subsequent improvements in classroom teaching. *Journal of Educational Psychology, 80*(1), 111–117.

Steele, C. M. (1992, April). Race and the schooling of Black Americans. *The Atlantic Monthly*, pp. 68–78.

Steele, C. M. (1997). A threat in the air: How stereotypes shape intellectual identity and performance. *American Psychologist, 52*(6), 613–629.

Steiner, R., Wiener, M., & Cromer, W. (1971). Comprehensive training and identification for poor and good readers. *Journal of Educational Psychology, 62*, 506–513.

Sternberg, R. (1985). *Beyond IQ: The triarchic theory of intelligence.* New York: Cambridge University Press.

Stevenson, H., & Lee, S. (1990). Contexts of achievement: A study of American, Chinese, and Japanese children. *Monographs of the Society for Research in Child Development, 55*(1–2), 1–119.

Stiggins, R. J., Frisbie, D. A., & Griswold, P. A. (1989). Inside high school grading practices: Building a research agenda. *Educational Measurement: Issues and Practice, 9*, 5–14.

Stipek, D. (1996). Motivation and instruction. In D. C. Berliner & R. C. Calfee (Eds.), *Handbook of educational psychology* (pp. 85–113). New York: Macmillan.

Stipek, D., & Mac Iver, D. (1989). Developmental change in children's assessment of intellectual competence. *Child Development, 60*, 521–538.

Stipek, D., & Ryan, R. H. (1997). Economically disadvantaged preschoolers: Ready to learn but further to go. *Journal of Educational Psychology, 33*, 711–723.

Suarez-Orozco, M. M. (1989). *Central American refugees and U.S. high schools: A psychological study of motivation and achievement.* Palo Alto, CA: Stanford University Press.

Tharp, R. G. (1989). Psychocultural variables and constants. *American Psychologist, 44*(2), 349–359.

Tinto, V. (1993). *Leaving college: Rethinking the causes and cures of student attrition.* Chicago: University of Chicago Press.

Tobias, S. (1985). Test anxiety: Interference, defective skills, and cognitive capacity. *Educational Psychologist, 20*, 135–142.

Toliver, K. (1993). The Kay Toliver mathematics program. *Journal of Negro Education, 62*, 35–46.

Tollefson, N., Melvin, J., & Thippavajjala, C. (1990). Teacher's attributions for students' low achievement: A validation of Cooper and Good's attributional categories. *Psychology in the Schools, 27*, 75–83.

Tollefson, N., Tracy, D. B., Johnsen, E. B., Farmer, A. W., & Buenning, M. (1984). Goal setting and personal responsibility training for LD adolescents. *Psychology in the Schools, 21*, 224–233.

Tomlinson, T. M. (1993). Education reform: The ups and downs of good intentions. In T. M. Tomlinson (Ed.), *Motivating students to learn* (pp. 3–20). Berkeley, CA: McCutchan.

Trawick, L. (1991). Volitional strategy training in students with a history of academic failure. *Dissertation Abstracts International, 52*, 165A. (University Microfilms No. 91–27, 987)

Turner, J. C., & Meyer, D. K. (1995). Motivating students to learn: Lessons from a fifth grade classroom. *Middle School Journal, 27*, 18–25.

Van Overwalle, F., Segarbarth, K., & Goldchstein, M. (1989). Improving performance of freshmen through attributional testimonies from fellow students. *British Journal of Educational Psychology, 59*, 75–85.

Veroff, J. (1969). Social comparison and the development of achievement motivation. In C. P. Smith (Ed.), *Achievement-related motives in children* (pp. 46–101). New York: Russell Sage.

Villegas, I. (1991). *Culturally responsive pedagogy*. Princeton, NJ: Educational Testing Service.

Vygotsky, L. S. (1962). *Thought and language*. Cambridge, MA: MIT Press.

Vygotsky, L. S. (1978). Mind in society. In M. Cole, V. John-Steiner, & E. Saberman (Eds.), Cambridge, MA: Harvard University Press.

Wade, S. (1992). How interest affects learning from text. In K. A. Renniger, S. Hidi, & A. Krapp (Eds.), *The role of interest in learning and development* (pp. 255–278). Hillsdale, NJ: Lawrence Erlbaum Associates.

Warren, L. L., & Payne, B. D. (1997). Impact of middle grades' organization on teacher efficacy and environmental perceptions. *Journal of Educational Research, 90*(5), 301–308.

Wehlage, G. G., Rutter, R. A., Smith, G. A., Lesko, N., & Fernandez, R. R. (1989). *Reducing the risk: Schools as communities of support*. Philadelphia: Falmer.

Weiner, B. (1979). A theory of motivation for some classroom experiences. *Journal of Educational Psychology, 71*, 3–25.

Weiner, B. (1985). An attributional theory of achievement motivation and emotion. *Psychological Review, 92*(4), 548–573.

Weiner, B. (1986). *An attributional theory of motivation and emotion*. New York: Springer-Verlag.

Weiner, B. (1990). History of research in motivation. *Journal of Educational Psychology, 82*, 616–622.

Weiner, B. (1992). *Human motivation: Metaphors, theories and research*. Newbury Park, CA: Sage.

Weiner, B., & Kukla, A. (1970). An achievement analysis of achievement motivation. *Journal of Personality and Social Psychology, 15*, 1–20.

Weinstein, C. E., & Mayer, R. (1986). The teaching of learning strategies. In M. C. Wittrock (Ed.), *Handbook of research on teaching* (pp. 315–327). New York: Macmillan.

Weinstein, R. S. (1993). Children's knowledge of differential treatment in schools: Implications for motivation. In T. M. Tomlinson (Ed.), *Motivating students to learn* (pp. 197–224). Berkeley, CA: McCutchan.

Welch, O. M., & Hodges, C. R. (1997). *Standing outside on the inside*. Albany, NY: SUNY Press.

Wentzel, K. R. (1989). Adolescent classroom goals, standards for performance, and academic achievement: An interactionist perspective. *Journal of Educational Psychology, 81*, 131–142.

Wentzel, K. R. (1991). *Social and academic goals at school: Motivation and achievement in context*. Greenwich, CT: JAI Press.

Wheelock, A. (1992). *Crossing the tracks*. New York: The New Press.

Wibrowski, C. R. (1992). Self-regulated learning processes of inner-city students: A social cognitive investigation. *Dissertation Abstracts International, 53*(4), AAI 9224865.

Wigfield, A., & Eccles, J. (1989). *Anxiety and worries about math and English before and after junior high transition*. Paper presented at the annual meeting of the American Educational Research Association, San Francisco.

Wiggins, G. (1993). *Assessing student performance*. San Francisco: Jossey-Bass.

Wilson, J. D. (1996). An evaluation of the field experiences of the innovative model for the preparation of elementary teachers for science, mathematics, and technology. *Journal of Teacher Education, 47*(1), 53–59.

Wolleat, P. L., Pedro, J. D., Becker, A. D., & Fennema, E. (1980). Sex differences in high school students' causal attributions of performance in mathematics. *Journal for Research in Mathematics Education, 11*, 356–366.

Wood, E., & Woloshyn, V. (1995). *Cognitive strategy instruction for middle and high schools*. Cambridge, MA: Brookline Books.

Yee, D. K., & Eccles, J. S. (1988). Parent perceptions and attributions for children's math achievement. *Sex Roles, 19*, 317–333.

Zimmerman, B. J. (1994). Dimensions of academic self-regulation: A conceptual framework for education. In B. J. Zimmerman & D. H. Schunk (Eds.), *Self-regulation of learning and performance* (pp. 3–24). Hillsdale, NJ: Lawrence Erlbaum Associates.

Zimmerman, B. J. (1995). Self-monitoring during collegiate studying: An invaluable tool for academic self-regulation. In P. Pintrich (Ed.), *Understanding self-regulated learning number 63* (pp. 13–26). San Francisco: Jossey-Bass.

Zimmerman, B. J., Bandura, A., & Martinez-Pons, M. (1992). Self-motivation for academic attainment: The role of self-efficacy beliefs and personal goal setting. *American Educational Research Journal, 29*, 663–676.

Zimmerman, B. J., Greenberg, D., & Weinstein, C. E. (1994). Self-regulated academic study time: A strategy approach. In B. J. Zimmerman & D. H.

Schunk (Eds.), *Self-regulation of learning and performance* (pp. 181–202). Hillsdale, NJ: Lawrence Erlbaum Associates.

Zimmerman, B. J., & Martinez-Pons, M. (1986). Development of a structured interview for assessing student use of self-regulated learning strategies. *American Educational Research Journal, 23,* 614–628.

Zimmerman, B. J., & Martinez-Pons, M. (1990). Student differences in self-regulated learning: Relating grade, sex, and giftedness to self-efficacy and strategy use. *Journal of Educational Psychology, 82*(1), 51–59.

Author Index

Subject Index

275